Monkey Business

MONKEY BUSINESS

The Disturbing Case That Launched the Animal Rights Movement

Kathy Snow Guillermo

People for the Ethical Treatment of Animals

National
Press
Books

Washington, D.C.

Library of Congress Cataloging-in-Publication Data

Guillermo, Kathy Snow.

Monkey business: the disturbing case that launched the animal rights movement

by Kathy Snow Guillermo

256 pp., 156 x 22.5 cm.

Includes index.

ISBN 1-882605-04-7 : $23.95

1. People for the Ethical Treatment of Animals.

2. Animal Experimentation—United States—Moral and ethical aspects.

3. Animal rights—United States.

4. Animal welfare—United States.
I. Title.

HV4926.P46G85   1993

179'.3—dc20

93-25693

CIP

PRINTED IN THE UNITED STATES OF AMERICA

1 2 3 4 5 6 7 8 9 10

Acknowledgments

Thanks first and foremost to Ingrid Newkirk and Alex Pacheco, who opened their voluminous files on the Silver Spring Monkeys case without hesitation. This vastly simplified the daunting task of gathering a decade's worth of police documents, court transcripts and briefs, correspondence and media coverage. They also found time they really didn't have to answer dozens of questions, sometimes in the middle of a hectic day, but often by telephone well past midnight.

Many others were generous with their time. Senator Robert Smith was particularly helpful; in addition to sharing his story with me, he supplied copies of all his correspondence on the case. His legislative assistant Darwin Cusack was kind enough to organize the dozens of letters. I am grateful to all those who granted interviews: Neal Barnard, Donald Barnes, Michael Fox, Gary Francione, Roger Galvin, Peter Gerone, Ronnie Hawkins, Annette Lantos, Lori Lehner, John McArdle, Shirley McGreal, Olive Nash, Dave Rehnquist, Ken Shapiro, Richard Swain, Geza Teleki, Robert Weitzman, and Margaret Woodward. (Edward Taub refused to comment on the case; William Raub chose not to return my numerous telephone calls to his office.)

Special thanks to Joel Joseph, Alan Sultan, Shawn Ortiz and Talia Greenberg at National Press Books; to my friends Mabs Mango and Ed Duvin; to my family, the Sorrells and the Guillermos; and especially to my husband and daughter, who shared me with the ghosts of the Silver Spring Monkeys for more than a year.

Chronology

1980

March: Alex Pacheco and Ingrid Newkirk found People for the Ethical Treatment of Animals.

1981

May: IBR Principal Investigator Edward Taub hires Pacheco for volunteer position.

September: Montgomery County Police raid IBR and seize the 17 Silver Spring Monkeys.

October: The monkeys are returned to IBR pending Taub's trial. When Charlie dies following a fight with another monkey, the 16 remaining monkeys are moved to NIH's animal center in Poolesville, Md.

November: Taub is convicted on six counts of animal cruelty. Representative Tom Lantos and 20 members of Congress ask NIH not to return the monkeys to Taub.

December: In an effort to block the return of the monkeys to Taub, PETA files suit against IBR, asking to be named the monkeys' guardians.

1982

February: Hard Times becomes paralyzed from the neck down and is destroyed by NIH staff.

July: Taub's appeal trial. After three days of deliberation, the jury at Taub's appeal trial finds Taub guilty on one count of animal cruelty.

1983

August: Maryland Court of Appeals overturns Taub's conviction, ruling that state law does not cover federally funded research.

1985

April: PETA's lawsuit seeking guardianship of the Silver Spring Monkeys is dismissed by the U.S. District Court without oral arguments. PETA files appeal.

1986

May: PETA's lawsuit is heard by the Fourth Circuit Court of Appeals. 256 members of Congress and 58 Senators ask NIH to release the monkeys to a sanctuary.

June: Representative Robert Smith introduces "Sense of Congress" resolution calling for release of the monkeys. Two weeks later, with no advance warning, NIH secretly moves the monkeys to Delta Regional Primate Research Center in Covington, La.

September: Fourth Circuit Court of Appeals dismisses PETA's lawsuit.

November: Brooks is found dead in his cage at Delta. Cause of death cannot be independently confirmed, as his body is incinerated.

1987

March: Secret memo outlining plan by the American Psychological Society to buy monkeys, complete Taub's experiment and then destroy the animals, is leaked to PETA.

July: Representative Smith introduces bill mandating release of the monkeys to a sanctuary. Later, Steve Symms introduces identical bill in Senate.

September: Five of the monkeys are transferred to the San Diego Zoo.

1988

July: Dismissing its earlier promise not to experiment on the monkeys, NIH recommends final invasive procedures for monkeys "requiring" euthanasia.

December: NIH announces that three of the monkeys will be experimented on and killed. PETA obtains temporary restraining order to prevent killings.

1989

January: PETA files lawsuit against NIH and Delta's overseer, Tulane University, seeking custody of the monkeys.

August: Paul dies at Delta. His body is incinerated the same day.

1990

January: Billy is subjected to a four-hour experiment and killed.

March: Fifth Circuit Court of Appeals dismisses PETA's lawsuit. PETA appeals decision to United States Supreme Court.

July: Domitian, Big Boy and Augustus are experimented on and killed.

1991

March: U.S. Supreme Court hears arguments in Silver Spring Monkeys case.

April: Before U.S. Supreme Court rules, Titus and Allen are experimented on and destroyed.

May: U.S. Supreme Court rules unanimously in PETA's favor. The suit is remanded to State Court for trial.

For Emil and Jillian

Contents

Foreword

by Oliver Stone

Monkey Business is the story of an injustice and of the two people who took on the federal government, the justice system and the ivory towers of biomedical research to set it right. What makes the story different is not the form of the injustice—the exploitation of others—but the victims, whose suffering is all the more poignant because they cannot speak for themselves.

Alex Pacheco's and Ingrid Newkirk's decade-long struggle to free a handful of crippled and neglected monkeys from a world of science gone awry has been a search for truth among the broken promises, cover-ups and outright lies of a government agency whose multi-billion dollar budget has financed decades of secret suffering. It is a tale of frustration and heartbreak, disillusionment and bitterness. But it is also about perseverance and hope. Out of the sad saga of the Silver Spring Monkeys grew one of the most important social movements of our time.

There is no doubt in my mind that the compassion Newkirk and Pacheco feel for others, whatever species they may be, is genuine. Nor do I doubt that they will spend the rest of their lives helping the rest of us see what is so obvious to them—that the recognition of others' feelings and respect for others' desires to lead their own lives should be extended to all beings.

You will come to understand this is in *Monkey Business*, because it is their story, told from their point of view.

I'm always fascinated by the contest that develops between individuals and the rigid institutions they confront; the good guys don't always win. But in *Monkey Business*, the strength and indomitable will of Ingrid Newkirk and Alex Pacheco make this true story one of personal triumph amid moral chaos.

After reading this compelling tale, people confused by the concept of animal rights will begin to understand the passion of the movement, the people behind it and the animals for whom they vigorously advocate.

Introduction

"Scientists . . . have moved away from animal research because of fear of being harassed by animal activists."
—Louis Sullivan, former Secretary, Department of Health and Human Services, the Washington Times, *July 31, 1992*

Justice Thurgood Marshall delivered the ruling on May 20, 1991, a warm, sunny day in Washington, D.C. Attorneys for both sides—the National Institutes of Health and People for the Ethical Treatment of Animals—waited anxiously in the broad hallways of the Supreme Court building.

Although Justice Marshall would claim that the decision dealt with only a "narrow jurisdictional question," NIH and PETA knew the stakes were much higher. A ruling in PETA's favor would not only put the powerful government agency on trial, but would clear the way for penetration of the legal shield surrounding the $10 billion world of federally funded medical research.

The case began exactly a decade earlier, when a college student named Alex Pacheco took a volunteer job at a primate research laboratory in the D.C. suburb of Silver Spring, Md. The subsequent arrest of an NIH grant recipient on animal cruelty charges jolted the animal experimentation community out of its sleepy complacency and set the gears of change violently into motion.

Within months, Congress would hear the story of the Silver Spring Monkeys, as the research animals came to be known, and legislation requiring better treatment of lab animals would be introduced. In coming years the case would also be discussed in countless criminal and civil courtrooms, the Justice Department, the White House, and eventually, in the Highest Court of the Land.

But most significantly, the sad story of the Silver Spring Monkeys would catapult the newly-formed People for the Ethical Treatment of Animals out of obscurity. PETA grabbed the opportunity and with a growing number of supporters, launched a movement that would add the words "animal rights" to the American vocabulary. PETA condemned not only painful research on animals, it denounced all experimentation on animals, regardless of the reason. PETA also protested the use of animals for food, for clothing and for entertainment such as circuses and traveling zoo shows.

Throughout the next decade, while a battle raged for the custody of the Silver Spring Monkeys, PETA's membership grew to more than 400,000, and its budget increased to nearly $10 million. Politicians as diverse as Barry Goldwater and Alan Cranston would join the fight for the release of the animals. Doris Day, Sir John Gielgud, Paul McCartney and dozens of celebrities would petition Presidents Reagan and Bush to intercede on behalf of the monkeys.

But the opponents of animal rights were growing more vocal, too. Health and Human Services Secretary Louis Sullivan would label animal rights activists "terrorists." Surgeon General C. Everett Koop would appear in commercials promoting the use of animals for medical research. The American Medical Association would author a "white" paper outlining a plan to defeat animal rights. NIH would design and sell T-shirts with the message: "Warning: Insufficient Medical Research Can Be Hazardous to Your Health."

Through it all, the Silver Spring Monkeys would remain the most important symbol of the growing animal rights movement. Sarah, Billy, Hard Times and the rest of the monkeys would lead a college student from an obscure laboratory in the suburbs all the way to the Supreme Court. The story of the student's fight to free these animals from the lab is the story of a new struggle against an old oppression.

Chapter One

The Laboratory

*"It shocks me now to think how easily we fell upon the atrocities
at the Institute for Behavioral Research."*
—Alex Pacheco, PETA co-founder and president

The stench was unbelievable.

As Alex Pacheco was led from the front offices toward the
monkey colony in the rear of the building the odor became almost
unbearable, but even the stink of urine and animal waste didn't
prepare him for what he would find on that sunny May morning
in 1981. Not that his expectations were great. He applied for a job
at the Institute for Behavioral Research because he wanted to
argue his case against animal experimentation from an informed
position.

What he saw in IBR's monkey room, though, was closer to a
nightmare than a research laboratory.

The deafening screams of 17 frenzied primates assaulted
Pacheco as he crossed the threshold, but the sight overwhelmed
him. Bloody stumps poked through the wire cages and it took
him a moment to realize these had once been fingers. Oozing
untreated wounds covered the limbs and torsos of many of the
monkeys. Decaying bandages that appeared to have been applied
weeks earlier hung in shreds from the arms and hands of others.

He watched one monkey spin around and around in her barren cage, then stop abruptly and viciously rip at the flesh on her own foot.

Pacheco realized immediately that the room was unventilated, although someone had hand-cut a square of plaster board from the ceiling and thumb-tacked a bit of screen over it. But this was only part of the reason for the stench. More than two dozen individual cages were crammed into the tiny square space measuring only 15 feet across and deep. Filth encrusted the wire walls and floors of the cages and several inches of waste loaded the pans beneath. Pacheco noticed one of the monkeys digging in his own excrement through the wire floor. He watched as the monkey retrieved a urine-soaked food pellet and greedily stuffed it into his mouth; there were no food dishes to prevent the dry biscuits from falling through the wire grid.

The monkeys had flung blood and feces at the walls, which had dried into a kind of gruesome modern art, illuminated by the greenish light of an uncovered fluorescent bulb. There were no windows in the room.

How, Pacheco wondered, could any relevant experimental data come from this pathetic group of maimed creatures?

The chaos and suffering in the monkey room didn't seem to bother Pacheco's guide for the grim tour. Of course, Dr. Edward Taub, IBR's principal investigator, and his staff had created it.

Pacheco's choice of IBR was accidental. As he flipped through the U.S. Department of Agriculture's directory of registered animal research facilities, he noticed one conveniently close to his home in Takoma Park, Md.

Pacheco was a startlingly handsome 22-year-old in 1981, of medium height, slender, with thick dark hair, brown eyes and a serious demeanor. He had just finished his third year of college at George Washington University. Though his major subjects were political science and environmental studies, he had already decided his vocation was animal protection. Just the year before, he and a young woman named Ingrid Newkirk had formed a new organization they called People for the Ethical Treatment of Animals. Newkirk was the chief of animal disease control for Washington, D.C.'s Commission on Public Health—the first woman and first non-veterinarian to hold this position. Only 31, the tall, blondish Newkirk had already reformed the decaying

D.C. city pound and instituted innovative programs to deal with the district's stray animal problems.

Newkirk and Pacheco agreed a new grassroots organization was needed to expose what they believed was the institutionalized abuse of animals used for food production and experimentation. Soon after, with just a few members, PETA took its campaigns to the streets and before the year was out was regularly protesting the government agencies that oversee animal agriculture and research.

They also picketed D.C. area slaughterhouses. Pacheco had visited a slaughtering facility in 1978. The violence of the animals' deaths and the fear in the eyes of the cows and pigs as they were led to the stun gun and knife were images he couldn't forget; he knew exactly what he was protesting at meat packing plants.

The world of animal research was more mysterious. Pacheco had read dozens of accounts of painful and apparently pointless experiments. He had seen graphic photographs and film footage and had even visited several laboratories. But experiments were conducted privately; if he wanted to know what happened in laboratories once the doors to the public were closed, he would have to work in one. Now that his semester's work was complete, he decided to spend his summer gaining first-hand knowledge.

By fall, Pacheco would be embroiled in the case that would dominate his life for years to come. He never returned to school.

Dr. Taub led the eager, but slightly nervous, young student to his office. Pacheco had dropped by unannounced after choosing IBR from the directory. He had no idea what kind of research was conducted at the lab or even what kinds of animals were used. He was lucky, he thought, to catch the head researcher in a free moment.

Pacheco sat opposite the dark-haired, portly Taub, who looked to be about 50, and explained that he was looking for a summer job. As he spoke, Pacheco couldn't help but notice that the severed hand of a monkey, fingers curled toward palm, held papers in place on Taub's desk. A skull, also from a monkey, grinned down at Pacheco from a book shelf.

Taub, who smiled at Pacheco throughout the half-hour interview, was obviously pleased to discuss his work with such a willing listener. Deafferentation, he explained, was the surgical procedure he performed on monkeys. It involved cutting the dorsal roots of the spinal nerves that carry sensory input from the limbs to the central nervous system. Once the nerves were snipped, the monkeys lost all feeling in the affected limbs and stopped using them, even though they were still physically capable of movement. The point of the experiment was to learn more about sensation and motor function in these damaged primates. Perhaps one day his work would lead to techniques that could help people who were similarly maimed: if he could force the monkeys to use their crippled arms, it may be possible for humans to learn to as well.

Pacheco asked how the monkeys could be made to use hands they couldn't feel.

There were several methods, Taub answered. He could bind the good arm to the monkey's body, for example, and restrain his head. After a few days without food he may get hungry enough to pick up one or two raisins with his numb fingers.

Unfortunately there were no paid jobs available. Taub offered to check into the possibility of a volunteer position and asked Pacheco to call later that day.

Pacheco called Taub that afternoon and was told that a student assistant, Georgette Yakalis, was interested in his help. Taub gave Pacheco her number. After another brief phone call to Yakalis, Pacheco was officially hired as a volunteer at IBR.

Pacheco was both excited and nervous when he awoke on May 11, the morning he was to begin his new unpaid job. He drank his usual three cups of coffee and wondered what he would find in the laboratory. The monkeys were difficult to imagine. Some of them would be hungry and crippled—not a pleasant thought. The rest was probably pretty standard: shiny stainless steel cages, gleaming surgical instruments, cabinets of neatly filed research data.

The tour of the facility wiped these pictures from his mind.

Pacheco followed Taub's assistant, a tall, quiet young man named John Kunz, to the monkey room where they were joined by Taub. Pacheco was astounded that Taub, who chatted about the monkeys, and Kunz, who stood silently behind them, didn't appear to notice the condition of the room, as though the chaos before them was completely normal.

Kunz silently left the room and returned a few minutes later with a compact, short-haired woman in her twenties who introduced herself as Georgette Yakalis. She, too, was a volunteer, she had explained to Pacheco during their phone conversation, a graduate student working on her Master's thesis. She was conducting her own experiments on the monkeys.

"Shouldn't some of the monkeys be bandaged?" Pacheco asked, noticing that at least five of the animals had large open wounds.

"They're doing all right," Taub replied.

Pacheco stepped over several piles of feces as he was led out of the colony toward the surgery area.

As he entered the room he was sure Taub must have noticed his shocked reaction. Dirty clothes and discarded shoes littered the floor. The records Pacheco had imagined neatly tucked into file drawers were scattered across the operating table and counter tops. Hours of scrubbing and disinfecting would be needed to make the area sterile. Even the rat droppings in the corners of the room and the scrub sink hadn't been swept up.

He followed Taub into yet another dismal room, this one a storage space by the look of its contents. A half-size beat up refrigerator served as the medicine cabinet though the contents of the bottles were spilled across its floor and frozen into a multi-colored mass. Next to this lay a bag of rotting apples, probably meant for the monkeys at one time.

Taub pointed out the shell of a refrigerator next to the first one. It had been converted into an immobilizing chamber with a plexiglass chair. The researcher described the procedure used with this device. The monkey, he explained, was placed securely in the seat with electrodes fastened to various points on his body. His crippled hand was placed around a small, fluid-filled bottle. If the monkey squeezed the bottle with his numb hand he could stop the electric shock that coursed through his body.

Dried blood coated the walls of the chamber.

Sacks of monkey chow were stacked on one side of the room. The most recent visible mill date on all the bags was February, 1981—four months earlier. Pacheco knew that after three months the crucial vitamin C content began to degrade. A wedge of peeled wallpaper hung over the stale food.

Pacheco followed Taub through several other rooms in similar disarray. Electrical equipment, spray bottles, loose papers and trash covered every surface. The brown tile floors looked as if they hadn't been mopped in months. The plasterboard walls were stripped in places and covered with grimy fingerprints and smudges of blood. In one of the experimental rooms a poster of an orangutan's face had been tacked up over the unrepaired wall. The words on the poster read: "When I want your opinion, I'll beat it out of you."

There didn't appear to be anyone cleaning cages or caring for the monkeys. Pacheco wondered where the staff veterinarian's office was and why he hadn't bandaged his patients. Why didn't the veterinary technicians pick the dead cockroaches out of the scrub sink? For that matter, where were the technicians?

Pacheco asked few questions initially, as he didn't want to arouse suspicion in Taub and the others, but he marvelled at how oblivious they were to their surroundings. Perhaps he was particularly sensitive to the conditions of the animals and the lab, but surely even the average believer in the benefits of animal experimentation would be appalled.

That evening, Pacheco described IBR to Newkirk. He felt sick to his stomach and couldn't manage dinner, but his shock had been replaced by a need to talk about everything he had seen. He sat at the kitchen table drinking cup after cup of coffee, jumping up every few minutes to pace the scuffed floor. They had spent many long nights this way, sitting up late, planning protests and campaigns for their fledgling organization while Newkirk put together a quick vegetarian meal. She discovered the day they met, when Pacheco showed up at the D.C. animal shelter and offered to volunteer, that although he was gregarious, charming and obviously very bright, he was so intent on his work that he neglected to care for himself. His shoes had holes in them and he seemed to live in a pair of white painter's overalls. As far as Newkirk could tell, his entire diet consisted of vegetarian hot dogs eaten cold from the can.

They were opposites in many ways. Newkirk was older by a decade, practical, straightforward and intensely private. She hated clutter or disarray and was as organized in her home as in her office. Pacheco, however, was professorially absent-minded. His fraternity house room was littered with scraps of paper, "to do" lists, receipts and empty soft drink cans.

But they shared a single-mindedness when it came to animals. Newkirk had scrambled over rooftops and down storm drains to rescue cats; she had walked into crack houses in inner D.C., sometimes well past midnight, to respond to cruelty calls. Few of her colleagues were willing to take these kinds of risks, and her work was sometimes lonely. In Pacheco she found a kindred spirit.

One afternoon not long after they met, they sat together in his frat house working on a flyer to announce the showing of an animal rights film on campus. Pacheco glanced out the open window just as a delivery van pulled up in front of the laboratory located in a building across the street. Without a word, he dashed out the door and down the steps. When Newkirk looked out the window she saw Pacheco running up the street with a large box, his shoulder-length hair flowing behind him, the UPS driver in hot pursuit. When Pacheco returned two hours later, his hair was cut short and he wore a red checked shirt he'd bought from the back of a man on the street. UPS and its enraged driver never recovered the box of rats.

At the time she met Pacheco, Newkirk had just broken up with a man she deeply cared for because they couldn't reconcile their different views of animals, and she wasn't looking for a romantic relationship. She found Pacheco good company and she liked spending time with someone who shared her ideology. When Pacheco made it clear his feelings for her were growing stronger, Newkirk didn't take it seriously until some months later, just before Pacheco happened on IBR.

He had finished his final exams just as Newkirk and a female friend were preparing to leave for a long weekend in Mexico. He looked so wistful as Newkirk told him of her plans that she decided to invite him. It was during those days lying on the hot sand and swimming along the reef in the turquoise-colored water that Newkirk found, to her surprise, that she had fallen in love. By the time Pacheco decided he would spend his summer break in the laboratory in Silver Spring, he and Newkirk were living together.

On this night, Pacheco and Newkirk tried to sort out their options. The first and most important task was to make the monkeys more comfortable. Pacheco decided to smuggle fresh fruit into the lab and hoped he would be left unsupervised long enough to give it to the animals. There didn't seem to be much he could do right away about their cages, which were less than two feet wide. The monkeys' daily lives could be improved immensely by the addition of a few simple items—food dishes, toys to manipulate, and smooth platforms to sit on so they could escape the uneven wire grid floors. Pacheco hoped he would have the opportunity to suggest these improvements to Taub.

Finally, they decided that Pacheco must keep a written record of everything he saw.

Pacheco's first assignment was to familiarize himself with the animals. Yakalis gave him a dexterity board, a small piece of wood with tiny holes in it, and asked him to place raisins on it and offer them to the monkeys through the wires. Since there were no charts on the cages she named the animals one by one. Pacheco later learned she had identified them incorrectly and didn't seem to be able to tell them apart. He wondered if this affected the accuracy of her reports.

Over the next few days, as he fed the monkeys both the raisins and the fresh oranges from his pockets, he came to know each of them as individuals with personalities as different from one another as would be those in any group of 17 humans. They were small animals, no more than a foot tall, with furry apple-sized heads and reddish-brown coats. Chester, the self-appointed leader of the colony, screamed in rage at his inability to defend his troupe. Paul, gray-haired and elderly, eventually chewed all the fingers from his deafferented limb and then ripped the skin and muscle from his palm, exposing the bone. Domitian was placating and docile, always ready to offer his good arm to Pacheco in a gesture of friendliness and curiosity. Sarah was a rhesus monkey and the lone female in the colony, whose pitiful childlike cries echoed through the lab. As a control subject, Sarah had not been physically crippled, and Pacheco learned she was purchased from a breeding lab when she was just 24-hours-old and had lived her entire eight years alone in the barren steel wires of cage #15. Hard Times shifted from one foot to the other, over and over again, trying to relieve his constant back pain. And Billy, the gentlest and most socialized of the monkeys, had undergone a bilateral surgery and was crippled in both arms. When food was tossed into his cage he bent over and frantically tried to eat it directly from the floor before it fell through the wires. He used his feet to pick through the waste below for stray pellets.

These and the other monkeys—Allen, Nero, Titus, Augustus, Haydn, Big Boy, Montaigne, Charlie, Brooks, Adidas and Sisyphus—were all that was left of an original group of 30 animals. The 16 males were crab-eating macaques born in the Philippine jungles and trapped by dealers who sell to laboratories. It was therefore impossible to know how old they were, but it was safe to assume most of them were quite young when caught. Trappers usually shoot nursing mother monkeys in the head and then pull the clinging infants from their fallen bodies.

Twelve of the remaining monkeys had undergone deafferentation, leaving at least one of their limbs disabled and supposedly without feeling. In their boredom and caged frustration they mutilated their useless limbs, which must have seemed like dead heavy weights hanging from their shoulders. By Pacheco's count, 39 fingers were either partially or completely missing, and there didn't seem to be any regular system for treating the wounds; some had been bandaged, most left exposed. During his first week, he saw no medication administered—though it was probably just as well. When he took a closer look at the scattered bottles in the refrigerator he found that none of the drugs were less than two years past expiration, while some dated from as far back as 1969.

Pacheco gradually earned the monkeys' trust. His surreptitious gifts of fruit were hungrily accepted and his presence in the tiny room calmed the animals. They thrust their disfigured arms through the bars when he approached and grasped his fingers in their small hands, as hungry for physical affection as for food. Billy loved to sit quietly in his cage, using his numb hands as pillows to cushion him from the wire floor, while Pacheco groomed him with his fingers—a ritual monkeys perform on one another if allowed to live in groups.

But as the primates opened up to him, Pacheco found himself growing attached to them—so much so that he felt he betrayed them when he went home at night and left them alone in their metal prisons.

Taub also seemed to take to the polite dark-haired student, even though he didn't say much. Pacheco heard from others in the laboratory that the principal investigator was married, but he had the feeling that Taub's interest in him was a bit too intimate. The few meetings they had had were uncomfortable for Pacheco. On May 19, just nine days after Pacheco's first visit to IBR, Taub put him in charge of a pilot study.

The "displacement experiment," as Taub described it, involved two of the monkeys—Augustus, who was deafferented, and Haydn, who had not been crippled. Pacheco was instructed to remove them from the colony and place them in individual cages in Experiment Room A, where they would be deprived of all food for two or three days. Pacheco was then to feed them each 50 raisins and record their reactions on videotape. After a few weeks of this pattern, he was to withhold food for three days but then, instead of giving them the raisins, he was only to show them the food and observe their reactions, noting any differences between the physically normal primate and the crippled monkey.

Pacheco's heart pounded at the thought of deliberately starving the very animals he'd just spent a week getting to know. He pointed out that he had no experience and wasn't really familiar with experimental procedure. Taub dismissed Pacheco's lack of credentials, and at Taub's insistence Pacheco finally accepted. At least, since he would be working on his own, he an would be able to check out the rest of the laboratory more fully without Yakalis and Kunz watching over him.

He asked Taub to explain the purpose of the experiment. Taub suggested that he might find some interesting results—something intriguing enough to generate another grant proposal. He also instructed Pacheco not to talk about the procedure, or about any of the experiments at IBR. You never could tell, another researcher might co-opt the study and publish the results first, he said.

Pacheco wondered if his confusion about the purpose of the study was due to his lack of scientific training. Or maybe researchers had some fundamental understanding about animal experimentation he would never have. Either way, the displacement study sounded sadistic rather that scientific.

Fortunately for Augustus and Haydn, if not for Taub's coffers, Pacheco's independence meant that he did not have to follow the protocol. Working at IBR was difficult enough without starving the animals.

In fact, Pacheco's life after hours was becoming just as trying as his days in the lab. Each evening, as he left IBR, he could hear the monkeys crying out softly from their cages. The sound was so human-like that the first time he heard it he went back into the colony room to make sure nothing unusual had happened. The tiny animals stood at the backs of their filth-encrusted cages, their good hands clinging to the wire, crying and cooing in their loneliness. It was a sound Pacheco would never forget.

At home, in the house he shared with Newkirk in Takoma Park, he stood under a scalding shower and scrubbed his skin raw to get rid of the odor, but still he seemed to reek of the rotting smell. When he closed his eyes at night he saw Billy's sad eyes and heard the infantile crying. He began smoking and drank even more coffee. He felt terribly guilty that he could leave IBR, could come home, wash, eat a fresh salad for supper and stretch out on his bed, while the monkeys were trapped in their dark bank of cages.

He was frustrated that he didn't have a plan to rescue the macaques. He considered just taking them—backing up a van one night and driving away with them. But aside from the obvious problem of breaking the law, this course of action wouldn't stop Taub from buying another colony of monkeys and starting over.

The best he could do for now was to continue to document the conditions at IBR. If he could take photographs, maybe he and Newkirk could show them to someone who could help. But who? And how could he bring a camera in without arousing suspicion? Although he didn't have an answer for the first question, he solved the second problem by requesting a set of keys so that he could work at night. He told Taub that he had a paying job during the day.

During the first few nighttime visits, he photographed the conditions that were familiar, if still shocking, to him. Then he began to look in areas he had not had a chance to investigate. One evening he opened the door of a freezer to find two plastic bundles labeled "Herbie" and "Caligula." He guessed they were the bodies of monkeys who hadn't survived IBR and made a note to ask Yakalis what had happened to them.

As he lifted his camera to photograph the bundles, he heard a door in the next room open. He started and dropped the camera, then quickly shoved it into the pocket of his jacket and closed the freezer. He was sure it was Taub. He walked calmly from the room and tried to think of what he could say, how he could excuse his midnight snooping without raising suspicions and getting thrown out.

But the young man in the shorts and T-shirt who faced Pacheco in the next room wasn't Taub. He wasn't even anybody Pacheco knew. The stranger introduced himself as a student caretaker—one of two who were paid to clean the lab and feed the monkeys.

That was one mystery solved. Now he knew who was supposed to be responsible for these tasks—and who was doing such a terrible job. The caretakers, he was told, were not paid on an hourly basis but were simply given $10 a day. No one checked to see when or even if they showed up. Pacheco suspected they often didn't come in at all and that the monkeys went without food much of the time. Eventually he proved this to himself by placing markers in the food bins and counting the number of days that elapsed before the level dropped.

The next morning he asked Yakalis what had happened to Herbie and Caligula. She could tell him nothing about the first monkey, but Pacheco would never forget what she said about Caligula. He was one of the most disgusting subjects they had ever experimented on. The monkey had mutilated his own chest cavity and eventually developed gangrene. When it was obvious he wasn't going to live much longer, he was strapped into a restraint chair and a final noxious stimuli—or acute pain—test was performed. The smell of his rotting flesh was overpowering. After the test he was destroyed.

While Pacheco carefully recorded and photographed all he saw, Newkirk was busy with her own investigation of IBR.

She learned that the president of Washington D.C. Humane Society, Jean Goldenberg, who was also a friend and colleague, had visited IBR long before Newkirk and Pacheco had ever heard of it. Goldenberg used to pass by the lab on her way to work each day and she often wondered what kind of research was being done. In January of 1977, she saw a bank of cages in the parking lot outside and decided to stop by. She explained that she was a state humane officer and asked to have a look at the place.

The lab was dirty enough to disturb Goldenberg and she reported it to the U.S. Department of Agriculture, the government agency responsible for enforcing the few laws on the books concerning animals in laboratories. She also discovered that IBR was not registered with the USDA, a mandatory procedure for federally funded animal research facilities. As far as Goldenberg knew, the USDA later inspected IBR, as did its funding agency, the National Institutes of Health (NIH), a branch of the Department of Health and Human Services (HHS). Presumably, improvements were made and business as usual continued.

Newkirk delved into the world of somatosensory research during this time as well. After several afternoons at NIH's scientific library, she had a pretty good idea what deafferentation involved: the monkey was anesthetized, stretched out on a surgery table and his spine opened up with a scalpel. The nerves that sent sensory input—feelings—to the brain were severed, or in some cases, a tiny portion was snipped out. When the monkey awoke, what had once been an arm was now an unfeeling dead weight hanging from the shoulder, and the deafferented animal usually bit or chewed it, just as he might attack any foreign object he suddenly discovered attached to his body.

There were differing views about how to treat these self-inflicting wounds. Some experimenters believed they should always be bandaged; others felt that the bandage actually encouraged the monkey to play with his arm. Most agreed, however, that deafferented monkeys required consistent veterinary and nursing care.

Newkirk photocopied as many of Taub's published articles as she could find, and Pacheco pored over them each morning.

Like Pacheco, Newkirk spent her evenings at IBR, but outside rather than in. The caretaker's unexpected intrusion had unnerved Pacheco, so to avoid future surprises he purchased a pair of inexpensive walkie-talkies from a toy store and had Newkirk act as lookout, warning Pacheco if someone arrived. During the weekend daylight hours, when she didn't have the discretion provided by the dark, she sat in the back of her car under a large box. Small viewing holes allowed her to see without being seen.

She felt ridiculous, hunched beneath the cardboard, and would have found the situation hilarious if she could have stopped thinking of the macaques inside IBR, who spent their lives in cages about the same size.

After several weeks, Pacheco was asked to oversee another experiment. This one was called an "acute noxious stimuli test"—the same kind earlier applied to Caligula. He was beginning to understand that the titles of the experiments masked the reality of the procedures. "Noxious stimuli" actually meant purposely inflicted pain.

Yakalis instructed him to pinch parts of the monkeys' bodies with surgical pliers to see where they experienced pain and where they had no feeling. To demonstrate, she had Kunz remove Domitian from his cage and place him in a restraint chair. The monkey was taped spread-eagled into the upright device. To keep his head immobilized, a plexiglass sheet with a wedge cut from it was placed at the back of his neck, and a pipe was placed at his throat.

Domitian struggled against the restraint and gagged as he pressed against the hard metal at his neck, flinging saliva from his open jaws. When some of his spit landed on Yakalis's arm, Pacheco remembers watching in amazement as she went into a rage, yelling and cursing at the choking monkey.

Pacheco had developed a particularly close relationship with Domitian and it was nearly impossible for him to keep quiet and not avert his eyes as Yakalis clamped the surgical pliers tightly on the monkey's testicles to demonstrate a "positive reaction" to the pain test. Domitian screamed and tried to escape but the chair held him fast.

Don't blow it now, Pacheco silently told himself. Concentrate on stopping *all* of it, not just one test.

The same procedure was repeated three times in less than an hour before Domitian was returned to his cage.

Again, Pacheco decided he would pretend to follow his instructions, rather than hurt the macaques. He would write in data that seemed reasonable. But he faced a significant problem: the room in which he was to conduct this procedure on the arms and chests of the monkeys had a door with a two-way mirror in it, so that Taub, Kunz and Yakalis could watch him without his knowledge. After fumbling through his first day at this new task, he told Taub that the monkeys could tell by a change in the light from the mirror that someone was walking past; could he tack a piece of cloth over the door to keep them calm?

Taub agreed and Pacheco heaved a sigh of relief.

Even though Pacheco never knew when someone would walk in unannounced, he used this time to photograph the monkeys. He kept a box at his feet and when he heard the door opening he quickly slammed the camera into it and shoved papers on top.

The evenings Pacheco didn't spend at the lab, he and Newkirk continued to agonize over possible solutions. Should they take the photos to NIH and ask for a complete investigation? Or would NIH close its ranks around IBR, shielding the institution it financially supported? Maybe they should go to the *Washington Post*. But there was no guarantee the *Post* would run a story, and if they didn't, would they blow the whistle on the whistleblowers? One thing was certain: once they made their case public they would lose their inside track. They would no longer be able to help the monkeys in any way and would have no say in their disposition. If they acted prematurely or unwisely, the animals might never be rescued.

As the monkeys' condition worsened, through neglect and self-mutilation, Pacheco became almost frantic. Old and fresh wounds alike were ignored or at best treated with a single dose of antibiotic. He worried that if he questioned Kunz or Taub too much about this they would become suspicious.

One morning Pacheco came in to find Billy's arm swollen to four times its normal size. He guessed it was broken and couldn't stop himself from suggesting to Kunz they call in a veterinarian to look at it. He had long since learned IBR had no staff vet. Now he was told there wasn't even one on-call.

"We really don't have a vet to come in. It's hard to get a vet to come in," Kunz answered quietly. It seemed to Pacheco that Kunz never spoke above a whisper.

"We can take him down to a vet nearby," Pacheco suggested. It's just a few blocks."

"I'll put a bandage on it. I'll take care of it."

Finally, in early August, Pacheco and Newkirk decided to meet with a member of the Montgomery County Council named David Scull. In the early 1970s, Scull, then a Maryland legislator, had worked with Newkirk to revise the state humane laws. Animal experimenters in this state, unlike many others, Scull told them, were not exempt from anti-cruelty statutes.

Newkirk was disbelieving. She knew the cruelty codes backwards and forwards, and she had always been told that federally funded research facilities were exempt from state law. "They're not," Scull said. "Look it up."

At last Newkirk and Pacheco had their solution. With a new rush of energy they began to prepare a criminal case against Edward Taub.

Chapter Two

Beginnings

" . . . I was a victim of the animal rights movement . . . "
—Edward Taub, in a lecture given on September 6, 1990

He's the spitting image of the Birdman, Pacheco thought, the first time he met Taub.

The Birdman earned his living by netting parrots and other exotic birds from tropical areas of the country. He often passed by Pacheco's childhood home in Mexico with as many as 20 cages on his back, each crammed full of birds captured in the jungles. The scarlet feathers and tiny gold beaks protruding from the bamboo slats intrigued the three Pacheco children. The first time they saw him, Alex, Jimmy and Mary stopped him to ask what he was going to do with the dozens of colorful animals on his back. When they learned the birds were going to be sold to dealers who in turn sell to pet shops, they purchased two very young parrots.

The Birdman extracted the small birds from one of the cages, then reached into his pocket and retrieved a pair of ancient rusty scissors. The children were puzzled. The Birdman extended one of the bird's wings between his first and second fingers, and the young Pachecos realized he was going to cut off the animals' means of escape.

"Don't do that!" Alex cried out, and the Birdman, willing to please his customers, put the battered shears back into his pocket.

The children happily took their new—and intact—pets inside to show their parents.

Alexander Fernando Pacheco may have been born into the comfortable middle-class world of Joliet, Illinois, in August of 1958, but he grew up in more primitive surroundings. His father was a medical doctor and a native of Mexico, and his mother was an American nurse. The couple moved their family, two boys and girl, to Mexico when Alex was still young.

The nicest home of the several his family lived in had cement floors and corrugated steel walls. The walls didn't meet in the corners and when there were sand storms, the Pachecos covered their heads with towels to protect their eyes. Eventually, the two tiny parrots escaped through the gaps between the sheets of metal.

Pacheco's father's relatives lived in homes with dirt floors and with only a single faucet to supply water for cooking and washing, but by local standards they were better off than many. The streets near his house were filled with beggars: women with babies and young barefoot children who urinated in the dusty streets, paraplegics and amputees who could not afford wheelchairs and moved laboriously through the alleys on carts made of wooden planks with wheels on the bottom.

His life was filled with animals of all sorts. Huge bats with wing spans of three feet hung from the rubber trees in his front yard. Dozens of species of snakes slept in the sun and hid behind the rocks near his house. When the Pachecos lived near the ocean, Alex watched the fishermen idling their motor boats behind the boulders at the edge of the inlet, waiting for the dolphins who, unaware, swam toward them in large groups. The fishermen would then zoom out and surround the mammals with their nets.

Other times the fishermen would set out enormous nets, hundreds of feet long, in the bay. After several days, dozens of villagers would gather and haul them in by hand. Pacheco watched the tens of thousands of creatures dragged up to the shore, gasping and dying in the bright sunlight.

Since slaughtering animals for food was not hidden away in closed buildings as it is in the United States, Pacheco regularly saw hogs, steers and chickens killed and butchered in the backyards of his neighbors and relatives. His uncle once raised a turkey the young Alex came to know as a pet and as a friend. He watched in horror one afternoon as his uncle hung the bird upside down and slowly cut away the top of the skull, letting the blood drain into a bucket beneath. There must be a better way, the seven-year-old thought.

Pacheco filled his home and his yard with dozens of cages he built himself, taking pride in making them roomy and comfortable for the wild animals he caught. Much later, he would regret taking these frightened creatures from their natural homes, even though he treated them well and eventually released them. But at the time, his fascination with animals guided his behavior. Like most children, he grew up believing that eating domestic animals and capturing wild animals for fun was acceptable behavior.

The Pachecos left Mexico when Alex was in junior high school and for the next several years moved between Ohio, Indiana and Illinois. Alex's interest in animals continued to grow in this country. He often bought turtles and birds from local pet stores and one day, when he was in high school, he purchased an infant crab-eating macaque.

What he learned about monkeys from Chi Chi, as he named the tiny, velvety-soft animal, would later help him understand and befriend the macaques at IBR. He soon realized—it hadn't occurred to him when he bought her—that Chi Chi was an orphan. She had been taken from her mother, probably in the jungles of the Philippines, much sooner than she would have left on her own, and was frightened and lonely in the unfamiliar surroundings. He spent weeks gaining her trust, gradually introducing her to larger cages until she felt comfortable perching on his shoulder as he walked around the house. Eventually he took her outdoors so she could leap and play in the trees until she was tired and climbed down to return indoors.

By the time Pacheco visited the slaughterhouse in Canada that was to bring about the first significant change in the course of his life, he was an enthusiastic college student with dark good looks. He had completed his freshman year and, always a deep thinker, was considering the priesthood.

He wasn't thinking about animals during his vacation in Canada that summer. He was having a good time seeing friends, one of whom suggested stopping by to see a fellow he knew who happened to work at a meat packing plant. Pacheco had nothing better to do and agreed to go along.

Since he had seen so many animals slaughtered in Mexico, it didn't occur to him that he might see anything troubling or unusual that afternoon. He was completely unprepared for the sight of two men, drenched in blood, heaving a newborn calf, cut from the belly of a slaughtered cow, over the side of a dumpster.

All around him were terrified pigs and cows, blood and disemboweled organs, the noise of the conveyor belt and the screams of the animals. Pacheco was sickened, but more than that, felt an overwhelming pity for the animals.

Later in the week, a friend handed him a beat-up paperback copy of *Animal Liberation*, by Australian philosopher Peter Singer. Singer's ideas were new to Pacheco, but they immediately felt right to him.

"I argue," Singer writes, "that there can be no reason—except the selfish desire to preserve the privileges of the exploiting group—for refusing to extend the basic principle of equality of consideration to members of other species. I ask you to recognize that your attitudes to members of other species are a form of prejudice no less objectionable than prejudice about a person's race or sex."

Animals don't belong to people, Singer argues, anymore than blacks belong to whites or women to men. They are thinking, feeling individuals who would like to go about leading their own lives, just as Chi Chi, Pacheco realized, would have wished to remain in the jungle, with her mother.

Pacheco returned to his Catholic university in Ohio a vegetarian and set about trying to convert the brothers and priests. His lack of success was disillusioning. Although they were committed to serving people, most had no interest in the billions of animals whom he felt had no hope of defending themselves against the abuses heaped on them by humans. He knew there were people who desperately needed help—he had seen this throughout his childhood—and he was glad there were many organizations devoted to this, but his calling was to work for other-than-human beings, as he came to think of them.

He transferred to Ohio State University and organized students to protest everything from steel-jaw leghold traps to the common practice of castrating cattle and pigs without anesthetic. This didn't make him popular at an institution largely devoted to promoting agriculture. Pacheco was often awakened by phone calls in the early hours of the morning.

"We're gonna blow your head off!" one caller repeatedly threatened.

Soon after the school year ended, *Saturday Review* columnist and *TV Guide* critic Cleveland Amory gave a speech to a crowded hall in Columbus. Pacheco was in the audience because Amory was also the founder of the Fund for Animals, an active organization whose anti-whaling vessel, *Sea Shepherd*, was stirring up controversy in European waters.

Pacheco sought out the tall, gruff Amory after the talk and hungry for more direct action, begged to be taken on board the ship. Amory wasn't in the habit of signing up young college students he had known for less than an hour, but something about Pacheco's intensity moved him.

"Okay," he finally said, "we'll try you out."

Hard, sweaty work in the engine room and as a deckhand took up Pacheco's vacation during the summer of 1979 as the *Sea Shepherd* travelled from Boston to Portugal. He learned the habits of dolphins, sea turtles and whales, and developed what was to be an enduring belief in the importance of taking action against exploitation of animals. He also began keeping logs of his activities.

By the time the *Sea Shepherd* had rammed and sunk the Portuguese pirate whaling ship the *Sierra*, Pacheco was on his way to England, where he joined activists trying to stop fox hunts. He learned how to cover the ground with perfume and other scents to confuse the hounds, and he sat in front of dens to prevent the dogs from seizing and tearing the foxes apart. The husband-and-wife team who began the Hunt Sabateurs Association made a lasting impression on Pacheco; their commitment showed on their faces in the form of permanent scars from the whips of hunters on horseback.

"Look, do you still drink milk?" Pacheco asked the division chief for the D.C. Commission on Public Health.

"Yes," Ingrid Newkirk answered. "Why?"

"You don't eat veal."

"Yes," Newkirk agreed, curious about what this serious young man might say next. "What's it got to do with milk?"

"They take the calf away from the cow and make veal out of him so that you can steal his mother's milk and put it in your tea."

This wasn't the first disturbing realization Newkirk had since the arrival of this volunteer, fresh from Newkirk's native England. On his first day at the shelter, early in 1980, he presented Newkirk with a copy of *Animal Liberation*. She was already a vegetarian; she had recently rescued several abandoned pigs, skeletal and weak from starvation, and immediately decided she couldn't pay someone else to be cruel to them in a slaughterhouse. But until she read Singer's book, she had never been able to express what she intuitively felt to be true, that animals didn't really belong to people, that they weren't on earth simply for humans to use.

As they got to know each other, Pacheco spoke of what he had learned during the past year. He had an upbeat way of talking she found engaging, and though he didn't criticize her, he did poke fun at her for not having thought the philosophy through already.

"If you like animals," he would ask, "how can you wear leather?"

Newkirk began to examine her life.

"I thought, this is rather pathetic," she said of this time in a 1992 radio interview. "Here I am: I've been inspecting laboratories, going out on cruelty to animals cases, running two shelters, and I didn't know a lot of these things happened to animals. There must be a lot of people who are just as ignorant of these things as I am."

In those early days of friendship, as Newkirk read *Animal Liberation* and explored Peter Singer's philosophy of animal rights, she called Pacheco "Alex the Abdul," after the name traditionally given to messengers in Muslim stories. She was sure he could change, and soften, the hardest of hearts. In March of 1980, she and Pacheco began People for the Ethical Treatment of Animals, never guessing they would soon be on a collision course with the most powerful funders and guardians of animal experimentation.

That Newkirk and Pacheco were in sync in their beliefs on the need to take action is not entirely surprising. Though she was a decade older and as fair as he was dark, they shared an important experience. Like Pacheco, she had lived as a child in a developing country where suffering is a daily—and very public—part of life for many people and animals.

When Ingrid Newkirk was seven years old, her father, a navigational engineer, was loaned to the Indian government. The family left their home in the small English town of Ware, traveled by boat through the Suez Canal to the Bombay Gate, and settled in New Delhi.

Newkirk's parents believed that public service was an integral part of living, and her mother wasted no time finding charities to devote her energy to. She worked with Mother Teresa (who was not yet the world-famous figure she is today), in a leper colony, and at a home for unwed mothers. Ingrid, her only child, remembers spending her vacations rolling bandages, packing pills or making stuffed toys to take to a nearby orphanage.

Newkirk spent much of the next eight years at a boarding school in the Himalayas. Her classmates were the daughters of well-to-do Indians and other non-natives who, like her parents, had settled in the former British colony. When she arrived at the exotic schoolgrounds some of the students giggled at the strange sound of her foreign language. She remembered this much later when she heard people laugh at the non-human communication of animals in zoos.

Growing up among the vestiges of colonial India instilled in Newkirk an abhorrence for injustice of any kind. One afternoon when she was nine she heard laughter from the alley behind her New Delhi home. She slipped out the courtyard gate and found a dozen servants from neighboring houses leaning over the deep monsoon ditch and laughing at something at the bottom. When she peered over the edge she saw a dog, front and hind feet bound, a string wrapped tightly around his muzzle, pathetically struggling to escape.

Newkirk asked her family's cook and his son, who were laughing with the others, to bring the dog up to her and then to bring some water. She held the mongrel gently, pulled the bloody string from his muzzle and offered him a sip of water, only to find that someone had packed his throat with mud. As she scraped the mud from his mouth, the weakened animal died quietly in her arms.

"It doesn't matter who suffers," her mother often told her, "but how."

India's influence on Newkirk would surface years later, after she moved with her parents to the United States, when she brought some abandoned cats to a local shelter in Montgomery County, Md., outside Washington, D.C. She was in her early twenties and, having an aptitude for math and a desire for some sort of a career, had decided to become a stockbroker.

Her car, loaded with boxes of mewling cats, thumped over the rutted and seldom-used road that dead-ended at the doors of a decrepit building next to a leaf-mulch dump. It was a rude awakening for Newkirk. She expected a tidy office and spotless kennels, not these wretched animals in damp, dirty cells.

There really must be a better way to run things, she thought, and applied for a job. She was reluctantly hired to clean kennels.

Newkirk scrubbed and disinfected kennels by day, and by night, studied reams of information on animal care, cruelty investigation programs, adoption services and animal behavior. Much of what she'd witnessed as a child in India returned to her: the Jains, a sect whose respect for all life is so deep its monks wear masks over their mouths to avoid disturbing flying insects; the schoolmates whose religion taught them not to eat meat; her mother, who never hesitated to help anyone in need.

She was now certain of one thing: selling bonds was not her cup of tea.

Newkirk soon blew the whistle on the Montgomery County Animal Shelter, instituted reforms there and moved on to the D.C. pound, which was in no better shape. She persuaded the city to fund veterinary services, an adoption program, an investigations department and a pet sterilization clinic.

By the time Pacheco plunked *Animal Liberation* on her desk, Newkirk was locally well known for her work to protect animals. She had even been named "Washingtonian of the Year." But the nation's capital hadn't seen anything yet.

There were two things you could do if you wanted to help animals before 1981. You could volunteer to clean cages and groom dogs at a local animal shelter or you could donate money to one of the non-profit organizations who lobbied Congress and wrote exposés of animal abuse. Most of these animal welfare organizations did useful work to promote humane slaughter statutes and other legislation to bring comfort to animals raised for food, experimented on and kept as companions. Certainly they didn't question the human prerogative to use animals—as long as the animals were treated as kindly as possible under the circumstances.

The term "animal rights" was still new and puzzling to many who had devoted their careers to animal welfare in the United States. They were already working long hours to promote improvements on farms and in slaughterhouses for cattle and pigs. Was Peter Singer really suggesting they shouldn't eat a hamburger even if the steer had a pretty decent—if short—life?

And though many called for the development of non-animal alternatives, the use of anesthetics, and better living conditions in laboratories, few were willing to suggest animals shouldn't be used at all. The anti-vivisection organizations that did exist were relics from the late 1800s, whose newsletters railed about abuses in the labs but offered few practical solutions.

Newkirk and Pacheco wanted to give people who cared something more to do than donate money and moan over the sad state of affairs. They wanted to hand out vegetarian recipes and print lists of companies that manufactured non-leather shoes and wallets. They wanted to protest, loudly and publicly, against the slaughter of animals for food. And they wanted to find out what really went on behind the very thick, soundproof walls of animal laboratories.

Edward Taub knew none of this when Alex Pacheco asked for a job. It would never have occurred to him that some people might question his judgment in the care and treatment of the animals who belonged to him. For 23 years he had studied deafferented monkeys, and aside from the 1977 visit by a humane officer, had heard not so much as a whisper of complaint from anyone. Now, at age 50, Taub's entire life was about to be turned upside down.

Like many animal experimenters, Taub was not a medical doctor or veterinarian. He described himself as a physiological psychologist and held advanced degrees from Columbia University and New York University. From all outward signs, he was a scientist in good standing. By 1981 he had published more than a hundred papers, about half concerning his experiments on monkeys. He belonged to numerous scientific organizations including the American Psychological Association, the American Association for the Advancement of Science, and the Society for

Neuroscience, all of which would later rally round their troubled colleague.

He did his first deafferentation study in 1957, and though his work would eventually involve biofeedback studies with humans, monkeys would remain his focus for the next two decades.

Deafferentation studies on animals date back to 1895, and over the years cats, dogs, rats, insects, lizards, birds, mice and fish, in addition to monkeys, have been used. Taub's own work centered around whether or not deafferented monkeys could purposefully use their numb limbs. It was commonly believed they couldn't until Taub, working with two other researchers, showed that they could be trained to grasp and flex in order to avoid intense electric shocks.

Taub was doing research for its own sake; he wanted to see what he could learn. Whether or not these studies would be relevant to humans suffering from similar conditions as a result of stroke or accident wasn't clear, though he would later claim it was. He admitted in a chapter he drafted for a 1980 text on physiology that differences between people and monkeys made it difficult to know whether humans could do what his animal subjects had done. He suggested that "this issue will have to remain unresolved" until scientists learned new ways of studying humans.

If his techniques are to be applied to people suffering from central nervous system damage, Taub offers several pieces of advice, including: "Motivation level should be kept high. This can probably be accomplished without the use of electric shock."

Taub also began deafferenting primates before they were born. Pregnant monkeys were anesthetized and the infants were "exteriorized," that is, cut from the uterus. Their nerves were snipped, a plastic prosthesis was inserted to replace removed vertebrae, and they were put back in the womb. There was only one problem with this study of central nervous system development—80 percent of the babies died.

This was part of the reason NIH rejected one of Taub's grant applications in 1979. The statement of the review committee noted: "A major concern of previous reviewers was that the survival rate of the prenatally operated animals was so low (10-20%) that the considerable expense in funds and loss of animal life associated with the project did not justify its potential goals ... The applicant fails to make a strong case that the overall scientific goals of the project require monkeys and prenatal surgery ... "

In spite of this, for years Taub had been funded largely by grants from federal agencies like the National Institutes of Mental Health (NIMH) and the National Institutes of Health. As Pacheco would later point out, much of Taub's work was paid for by tax money. In fact, Taub had received more than a million and a half dollars in grants since 1970, when he became chief investigator at IBR, much of it for studies on surgically crippled monkeys.

A second grant application from 1979 was approved, and it was the money from that award, a total of $301,522 for the period from April 1, 1980, through March 31, 1983, that financed the experiment Taub was conducting in that summer of 1981.

For Taub and thousands of experimenters, federal grant monies were, and still are, a major source of income. The decision to award or deny funds is made by a peer review panel. In some ways this is sensible; who better to understand the validity of your work than those engaged in that very kind of research? But it can also lead to a favor system, a "you scratch my back, I'll scratch yours" framework in which the relevance of the work to the taxpayers supporting it is not even considered.

But it wasn't the relevance of Taub's experiment that would be questioned, at least not initially. It was the condition of his lab and the monkeys who were caged within its walls. Because aside from the problem of conflict of interest in the peer review process, Alex Pacheco had bumped into, and was about to expose, another troubling flaw in the world of federally funded research: once the agency cut the check, how the subjects—the live animals—were cared for was not an issue. True, there were guidelines for cleanliness and housing. There were annual inspections from the U.S. Department of Agriculture. There was an NIH site committee. IBR even had a perfunctory animal care and use committee of sorts, as required by NIH. But as Alex Pacheco's evidence was soon to prove, the system didn't work.

The words "animal rights" were about to become part of the American vocabulary.

Chapter Three

Nighttime Visits

"My first comment must be that I have never seen a laboratory as poorly maintained for animal subjects or human researchers. The premises were filthy . . . "
—*Geza Teleki, primatologist, from his affidavit after visiting IBR in 1981*

Of all the monkeys, Domitian was most like Chi Chi. He had the same way of puckering his velvety brown lips as if asking for a kiss. His golden eyes, set deep beneath the prominent line of his brow, showed acceptance of Pacheco and a desire to be protected. But the similarities ended there. Domitian's withered left arm ended in an oozing red stump where the fingers had been, and the three inch gash Pacheco saw on his first day at IBR was still, in mid-August, open and draining. The monkey's right hand, in sharp contrast to the mangled mess of his left, was perfectly formed, and when he stretched his normal fingers through the wires of his cage he seemed to Pacheco like a small human child, confused by his circumstances but trusting and willing to accept the kindness offered him.

In an odd way, Pacheco had come to see all the monkeys as his children. Having discovered the dark dungeon of their lives, he felt responsible for making sure they escaped it.

At least now he had some hope. His terrible feelings of guilt and helplessness had lifted since his meeting with David Scull. He felt confident that if he could document the conditions at IBR, the court would be as appalled as he had been and take the animals away from Taub.

The next three weeks, in late August and early September, were frenzied for Pacheco and Newkirk. Newkirk had compiled evidence for many cases of animal cruelty and she knew exactly what they needed, but there wasn't much time to do it. Taub was leaving for vacation on August 21 and they wanted to finish documenting the conditions in the lab before he returned on September 9. Then the photographs would have to be catalogued according to subject matter, the date taken and the date developed. What records there were on the monkeys had to be photocopied and catalogued. Pacheco's written log had to be typed and the entries accurately dated. And they would need testimony, in the form of notarized affidavits, from experts.

This last requisite put Pacheco and Newkirk in a quandary. There were many primate researchers in the Washington area, but most of them were funded by NIH, the same agency financing Taub's study. Many undoubtedly knew Taub personally. If word got back to NIH prematurely, the case might go no further. NIH had sanctioned Taub's work and clearly had an interest in protecting its own reputation as keeper of the research flame.

After some thought, Pacheco called Dr. Shirley McGreal of the International Primate Protection League (IPPL), the foremost primate conservation organization in the world. McGreal had already heard of Taub, Pacheco discovered, back in 1977 when the humane officer filed a complaint with the USDA. She ran a critique of his work and found it scientifically unsound. That same year, she "honored" him with IPPL's "Rubbish Research of the Month Award" and had heard nothing of him since.

She could think of two people, she said, and suggested Pacheco start with Geza Teleki.

Geza Teleki, at age 37, knew almost nothing about the world of animal welfare. He was a primatologist and a conservationist, and he hadn't really given much thought to the people who oppose the use of monkeys and apes in laboratories.

The tall, bearded Teleki was Hungarian by birth, but grew up and was educated in the United States. After studying anthropology in college, he dreamed of going to East Africa to dig in the ruins with the world's most famous anthropologist, Louis Leakey. Leakey already had more students than he could handle, so Teleki accepted another rather sudden offer from Tanzania. Instead of dusting off bones and artifacts, he found himself studying chimpanzees near Lake Tanganyika with Leakey's protégée, an animal behaviorist named Jane Goodall. It didn't take him long to decide he preferred living beings to dead.

He spent the next 15 years studying nonhuman primates, accumulating more than 4,000 hours in field and laboratory work. He earned a Ph.D. in anthropology with a specialty in primate behavior, and by 1981 was recognized as a global expert on primates. He divided his time between Africa, where he had undertaken a number of conservation projects, and the District of Columbia, where he was a lecturer at George Washington University.

Teleki had met Pacheco only once, when Pacheco stopped by to ask about a primatology course Teleki was teaching. He had no idea this polite student might be anything other than what he appeared—a bright young man with an interest in primates. Their conversation was brief, a bit formal, and Teleki thought no more about him until he received a telephone call one evening several months later.

"I've been working in a primate lab this summer," Pacheco told him, "and I wonder if you would be interested in coming to see it and giving me some pointers about the animals."

Teleki found nothing unusual in this request. Students often came to him for advice and feedback on their work. Pacheco gave no indication there was anything out of the ordinary at IBR, a lab Teleki had never heard of before now.

He did think it was a little strange that Pacheco asked him to visit IBR at 8 o'clock at night, and stranger still that they didn't immediately get out of the car and go into the building. But he said nothing, even when Pacheco spoke softly into his walkie-talkie. As odd as Pacheco's behavior was, Teleki figured he must have a pretty good reason for wanting to make sure no one was in the lab, so he waited quietly. Finally, he followed the obviously nervous student through the back door.

"My first response to entering the rear door and stepping into the hallway," Teleki later testified in court, "was that there was an incredible stench, a stench that I have not smelled in any laboratory that I've ever been in."

Pacheco asked him to wait in the hall while he made sure no one else was there.

For the next hour, Teleki toured the lab while Pacheco stood silently in the background, speaking only when Teleki questioned him about something. The colony room appalled him. He cautiously approached the cages, averting his eyes so the monkeys wouldn't feel threatened. He saw Billy's grossly swollen arm and wounds on other monkeys that were at least two inches long, "a serious matter on a 14-inch monkey," he later wrote.

He guessed the sizes of the tiny cages satisfied federal requirements (as inadequate as the regulations were), but he also noted the jagged wires sticking up through the floors, reducing the actual living space. The monkeys sat hunched within, trying to avoid both the sharp wires and the piles of excrement caked to the grid floors.

The timing device on the lights, which should have clicked the overhead fluorescent bulbs off in the evening to simulate nighttime, was broken, and consequently the monkeys lived in perpetual light. Teleki knew that this alone was enough to suppress the immune system and cause severe stress.

The barely-working ventilation system pumped stale air from an adjacent room into the colony. This not only deprived the monkeys of fresh air, but made the transmission of air-borne diseases, which could be lethal to both humans and animals, much more likely.

The rest of the lab didn't make Teleki feel any better. When he stepped back outside into the hot August evening, Teleki knew he would never be quite the same.

Not long before his clandestine visit to IBR, Teleki had decided to leave scientific research and focus on conservation. His two years in Tanzania had shown him that wild places like Gombe were disappearing fast. After 10 years of graduate and field studies, he had decided it was no longer possible to be a "scientist without a conscience." He would soon return to Sierra Leone in West Africa, where he had already conducted a population survey of primates, to spend four years setting up a national park.

But his conservation work concerned issues that were somewhat abstract—damage to the environment and entire populations of species. And though he had spent many hours in other primate facilities, he compared his visits to these sanitized places to a trip to communist Hungary: you saw what they wanted you to see, never what you would dislike.

He rarely dealt with individual animals who were suffering and never knew such places as IBR existed. The realization that they did affected him in a way he couldn't have expected. Though he had never heard of PETA and knew next to nothing about the student who brought him to Silver Spring that night, he decided then and there he would do what he could to help Pacheco.

Throughout the ordeal to come, Teleki would repeatedly ask himself one question: How can the mind of a person who tolerates such filth be organized enough to do science?

Pacheco led six startled people on nighttime tours through IBR during late August and early September. Though it hadn't been planned this way, those who submitted affidavits had expertise in animal behavior, veterinary medicine, primatology, psychology, anatomy and zoology—a well-qualified panel by any standards.

There were things they would never see, of course. The way the primates were netted and removed from their cages, for example. According to Pacheco, it was a violent, bloody process. The monkeys clung to the wires of their cages when John Kunz approached until the net was slammed down over them and they were forcibly dragged out, screaming and fighting.

What they did see was enough to convince them that Taub's work should not be supported by public funds, and one of them had spent 15 years doing animal experiments, courtesy of the government's expense account.

Donald Barnes, like Taub, was a research psychologist who never questioned the use of animals to further medical science. Since 1966 he had conducted radiation studies on primates for the U.S. Air Force at Brooks Air Force Base in Texas. (These experiments are depicted in the 1987 film "Project X," starring Matthew Broderick, for which Barnes was a consultant.)

He once severely reprimanded a young airman he caught with his fist drawn back, preparing to punch a feisty baboon in the face.

"But I wouldn't hesitate to ask the same person to put that baboon in a box and shock him a thousand times," he recalls.

In 1981, just before Pacheco went to work at IBR, Barnes was asked to conduct an animal experiment that seemed to him to have no scientific validity. As he pondered what to do, a troubling question kept flitting through his mind. Had any of his experiments really had any value? Eventually, he concluded that they hadn't, and was left with the disturbing realization that he had, with the best of intentions, caused incredible suffering for no good reason.

He refused to do the new study. When Air Force officials ordered him back to the laboratory he knew it would be impossible to return. He was tempted to call in sick, but it occurred to him that he wasn't sick at all. In fact, he never felt better in his life. So he phoned with another message.

"This is Don Barnes and I'm calling in well," he said. Then he resigned.

Barnes saw IBR three days before Teleki, and at that time did not believe all animal experimentation was wrong. His own experience had made him more critical of animal research, but he still felt there was good justification for much of it. Though he had been invited to speak at several animal welfare conferences and had accepted the invitations, he wasn't familiar with the sponsors or their work. The Fund for Animals was one of the organizations and it was Gretchen Wyler of the Fund who recommended Barnes to Pacheco.

Barnes wasn't familiar with Edward Taub or the Institute for Behavioral Research. But he had once worked with a primate researcher named Dr. Joseph Brady. He didn't know that Brady was now the chairman of IBR's board of directors.

Like Teleki, Barnes was appalled by what he saw. In his affidavit he wrote: " . . . this laboratory (IBR) appears to abuse blatantly its resources procured through Federal funding . . . The animals I observed appeared nothing more than reflections of experimenter callousness and abuse."

Late in the evening of August 28, Barnes sat in Newkirk's Takoma Park living room with Pacheco, Newkirk and another expert who had visited IBR earlier that night. Dr. Michael Fox was furious. In his 20 years as a veterinarian, animal researcher and behaviorist, he had never seen anything like Taub's lab.

At that time, Fox, like Newkirk a native of England, had authored more than 120 scientific journal articles and 20 books, including texts on laboratory animal care. He had worked with the National Academy of Sciences to update NIH standards for housing and behavioral needs of experimental animals. At 44, he was tall, slender and soft-spoken.

When Pacheco called and asked him to look at a lab, something Fox was often called on to do, he agreed without giving it much thought.

Unlike Barnes and Teleki, Fox was familiar with animal welfare issues. For the last six years he had served as scientific advisor to the Humane Society of the United States (HSUS), a national animal welfare organization that does not oppose the use of animals for medical research. Fox's own view was somewhat more radical. Though he had himself experimented on animals and did not object to all laboratory use of animals, he no longer believed it was a "necessary evil," but felt that inflicting pain on non-humans diminished human compassion—too large a price to pay for the perceived benefits.

Nevertheless, Fox was caught completely off guard by IBR. "It is my professional opinion that the monkeys I viewed . . . were, without exception, suffering unnecessarily from various causes, including physical and psychological deprivation, a lack of veterinary care and a failure to provide proper, basic environmental needs," he wrote that night.

Three days later, John McArdle left his home in Illinois and flew to Washington, D.C. because his friend Shirley McGreal had called and asked a favor.

"We need you to look at a situation," she said, "but I can't tell you what it is. We'll send you the tickets."

McArdle, a professor at Illinois Wesleyan University, frequently helped McGreal and the International Primate Protection League by providing scientific expertise. He had a Ph.D. in anatomy from the University of Chicago and at age 34 had worked with primates for more than a decade.

The soft-spoken McArdle also believed in animal rights. In graduate school he had been shocked by the callous attitude toward the experimental animals in the anatomy department.

When another student's animals were so poorly cared for they began dying from neglect, McArdle complained to a faculty advisor.

"Well, listen," he was told, "let 'em all die and when he loses his data he'll learn to take care of them."

He detested this attitude, but he wanted to be a scientist and felt he couldn't jeopardize his chances by creating conflict in the department. He kept quiet until he got his degree.

When his doctoral work was complete McArdle took a teaching position and began to introduce animal rights concepts to his students at Wesleyan. He eliminated dissection from his anatomy class and taught a lecture called "The Evolution of Intelligence: We are not alone." It wasn't long before he was in trouble with his supervisors, and by the fall of 1981 McArdle had already received two warnings.

Pacheco and Newkirk were waiting for him at the airport. McArdle had never met them before, never heard of PETA, and he found them as mysterious about the reason for his visit as McGreal. Pacheco was particularly guarded in his conversation, but McArdle found him polite and personable.

After introducing herself, Newkirk left for another appointment and Pacheco drove McArdle downtown to spend some time with Michael Fox, who McArdle knew well, at the Humane Society office on L Street. Still, they didn't discuss why he was in town.

"I think I know why you're here," Fox said, "but I can't say anything."

Pacheco spent the afternoon with McArdle and after dinner, just past sundown, finally took him to IBR. As soon as McArdle saw the colony room, he knew why he was there. He realized that Pacheco and McGreal had been careful not to prejudice him, but even if they had described IBR, he wouldn't have believed it could be as bad as what he saw in front of him. He had maintained his own primate colony for his own research and he knew what went into a sanitary facility, but IBR didn't even measure up to some of the worst places he had seen. He knew monkey importers who bought and sold primates for no other reason than to make money, and their animals were in better shape than IBR's.

What shocked him most, in a strange way, was the contrast between Taub's spotless, expensively furnished office and the grimy laboratory.

When Ronnie Hawkins was in her third year of medical school, one of her instructors asked her if she liked animals. Yes, she answered, her undergraduate degree was in zoology. Good, she was told, then she would like working in the primate lab.

For the next 18 months, Hawkins worked with stump-tailed macaques for the Department of Neurology at the University of Florida Medical School. But liking animals, she found, didn't make the job enjoyable at all. Quite the reverse. One of her early assignments was to tame and nurture four wild-caught infant macaques, who were just months old. After they learned to trust her and depend on her as a surrogate mother, after she taught them several simple tasks, she was to participate in a procedure she describes as "sucking out part of their brains and seeing what they couldn't do anymore." She participated because, like McArdle, she wanted to be a scientist, and scientists weren't supposed to become attached to their subjects.

Nevertheless, she did try to make the primates' lives as comfortable as possible. She often went into the lab on weekends and took the macaques out of their cages to stretch their cramped limbs. One Saturday afternoon, a senior researcher unexpectedly found her exercising a monkey outdoors and reprimanded her. He seemed threatened by her acknowledgment that his experimental subjects were living beings, and she wondered if he was suppressing something similar in himself. His defensive attitude was common among her supervisors. She wasn't even allowed to give the animals names; they were only to be identified by their numbers.

Hawkins had never heard of PETA, but she didn't hesitate when a friend who happened to know Newkirk asked her to visit a primate lab. She was going to be in Washington for a medical conference anyway.

Certainly it was the dirtiest facility she'd ever been in and her affidavit detailed what she saw late at night on September 4. But the obvious lack of concern for the animals, evident in their open wounds and poor psychological health, didn't surprise her much. It reflected an attitude she'd seen many times.

We say we experiment on animals to help humans, she thought after leaving IBR, and we use monkeys because they're so like people. But if they are so like us, why do we leave them out of our moral code?

Chapter Four

The Seizure

"*The animal handling devices were filthy and crudely constructed. Nets were filthy and bloodstained, and the pillory chairs were of cruel design, and appeared to be gerry-built beyond the limits of safety. The equipment is archaic. . .*"
—*Donald Barnes, former research psychologist, from his affidavit after visiting IBR, August 25, 1981*

By the end of August, Newkirk and Pacheco were beginning to show the strain of their efforts. In addition to the secret nighttime tours, which were nerve-racking for both, they were preparing to present their evidence to the Maryland state's attorney's office and to the Montgomery County police. PETA's legal counsel, Tom Heeney, had arranged for a meeting at the end of the month.

To complicate matters, they were running out of money. Long distance phone bills, film, film processing and legal fees had depleted Newkirk's savings, and even though Cleveland Amory's Fund for Animals had given them money for a new camera and walkie-talkies, they were facing the expense of air fares for the scientists who had agreed to come from out of state. In addition to putting together an airtight case, Newkirk and Pacheco had to raise some cash.

Neither had any experience at this and PETA, though incorporated as a non-profit organization, was little more than a group of a dozen or so volunteers. So they began asking people they knew to help and eventually small donations came dribbling in. Meeting the costs of the case was to be a continuing problem.

On a warm evening near the end of August in Rockville, Md., Pacheco, Newkirk and Tom Heeney spread their stacks of evidence on the table in front of Joseph Fitzpatrick, the assistant state's attorney, and two police officers.

One of the officers was Sergeant Richard Swain, a lean, good-looking investigative supervisor for Silver Spring. He had never met Newkirk or Pacheco, and wasn't aware that any animal protection organizations existed aside from the county animal control department. A few days earlier he'd received a call from Fitzpatrick, who asked to meet with him about the possibility of a warrant to enter a research facility.

In his ten years with the Montgomery County police department, Swain had never handled an animal cruelty case. Narcotics, homicide and sex—sudden death, murders, rapes and aggravated assaults—were his beat. But Fitzpatrick had asked, so Swain agreed to the meeting. He brought along the police detective he planned to assign to the case once they had looked at the evidence.

Pacheco liked Swain immediately. That night, of course, neither men had any idea their lives would be intertwined for the next year. Swain was businesslike and straightforward. He looked over the photographs and asked for the facts of the case.

After seven years in homicide little shocked Swain anymore, but he was disgusted enough by what he saw in the pictures to proceed with the case. The first step was to get a court-ordered search and seizure warrant. They would talk again soon about what else was needed.

"I probably should have told you before we went into the meeting," Swain's hand-picked detective said as they left the room, "but I'm going to be leaving in two weeks to take a job in the private sector."

Swain, who had never even read the state anti-cruelty statutes, had inherited the Silver Spring Monkeys case.

For Pacheco and Newkirk, already exhausted, there would be little sleep for the next week and a half. For four anxious months they had struggled with the problem of how best to help the monkeys. Newkirk had delegated as many of her responsibilities at the D.C. pound to other people as she could and spent every penny she had to get to this point. Pacheco had chain-smoked his way through long, tense nights and risked discovery by IBR's staff no less than dozens of times. He had missed fall registration for his college classes. They had spent endless hours sorting, labeling and copying evidence. But now was no time to slow down.

Swain soon made it clear that if the police were going to seize the primates, Newkirk and Pacheco were going to have to be responsible for them. Somehow, within a few days, they had to arrange transportation for the monkeys, find a place for them to go, build cages, hire veterinarians, and find people to help care for them. And they had to pay for it all.

Pacheco found help at Michael Fox's employer, the Humane Society of the United States, as well as at the Fund for Animals, the California-based Animal Protection Institute (API), which eventually hired Don Barnes as a consultant, the Animal Welfare Institute and several other groups. It was almost unheard of in 1981 for animal welfare organizations to work cooperatively, but it was clear to all involved that there had never been a case like this one.

Where to put the monkeys was as big a problem as how to pay to get them there. Since they would need to adapt a room, it would have to be a house owned by someone who wouldn't mind a remodeling job. They were also determined to provide round the clock care for the monkeys—a significant invasion of privacy for even the most sympathetic PETA supporter. On the spur of the moment, Lori Lehner, a cheerful 23-year-old adoption specialist at the Montgomery County Humane Society offered her tiny suburban Rockville home. Within hours, before Lehner could reconsider, Newkirk and Pacheco were rearranging her furniture and tossing out boxes. Bill Keneally, a Washington Humane Society volunteer and carpenter installed a sump pump, flooring that could be sterilized, and turned the basement into a temporary sanctuary. (Lehner and Keneally, who met for the first time that day in her basement, later married.)

From that point on, PETA's few volunteers would play an increasingly important role. Newkirk and Pacheco had turned to others to help finance the rescue; now they enlisted the help of a dozen trusted PETA members, including Pam Chapman, Jo Shoesmith, Bob and Loretta Hirsh, Virginia Bourquardez, Karen Anderson, Walt Rave, Olive Nash, Sheryl Thomas and Pacheco's brother Jimmy.

Another volunteer, Nat Miller, was skilled enough to build roomy cages for the monkeys, but the cost of the materials—$2,200—was staggering for PETA. Newkirk begged the Animal Protection Institute to come through with a check to cover this expense. Miller built perches and climbing ramps into these spacious new homes, and the volunteers found sturdy children's toys for the monkeys to manipulate and attached infant playboards with unbreakable mirrors and press-button horns to the sides of the cages.

When the caging was finally ready and transported to Lehner's house, an unexpected problem arose. Pacheco and Newkirk wanted large enclosures, at least compared to IBR's narrow wire cells, but had neglected to measure the entry way to the basement. Part of the door-frame would have to be cut away and the cinder blocks next to it moved to get the new cages through.

PETA also purchased surgical gowns and masks to prevent the possibility of disease transmission between the monkeys and their human caretakers, and placed a tub of sterile solution at the entrance of the room for workers to slosh through on their way in and out. Though these procedures are standard at most primate facilities, they were not followed at IBR.

On Tuesday evening, September 8, Pacheco, Newkirk, Jean Goldenberg (the humane officer who had complained about IBR in 1977), and Tom Heeney, met with Sergeant Swain and Joe Fitzpatrick at police headquarters on Shady Grove Road in Rockville. Swain was ready to put together a team of officers to execute a warrant as soon as it was authorized by the court.

If the last week had brought little sleep for Newkirk and Pacheco, the next 72 hours were to bring none. They couldn't risk any slip-ups. Though their primary focus was getting 17 monkeys out of the filth of IBR, they had begun to realize this case had other ramifications. The American government, through NIH, parcelled out $3.4 billion to animal experimenters every year. The scientists who comprised this taxpayer-funded club generally considered their methods beyond question. While there were critics of trivial and repetitive animal experiments, these "nutty animal people" were at most an annoyance. Certainly the police had never taken their animal subjects away. As long as experimenters claimed they "sacrificed" animals only to help people, who could seriously question their work?

But Pacheco and Newkirk knew this exclusive grant-dependant world would never again be quite as invulnerable once Taub's research subjects were seized. They had stumbled on IBR quite by accident; how many other facilities held similar secrets? IBR would be the first laboratory ever raided by police. If all went as planned, Taub would be the first animal experimenter ever charged with cruelty. But he wouldn't be the last held accountable for what he did to the animals in his care.

Of course, if nobody ever heard about the raid, what good would it do? If the public was to know, the media had to know, too. Pacheco and Newkirk were inexperienced with the press and too busy to deal with it, so when the Fund for Animals offered to help, Pacheco and Newkirk agreed and thought no more about it.

This is a different sort of case for me, Swain thought several times during the days before the raid. For one thing, Pacheco and Newkirk were the first animal rights activists he had ever met, and even if their ideas appeared strange to him, he still liked the earnest couple. Pacheco was quiet and deferential, and clearly committed to his beliefs. He impressed Swain as a very thoughtful and intelligent young man who nevertheless could seem quite naive. Newkirk, on the other hand, was more streetwise, he thought, and less willing to trust the legal process. Her commitment to animal rights matched Pacheco's and she was always ready to talk about it. When Swain showed up at a meeting with a bag of hamburgers, Newkirk sent him a vegetarian cookbook the following day. He had already seen her extraordinary energy in pursuing the case. Whatever he asked her to do she did, no questions asked.

The other major difference was that the alleged violations were misdemeanors, not the felony crimes he was used to dealing with. But then animals are "property" according to the law, not living beings. Even so, he treated it like any other case. And once the warrant was executed he would simply hand the evidence over to the assistant state's attorney and his work would be done. Or so he thought.

On Thursday, September 10, Swain left headquarters and drove south to Seven Locks District Police Station to meet with Judge John McAuliffe. He was ready to raid the lab the next morning. All he needed was the court's permission. After looking over the affidavit, McAuliffe picked up his pen and signed the warrant.

While Swain was at the Seven Locks station, Pacheco was giving a final secret tour of IBR to Robert Weitzman, a local veterinarian who had treated Newkirk's dogs and cats for many years, and who had assisted as an expert witness in Newkirk's Montgomery County prosecutions of animal abusers. Newkirk had shown him some of the photos Pacheco had taken, and he agreed without hesitation to see the lab.

Pacheco was particularly cautious that evening. Taub had returned from vacation the day before and had been in the lab that very morning. He didn't want to raise any suspicions when they were so close to getting the primates out.

Pacheco's eyes were underlined with dark smudges. He had not slept for more than 48 hours and somehow he had to get through this day. It had been a long haul, but finally, on Friday morning, September 11, the police were about to seize the monkeys from IBR. He was to lead the officers through the facility and show them the evidence they needed for the state's case against Taub.

He dressed neatly—for press interviews, in case there were any. Newkirk helped him carefully knot a wide tie at his throat. He combed his dark hair away from his face. His mind raced. Would Taub be there? How would the monkeys react to the new cages and the strange truck ride? Had he forgotten to do anything? He was jittery, on edge; confrontations were not easy for the 22-year-old.

Newkirk, who was known for her skill at managing complex situations, was less outwardly nervous. For weeks she had coped with the awful knowledge of the monkeys' suffering by setting her emotions aside and tackling the problem. On that Friday morning her defenses were still firmly in place. This was the last phase of a coordinated plan. Her guard wouldn't come down until afterward, when the primates were safely in Lehner's basement.

For Swain, it was a straightforward search and seizure. He'd executed hundreds and expected nothing out of the ordinary. True, the evidence was alive, but that could be handled easily enough. Earlier that morning he'd called Geza Teleki. Could he meet the police at IBR at 10:00 a.m. to supervise the removal and transport of the monkeys? Teleki agreed.

All together Swain put 20 people on the warrant team including Pacheco, Newkirk, Goldenberg, three police officers, two animal control officers and three detectives. One person he hadn't counted on needing was Nancy Moses, the Montgomery County police media relations officer. But then he hadn't counted on seeing Roger Caras from ABC network news and a reporter from the *Washington Post*, either. He understood why PETA wanted the press tipped off; a little public pressure wouldn't hurt their case. But it made Swain's work more difficult. He, too, would be under scrutiny now. Besides, it was technically illegal to tell anyone about a pending search warrant. He radioed HQ for Moses, who arrived within a few minutes.

The officers closed off the property with bright yellow police ribbon and Pacheco led the warrant team into IBR.

"I've served a lot of search warrants," Swain later recalled, "and I've been in a lot of crummy scenes, because I'd spent some time in narcotics, but that place was so incredibly dirty and the conditions were so foul that for the first time I felt a real health risk just being in the building."

When he saw the eight inches of feces and mold layered in the stopped-up utility sink in the tiny janitor's closet off the colony room, he sent his team outside the building and ordered face masks and plastic gloves for everyone. He didn't know what diseases they might be exposed to and he wasn't taking any chances.

He was glad he'd taken this precaution when he found the bodies of several monkeys floating in a formaldehyde-filled trash can. A board had been placed across the top and weighted down with greasy motor parts to keep the dead animals submerged.

As day stretched into night, the warrant team transferred the monkeys safely to the truck, photographed the conditions listed in the affidavits and gathered evidence. Taub showed up 20 minutes after the police cordoned off the property and was met by uniformed officers and TV cameras. He was outraged that his lab had been invaded by a swarm of people without his permission.

"I'm surprised, distressed and shocked by this," he told the *Washington Post* reporter. "There is no pain in these experiments."

He tried to disrupt a television interview with Teleki, who described IBR as "some kind of hell" to reporters. It was Teleki's first meeting with Taub, and he was struck by the disparity between Taub's neatly pressed suit and the filth inside his laboratory.

Within hours, IBR released its own press statement again claiming the monkeys felt no pain.

For Pacheco, the media interviews were the most difficult part of the day. He was worn out from lack of sleep and felt unable to organize his thoughts properly. He worried he might not be able to communicate how bad it had been, how much the monkeys had endured physically and psychologically.

When it was over and the macaques were at last sleeping on soft mats in clean cages in a darkened room, the volunteers headed out the door to celebrate. But they went without Pacheco and Newkirk. Pacheco had finally collapsed. He has no memory of that night. Newkirk went home, dragged herself upstairs to her room and let her defenses down. They had done it. She curled up on her bed and cried uncontrollably.

That evening, a shocked nation watched the ABC coverage of police officers removing the Silver Spring Monkeys from IBR. They heard Pacheco describe the self-mutilation. They saw the faces of the primates. For thousands of people, it was a turning point in their lives. Until now, most people had willingly looked the other way, not wanting to know exactly what happened to the 70 million rats, rabbits, dogs, mice, cats, pigs, birds, primates and other species in laboratories. They believed experimenters would do only what was necessary to help humans and to cause a minimum of suffering to the animals used. The Silver Spring Monkeys case shattered this trust. Within days they would rally support for PETA and within months grassroots animal rights organizations would spring up in cities around the country.

For animal researchers and NIH, the embarrassment of the front-page *Washington Post* article was acute. There were photos of Pacheco, Teleki and their colleague, Edward Taub.

And there was the photo of Domitian, stretched out and strapped in the restraint chair, his ankles and wrists taped to the frame.

Chapter Five

Losing Control

"Until 1981, it didn't occur to most folks that, over and above the research that was being done on them, animals—from mice to dogs to chimps—might be abused in scientific laboratories. Then came Alex Pacheco . . . "
—*The* Philadelphia Inquirer, *October 2, 1989*

By Monday morning media reports of the first-ever raid on an animal laboratory had exploded worldwide. In interview after interview an outraged Taub proclaimed his innocence and accused Pacheco of deceiving him with cloak and dagger tactics. Pacheco had no experience, Taub asserted, he was not qualified to judge the conditions at IBR.

"He thought I was qualified enough to do original research for him," Pacheco responded.

Taub's right to freedom as a scientist became his main defense. Rather than trying to explain the oozing wounds, missing fingers and filthy cages, Taub portrayed himself as the victim and compared himself to scientists burned at the stake during the middle ages. He claimed that his work shouldn't be questioned by lay people who knew nothing about science.

The public didn't buy it. They sent dozens of outraged letters to the editor, condemning Taub and calling for his prosecution.

In the coming weeks, letters from all over the world urging immediate action poured into the police department and the state's attorney's office. There was so much mail on some days the post office delivered it in bags.

Swain got his first inkling the Silver Spring Monkeys case might not wrap up as neatly as he had hoped when he returned to police headquarters on Monday morning after the raid. His desk was covered with phone messages from animal welfare groups, humane societies, scientific organizations, and outraged NIH officials.

Swain had some sympathy for NIH. The agency could be publicly embarrassed if they made a statement they would later have to recant. Besides, one of the detectives in his department had a brother who worked at NIH's Office for the Protection of Research Risks (OPRR) and Swain didn't mind giving him a piece of advice.

"Before you make any public statements," Swain cautioned him, "or before you take an official position, you ought to review the evidence."

A meeting was arranged for the next week, on September 19. On that Saturday morning, Swain and Joe Fitzpatrick passed the police photos around the table. OPRR's assistant director, William Dommel and two of his staff members looked at each one, but made no comment. It was clear to Swain they knew they had a real problem. NIH funded this lab and didn't even know what was going on there. How were they going to explain that to the press?

NIH's first response, thanks largely to Swain's advice, was cautious. "It was surprising," Dommel told the *Washington Post*. "We had received no complaint as to the conditions of this facility from any source." Dommel was either unaware of Goldenberg's report four years earlier, or chose not to cite it.

On September 14, the Monday after the raid, Dr. William Raub, NIH's Associate Director for Extramural Research and Training, instructed OPRR director Charles McCarthy to conduct an investigation of IBR. Raub, a 15-year veteran at NIH, couldn't have known that he would be dealing with the same case throughout the next decade.

McCarthy passed the responsibility to Dommel, who organized a committee including three OPRR staffers, an NIH attorney, an NIH auditor, the acting deputy director of NIH's

Neurological Disorders Program, the director of NIH's Laboratory Animal Sciences Program, and the director of East Carolina University's Animal Resources Center. Dommel chaired the committee.

The NIH Committee to Investigate Alleged Animal Care Violations at the Institute for Behavioral Research would take nearly three weeks to conduct its inquiry and make its recommendations. Though committee members visited IBR, questioned Taub, and reviewed the police evidence, they did not request a meeting with the state's chief witness, Alex Pacheco.

Swain also arranged a meeting with PETA and representatives of the other organizations involved. The constant calls from reporters and county residents convinced police officials they had better handle this situation right or they would look incompetent. Swain had already figured out he was going to be spending a lot of time on the case—and it was going to cost a lot of money. He didn't think it was fair for the state to pick up the tab on misdemeanor charges.

"We will control the investigation and prosecution," he told the group. "We will have the final say-so in every step in the case. But if you want us to do this, you have to pay for it. We'll tell you what we need and how much it's going to cost, but you all are going to have to get it for us."

It was the first and only time in Swain's career as an investigator that the state didn't pay for its own prosecution. But as Swain had already learned, this case just couldn't be made to fit the usual pattern.

The mood in Lehner's basement was jubilant in those first days after the primates were seized. Within 24 hours the monkeys were responding to their new surroundings and the people who cared for them began to notice differences in their personalities. Adidas and Sisyphus were playful within the confines of their new homes, and since they hadn't been deafferented, they could feel the touch of their fingertips through the wire mesh separating them. Sarah showed her preference for men and screeched and complained at the women who fed her and cleaned her cage.

Some of the animals were heartbreaking, in spite of the improvement in their circumstances. Paul's grey wrinkled face reminded Newkirk of old dogs she saw at the D.C. pound, whose troubled pasts showed in their sad faces. Billy, who could use neither of his arms, remained gentle and cheerful, in spite of his pathetic appearance.

The monkeys enjoyed fresh fruit and were mesmerized by the daytime soap operas on the TV installed for them. They were curious about the new humans in their lives, too. One afternoon Sisyphus looked on with fascination as Lehner scrubbed his cage. When she set down the sponge for a moment, he grabbed it and took over the job, mimicking her movements.

Teleki was a frequent visitor to the Rockville house. He offered advice on diet and appropriate cleaning techniques, and arranged for an independent exam by two veterinarians. On September 17, Dr. Phillip Robinson flew in from the San Diego Zoo, and Dr. Janis Ott came from the Brookville Zoo in Illinois.

One by one the primates were removed from their cages and carefully examined. Nero, Domitian, Paul and Billy were in the worst shape. Among them they had lost 23 fingers. Domitian had two pus-filled punctures on his arm. Another large self-inflicted wound would need skin grafting to heal properly.

Billy's right arm was fractured, as Pacheco had suspected, and was consequently shortened. But both arms were distorted from numerous injuries that hadn't healed properly. The bones of his right wrist moved abnormally, and had probably been dislocated or broken. One of his canine teeth was fractured and infected and needed pulling; the monkeys had never had dental care.

The tips of all five digits on Nero's left hand were missing and the bone stumps were infected. Both Nero and Paul had massive scars running the length of their deafferented arms, and both appeared to have fractured left wrists. They would need radiographs and immediate treatment.

It was on this day, while Ott and Robinson meticulously examined each of the damaged monkeys, that things began to go wrong. Pacheco and Newkirk were about to find out that prosecuting this animal abuse case, and consequently challenging the powerful world of government-funded animal research, was not going to be as straightforward as they had hoped.

While Dr. Robinson was soaking the dried feces off Hard Times's tail, Harvey Steinburg, one of IBR's attorneys, was arguing in court for the return of the monkeys to IBR. When Judge David Cahoon questioned IBR's chief investigator, Taub stated under oath that he was responsible for IBR and its conditions. He admitted that the animals hadn't been seen by a veterinarian in two years. He also said he feared that some of his monkeys might die in the care of people unfamiliar with his work.

To Pacheco, who had never even been inside a courtroom before, the situation seemed clear. He was certain the judge would review the affidavits and deny Taub's request. Then the state would formally file charges. He and Newkirk sat in a room down the hall with Michael Fox and Geza Teleki, who were waiting to testify.

But neither Fox nor Teleki were called to the witness stand. Joe Fitzpatrick had not been able to convince the judge to hear their testimonies. Only Rick Swain had been allowed to describe what he found.

Fitzpatrick, as assistant state's attorney, normally handled hundreds of cases a week in district court, none of which lasted more than an hour. It became obvious that afternoon that prosecuting Taub was going to take a lot of preparation, and Fitzpatrick didn't have time for that.

The next day, Judge Cahoon ordered all the monkeys returned to IBR.

Pacheco and Newkirk were devastated. It was now exactly a week since the monkeys were rescued. They were disappointed that despite Swain's assurances, no charges had yet been filed, but *nothing* could have prepared them for the blow Judge Cahoon delivered that Friday afternoon.

What they didn't know was that while they were in court, while Ott and Robinson worked in Lehner's basement, a USDA veterinarian was inspecting IBR. Just six days after the warrant team had photographed the inadequate ventilation, lighting, drainage, and waste disposal systems, the USDA inspector approved these very systems. And even though there were no animals in the facility, he okayed the "veterinary care," watering, feeding and separation of the primates.

Judge Cahoon ordered the return of the primates on the strength of this report.

It was incomprehensible to Pacheco that on the same day the monkeys' wounds were being catalogued and treated, the USDA could approve the facility responsible for their condition. One week was just not enough time to improve IBR that much.

But then Dr. Arthur Perry, the USDA veterinarian, had also inspected—and approved—IBR in April and again in July, while

Pacheco was documenting the foul conditions in the lab. On April 24, the record would show, Perry noted one deficiency—some loose floor tiles in the colony room. He recommended replacement within 45 days. Dr. Perry returned on July 13, halfway through Pacheco's four months at IBR. "Deficiencies Corrected," he wrote on the inspection form. "No deficiencies noted."

Four days after the monkeys were seized, Dr. Perry made his third inspection of IBR that year. This time he found "minor deficiencies." He recommended a thorough cleaning of the janitor's closet, painting the cracked walls, and providing food containers for the monkey chow.

Two days later, on September 17, Perry deemed IBR adequate and turned in his report.

Judge Cahoon's order was followed by a gloomy weekend at Lehner's house. Pacheco felt control of the primates slipping away, even though Fitzpatrick had promised to try to persuade the judge to hear all the testimony. It was normal, Swain explained, standard procedure for evidence to be returned to the owner until the trial; if the judge couldn't be persuaded to change his mind they had no choice but to comply with his ruling. But Pacheco and Newkirk couldn't accept the risk Judge Cahoon was taking with the monkeys' lives. It could be months before the case came to trial—if charges were ever filed.

For his part, Judge Cahoon had little reason to suspect the validity of the USDA report, and Taub's credentials were impressive. Finding himself at the center of a controversy that had no precedent, the judge did what many would have done at that time: he deferred to the scientist. After all, the world of science was supposed to be inexplicable to the average person.

Of course, Teleki, Fox, Barnes, Hawkins and McArdle were also scientists, but they weren't funded by the government. Pacheco and Newkirk suspected NIH was applying some behind-the-scenes pressure, probably arguing that a thorough internal investigation should preclude prosecution.

Pacheco and Newkirk planned to bring pressure, too, by rallying support from an already outraged public. On Sunday morning PETA ran a two column by five inch ad in the *Washington Post* asking for donations to help with expenses of the case. In the ad was a photo of a monkey held in a crouching position on the floor, one of his arms bound to his body with layers of gauze wrap. His head was tilted to one side, his mouth grimacing, his brows drawn together in a hauntingly human expression of agony.

Taub responded angrily to the ad, threatening to file suit against PETA. He claimed the photo was stolen from IBR. "I have become a representative of free inquiry and scientific research, against the forces of ignorance," he told a Maryland paper, the *Montgomery Journal.*

The same day the ad ran, PETA volunteers went silently about their work at Lehner's house, chopping fruit, disinfecting cages, grooming the monkeys. Pacheco, disillusioned and depressed, had left town that morning and planned to be away for the weekend.

Nobody wanted to send the monkeys back to Taub's lab, but how far were they willing to go to keep the animals? At least a few of the more than two dozen people who passed through Lehner's house that week were willing to put their own freedom on the line. Sometime during the inky black night of September 21, the monkeys were stealthily removed.

Chapter Six

Arrest Warrants

"There were those in the movement who envisioned an Entebbe-style raid to free the monkeys. They would pattern their actions after those of the hooded figures who descend on labs and kennels in Europe to sweep the animals to safety."
—*The* Washington Post, *October 11, 1981*

In Great Britain, a secret group known as the Animal Liberation Front had for years raided laboratories where inhumane experiments were conducted and slipped into the silent night with the rabbits or rats or dogs or other animals. In 1981, most people on this side of the Atlantic had never heard of the British ALF and there was nothing comparable to it in the United States—until the Silver Spring Monkeys disappeared from Rockville. Judge Cahoon's order spurred the formation of the American Animal Liberation Front, and the removal of the monkeys was their first act.

Direct action of this sort was unheard of in America. The usual method of protest for animal protection organizations consisted of telephone and letter writing campaigns targeting the elected officials who controlled funding for the National Institutes of Health. The few individuals who identified themselves as animal rights suppporters in 1981 might have demonstrated, as Pacheco or Newkirk had, against the use of animals for experimentation, but no one had ever kidnaped the victims to save them.

During the next decade, the American Animal Liberation Front broke into more than 100 laboratories and transported thousands of animals to safety by way of a modern "underground railway." Though the ALF injured neither human nor animal during their raids, they did destroy equipment used for experimental procedures and spray-painted slogans on laboratory walls. The FBI eventually listed the ALF as a "terrorist" group and pursued the shadowy figures with an increasing intensity.

Pacheco returned to town on Tuesday to find both the monkeys and their cages missing from the basement sanctuary. He didn't know who was responsible but knew it must have been one of the volunteers who had fed them, bathed their wounds and had come to know them as he had. He didn't doubt the monkeys were better off wherever they were than back at IBR.

That same day, Swain and Fitzpatrick, unaware that the monkeys were gone, were in court trying to convince Judge Cahoon to review the veterinary reports. When Newkirk and Pacheco didn't show up, Swain called Lehner's house. When he got no answer, he drove the short distance to the Rockville home. The house was silent and empty, the windows covered, the monkeys gone.

Swain was furious. The monkeys may have been legally in Newkirk's and Goldenberg's custody, but he was ultimately responsible for them.

"If you want to work with us," he told Pacheco when he caught up with him, "part of that agreement is you've got to play by our rules. If you're not willing to play by our rules, then don't expect us to work with you."

When Swain cooled off, he saw that Pacheco couldn't have been involved, and frankly, he didn't want the monkeys returned to IBR any more than PETA did. He understood why it happened, but that didn't change his strong conviction that enforcement of the law should never be taken out of the hands of the authorities. Besides that, it made his job uncomfortable for a while. He was in charge and it didn't take long for suspicions about his part in the kidnaping to surface. His character reference came from an unlikely source. Jimmy Miller, one of Taub's attorneys, a down-to-earth Rockville criminal lawyer, persuaded the judge that Swain couldn't have been involved.

On Wednesday afternoon Taub turned the tables by calling a press conference at IBR. Dressed in a white lab coat with his name stitched above the right breast pocket, Taub asked for the public's help in locating the monkeys. His second attorney, Edgar Brenner, from the high-profile Washington firm Arnold & Porter, stood to Taub's left.

"As of this time," Taub stated, "We have received no word as to the whereabouts of the monkeys, and we are greatly concerned for their safety." He then offered a $450 reward for the return of the primates he had earlier valued at $100,000.

Pacheco, dressed in a suit and tie, also showed up at the news conference. "I'm glad that I don't know who took them," he told reporters, "but I'm *damned* glad they're gone."

Exactly what happened to the monkeys remains a mystery. If Newkirk or Goldenberg knew anything, they weren't saying. Lehner had heeded a suggestion to spend the night away from her home on the date of the disappearance. When she returned home on Wednesday evening she was arrested and taken to Montgomery County's detention center.

The next 24 hours were traumatic for Lehner. Though she was glad to do all she could to help the monkeys, there was no denying that the last two weeks had been difficult. Her home was filled with people, many of whom she didn't know, at all hours of the day and night. Her neighbors already disapproved of her eight dogs and some of them didn't appreciate the strange cars and constant activity at Lehner's house.

Suddenly she was handcuffed, carted to jail and strip-searched. She spent the night in a cell without ever being told what she was charged with. By the time she got an attorney and was released, Lehner's anger matched Swain's. If he hoped to intimidate her into confessing something, he had miscalculated. She knew nothing about the disappearance, and even if she did, she probably wouldn't have shared it with the police after the way they treated her. (Lehner was later part of a successful class action suit against the police department's strip-search and detainment practices.)

Warrants had also been issued for Newkirk and Goldenberg, but they were both staying in the District of Columbia at the time, didn't know about the warrants and weren't apprehended. They turned themselves in the next day. It was rather ironic, Newkirk thought, as the booking officer fingerprinted her, that she was standing there instead of Taub.

All three women were released on their own recognizance that afternoon. No charges were ever filed and the authorities were no closer to finding the monkeys than they had been on Tuesday. It would have been completely pointless had Newkirk not met Edward Genn, an attorney recommended by a friend who worked in District Court. Tom Heeney, the lawyer who helped PETA put their evidence together, had angrily backed out of the case when he heard the monkeys had vanished, leaving Newkirk facing an arrest warrant and suddenly in need of a new attorney.

Fortunately, Newkirk didn't need Genn to defend her against a theft charge, but she would call on him again sooner than she expected.

From Geza Teleki's point of view, the disappearance of the monkeys jeopardized the credibility of those involved and he was pretty angry about it. It seemed to be a no-win situation. If the monkeys were found, the wrong people—the people who wanted the monkeys out of the lab—would be prosecuted, and the primates would be sent back to IBR for good. And if the monkeys didn't return, Taub would never stand trial. He could simply buy more primates and continue his experiments.

Thinking there must be *some* way to reach a solution, Teleki offered to mediate. What would satisfy Swain and Fitzpatrick as well as Pacheco, Newkirk and the shadowy rescuers?

Two days of hushed negotiations followed and the details of a plan proposed by Teleki were gradually agreed to by both sides. The monkeys would return to Rockville, with no questions asked about where they had gone or who took them. In exchange, charges against Taub and his assistant John Kunz would be formally filed, and a more experienced prosecutor, with more time to prepare, would be assigned to the case. Where the monkeys would live pending trial was still to be decided, and a new hearing would be scheduled.

On Saturday, September 26, five days after they were mysteriously spirited away from Lehner's house, the Silver Spring Monkeys reappeared. They were greeted by Newkirk, Pacheco, some of the PETA volunteers, the armed police officers who would guard them 24 hours a day and the press. As the cameras clicked, the cages were removed from the van one by one and carried back to the basement.

Sunday readers of the *Washington Post* opened their papers the next day to a photo of Sisyphus, standing erect in his large mesh cage, and the headline, "After Delicate Negotiations, the 17 Missing Monkeys Are Back." By now there were few people in the Washington area who hadn't heard of the primates.

Later that morning, Newkirk stopped at a market near Lehner's house to stock up on the primates' favorite treats—pounds of bananas, apples, grapes and Donald Duck orange juice.

"The Silver Spring Monkeys are back," she explained to the clerk, who seemed puzzled by the unlikely purchase.

"Hey!" the clerk shouted to the other employees at the back of the store, "The Silver Spring Monkeys are back!"

Within 24 hours of the monkeys' return, arrest warrants were issued for Edward Taub and John Kunz. The charges were inflicting unnecessary suffering and failure to provide adequate food, water, space, protection from weather and veterinary care for each of the 17 monkeys. Each charge carried a maximum penalty of $1,000 fine, 90 days in jail, or both. Because she was not an employee of the lab, and not legally responsible for the animals, Georgette Yakalis was not charged.

On Monday Taub and Kunz surrendered to Montgomery County police. Swain remembers talking with Taub in the elevator at police headquarters that morning as they headed upstairs to the booking office.

"I am a scientist," Taub said. "Nobody but other scientists has a right to review and decide whether my work is good, just, appropriate or legal."

Taub really believed he was above the law, Swain thought. Maybe he'd change his mind on October 27, when the trial would begin.

The first animal experimenter ever charged with cruelty triggered a barrage of new phone calls to police, the state's attorney's office and PETA. *Life* magazine, *Science*, the *London Times*, the *Montreal Globe*, and dozens of newspapers and wire services wanted interviews with Swain and Pacheco. Taub's arrest opened a Pandora's box of possibilities. Is IBR typical of research laboratories? the reporters asked. How can we find out what's really happening inside these places?

The news articles pushed PETA to the forefront of the animal protection movement, and Pacheco and the monkeys stood out as the most visible proof that the priesthood of animal experimentation was due for reformation. Small donations began flowing in to PETA's Washington post office box from people who were shocked by the photos and stories of the Silver Spring Monkeys.

This new wave of support confirmed Pacheco's and Newkirk's belief that many people were ready for animal rights, and they made time to respond personally to each letter. This wasn't easy in the week following the monkeys' return. Though the primates were safely in the basement for the moment there was no guarantee how long they would be allowed to stay. A new hearing was scheduled for Friday, October 2.

Three days before this, Fitzpatrick, who was still handling the case until another prosecutor was appointed, asked Geza Teleki, Michael Fox, and Swain to reinspect IBR. They met at IBR at 8 o'clock in the evening, as scheduled, and were greeted by Taub, who asked them to wait a moment in the front office. Nearly an hour passed before Taub led them to the colony room.

As far as Teleki and Fox could see, no real changes had been made. The light-timer had been fixed, the walls and rusted cages had been touched up with paint and the rodent excrement was cleaned off the floor. But feces were still splattered on the ceiling, the ventilation system hadn't been improved, and some of the cage doors couldn't be opened; when Teleki ran his hand over the interiors of several cages, which had been ineffectively cleaned, he found matted hair, bits of old bandage and mouse feces. Fox scraped encrusted urine off the doors and wire walls of each cage he inspected.

"The 17 macaques now in State custody should under no circumstances whatsoever be returned to substandard conditions at the Institute for Behavioral Research," Teleki concluded in his detailed six-page affidavit.

Fox wrote, "In their present holding facility [Lehner's basement], the monkeys are calm, healthier than when first seen in the laboratory prior to seizure, less defensively aggressive and more sociable."

Taub's attorneys abruptly ended the inspection before Fox and Teleki could see the rest of the laboratory.

In the end, the second inspection, the second set of affidavits, and Fitzpatrick's arguments did no good. On October 2, Judge Cahoon again ordered the monkeys back to IBR. Rick Swain was appointed guardian and James Stunkard, a veterinarian who had briefly consulted with IBR years earlier, was to ensure the cleanliness of the lab and the good health of the macaques. The judge instructed IBR to correct the deficiencies Fox and Teleki observed a few days earlier. For the moment, Taub was to conduct no further experiments on the animals.

Cahoon's detailed orders did nothing to alleviate Pacheco's fears. For the second time in as many weeks, he was appalled by the court's apparent deference to Taub simply because he was a scientist, as though his Ph.D. exempted him from the law. He felt a twinge of guilt for playing a part in bringing the monkeys back to Maryland. Their last hope was an appeal, which Fitzpatrick filed that afternoon. His request for a stay had already been denied.

Despite the feeling of impending doom among the humans at Lehner's house on Saturday afternoon, Billy still wanted to be groomed, Adidas wanted to watch TV, and all the monkeys needed to be fed. Teleki had stopped by to review the detailed charts that were being kept on each animal. The tiny house was quiet except for the chattering of the primates and the responses of the volunteers who looked after them. A warm breeze blew through the open windows.

Newkirk was the first to hear the van pull up in front of the house.

"Quick, shut the windows!" she ordered, striding across the tiny living room to lock the front door. "Pull the blinds. Shut off that TV. Everyone quiet!"

Taub's assistants had come for the monkeys, but she wasn't going to give them up without a struggle. She began moving furniture in front of the door.

A police officer stood on the other side of the door, pounding it with his fist. He knew there were people inside but the house had been effectively barricaded within seconds of his arrival.

Teleki, with chart in one hand and pen poised to write in the other, stood dumbfounded in the kitchen. He couldn't help but feel respect for Newkirk's decisive action, but he was stuck in Lehner's house, too. What if the police returned with a search warrant and they were all held responsible for obstructing justice?

The stand-off was short-lived. Two hours later, Yakalis and Kunz draped the cages in white cloths and loaded the monkeys into a rented U-Haul van.

Four days later, on October 7, the NIH Committee to Investigate Alleged Animal Care Violations at the Institute for Behavioral Research issued its 18-page report. The same day, NIH suspended Taub's funding.

The committee visited IBR on September 21, just four days after the USDA inspector pronounced the facility acceptable, and found many of the same violations Teleki, Fox, Barnes, McArdle and Hawkins had cited in their affidavits. The ventilation was inadequate; the cages were too poorly constructed to be sanitized properly; there were no coverings for the florescent light bulbs; feces and urine crusted the bottom wires of the cages; there was no drainage system in the colony room and the plasterboard walls were difficult to disinfect.

Taub admitted the monkeys were not tested for disease like tuberculosis or parasites, and that weight gain and loss records were not kept. Moreover, there was no occupational health system in place, as required, to protect employees from diseases transmissible to humans.

IBR's Animal Care and Use Committee, which is supposed to ensure compliance with the NIH Guide for the Care and Use of Laboratory Animals, did meet and tour the facility once a year. But the NIH report concluded that its "members present at the site-visit interview appeared unfamiliar with the substance of the Guide, with its underlying purpose, and their review role."

IBR's only consulting veterinarian, Paul Hildebrandt, who had never been called upon to examine or treat an animal, "conceded that, as a pathologist, he had little experience with research animals of any sort, or with primates in or out of the laboratory."

Taub took responsibility for the conditions of the lab, but pointed out that it was John Kunz's job to make sure that all was running smoothly and to report any problems to Taub. As for the lack of veterinary care, IBR's animal care committee agreed that only Taub was qualified to deal with the special needs of deafferented animals.

Not surprisingly, Taub had few kind words for Pacheco. He had no interest in the experiments assigned to him, Taub complained, and he didn't properly care for the two monkeys assigned to him. Taub had no idea Pacheco was photographing his animals. Furthermore, Taub claimed, in direct contrast to Pacheco's later court testimony, the disinterested student had never uttered a word of protest about the condition of the animals or the facility. Taub acknowledged the lab didn't look its best on September 11, but he had been on vacation for three weeks prior to that. It had obviously deteriorated during that period.

The investigation committee listened patiently to Taub's explanations and appreciated his forthright responses to their questions. Nevertheless, IBR did not meet their standards. In spite of the USDA inspection reports, the committee could not sanction the lab as it was.

If the raid on IBR had unnerved Taub's colleagues, the suspension of his funds horrified them. "NIH Cuts Off 'Monkey Lab' Federal Fund" was a headline they never expected to see in the *Washington Post*, and it sent a tornado of fear ripping through the research community. If NIH could take such drastic steps against one of its own, how safe could any of them be?

Before long, animal experimenters would begin to organize against this new and, to their great surprise, effective new group of animal activists. Instead of rejecting Taub as an aberration, they would eventually close their ranks about him, and just as the Silver Spring Monkeys would become the symbol of the new animal rights movement, Taub would be a constant reminder to researchers of their own vulnerability. By protecting him, they protected themselves.

Taub immediately issued a press release in response to NIH's decision, calling half their findings legal technicalities. "Their findings are badly unbalanced and present a grossly inaccurate picture," he asserted.

NIH director Thomas Malone acknowledged the suspension was unprecedented, but stated that IBR had "failed in significant ways" to comply with NIH policies on lab animal care.

Pacheco felt the suspension was the least NIH could do. What they should do, he told reporters, is take the monkeys away; they weren't safe at IBR. Tragically, it didn't take long for Pacheco's fears to be proven valid. Just two days after NIH's suspension of

Taub's grant money—six days after the macaques were returned to Taub—one of the monkeys died.

Chapter Seven

An Invitation From Congress

"There is a high probability, on the basis of extensive research documentation, that the monkeys will be under severe psychological stress as soon as they are put back in the IBR's animal room . . . This will delay the recovery of sick animals, retard wound healing and in some may also cause a resurgence of self-mutilative behavior, leading to further physical injury."
—*Michael Fox, from his affidavit after revisiting IBR on September 29, 1981*

Charlie died on Friday morning at 10:15 a.m. while the court appointed veterinarian, James Stunkard, was operating on him. According to Stunkard, Charlie had been removed from one cage so it could be cleaned and was placed in another next to Nero. The monkeys began to fight, and since the wires were large enough for the animals to reach through, Charlie was wounded. Stunkard felt a general anesthetic was required to suture the rips in the monkey's flesh. The cause of death, Stunkard said, was cardiac arrest.

Stunkard performed an autopsy and turned Charlie's body over to the police, who then sent the remains to Cornell University for an independent exam. To the amazement of Pacheco, Newkirk and Swain, the Cornell report showed that Charlie's heart, lungs, kidneys and other vital organs were missing. Naturally, they had been unable to confirm cardiac arrest, or anything else for that matter, as the cause of death. Cornell also found several conditions that weren't mentioned in Stunkard's report: a recent seriously fractured wrist and multiple bite wounds.

Stunkard never explained these inconsistencies, but he did recommend to Judge Cahoon that the monkeys be removed from IBR. A few months later he resigned from his newly appointed position on IBR's animal care and use committee, and eventually sued IBR for nonpayment of veterinary fees.

Taub told a *Baltimore Sun* reporter that Charlie's death was "one of those bizarre, rare accidents—and this whole situation has been full of them."

Swain couldn't agree more. Every time he thought he had the situation under control, something unexpected happened to foul everything up. Sending the macaques back to Taub was in accordance with the standard practice concerning state's evidence. But once again, standard procedure didn't work.

The same day Charlie died, Judge Cahoon ordered Swain to move the monkeys to an NIH animal breeding facility in Poolesville, Md.

Charlie's death reinforced Pacheco's growing conviction that the justice system didn't protect the voiceless members of society. He felt he couldn't have provided more concrete evidence of Taub's inability to care for the animals, but it took the loss of a life to convince the judge. Pacheco had been supremely confident when the monkeys were seized. Now bitter disillusionment began to creep in, and with it, the resolve to do whatever it took to keep the monkeys away from Taub.

Then, while he was at his lowest point since the case began, Pacheco was invited to tell his story to Congress.

The hearings before the House Science, Research and Technology subcommittee had been scheduled for some months, but when the Silver Spring Monkeys case blasted its way into the headlines, committee chairman Doug Walgren of Pennsylvania invited Pacheco to speak. He offered Taub equal time, but IBR's chief investigator declined.

According to Walgren's legislative assistant, Congress had received more mail on the upcoming hearings than any other issue, including the other current hot potato, the Reagan budget cuts. Several bills providing for better care of animals in laboratories had been introduced already, and the Animal Welfare Institute, Friends of Animals and other groups were lobbying heavily with their limited resources. These organizations had been pushing for new laws for years, charging that the 1966 Animal Welfare Act was inadequate. The IBR case gave them the evidence they needed to prove their point.

Pacheco led the testimony on Tuesday, October 13. The hearing room was crowded with legislators, NIH officials, and representatives from both animal welfare and scientific organizations. The spectators spilled out into the hallway. Pacheco was warm beneath his suit coat.

"No one needs a Ph.D. or any other credentials to recognize blatant violations of the Animal Welfare Act," Pacheco argued. "No one needs a degree to recognize when an animal's cage should be cleaned or that an animal who has just chewed off all his fingers should be seen by a veterinarian."

Committee members examined the enlarged color photographs of IBR. Pacheco described the blood on the experimental equipment, the holes in the walls, the piles of molding feces, the dirty laundry and discarded tennis shoes.

It was a tough act for NIH's William Raub to follow, but his line of defense was remarkably similar to Taub's. Scientists must be free to use animals if they are to find cures for heart disease, diabetes, cancer and other disorders, he claimed. If their ability to use animals as they deem necessary is too severely restricted, their research would virtually stop.

But when questioned about the Silver Spring Monkeys case, Raub admitted NIH's policies to protect animals had failed. One committee member, quoted in the *Baltimore Sun*, called NIH's self-policing procedures a "non-system hiding behind a paper curtain."

It was clear that NIH officials were embarrassed by IBR, but it was equally apparent they wanted no interference from Congress. To placate the committee, Raub unveiled NIH's plan to begin unannounced visits to federally funded laboratories.

Pacheco and Newkirk realized this was a concession for an agency that often operated as though it had no obligation or accountability to the taxpayers who funded it (AIDS activists would later challenge and embarrass NIH on this issue). They had succeeded in driving NIH temporarily out of its fortress. But they weren't convinced that stepped-up self-policing would make any difference. The USDA's inspections of IBR illustrated the flaws in that system.

The problem was much deeper. Surprise visits from NIH were little more than a bandaid on a gaping wound. The real problem, as Newkirk and Pacheco saw it, was that monkeys and dogs and rats and rabbits and other animals were viewed by many experimenters as disposable objects to be used and killed and tossed out. This attitude was what Ronnie Hawkins butted her head against when she merely wanted to let some stump-tailed macaques stretch their legs; this was what John McArdle had struggled with at the University of Chicago; this was what drove Don Barnes and Michael Fox away from careers in animal experimentation. And it was this view of animals, in its extreme form, that allowed Taub and Kunz and Yakalis and the other employees of IBR to go about their work in the midst of so much filth and pain.

The Animal Welfare Act didn't help much either. It was designed to give some protection to animals used in laboratories, but it mandated only minimal standards. Researchers who put macaques, baboons, squirrel monkeys and chimpanzees in steel boxes barely big enough for them to stand up and turn around in, with nothing to do, no one to look at, nothing but cold metal to touch year after year after year, were well within the law. Rats and mice, birds and reptiles weren't even covered by the Act. Analgesics were not (and still aren't) mandatory for animals who have undergone painful procedures.

Representative Patricia Schroeder, the next speaker at the hearings, tackled these last two inadequacies. She had introduced a bill that attempted to define pain and required the use of painkillers for all vertebrates, including rodents.

Congressman Robert Roe of New Jersey threw the final curve at NIH that day. His Research Modernization Act would force NIH to establish a Center for Alternative Research and spend some of their grant money to develop non-animal tests.

For two days, the media focused on the testimony on Capitol Hill and a flurry of editorials and debates followed. Columnist

William Raspberry questioned the priorities of activists who spent so much time worrying about 17 monkeys when millions of people were suffering. In a follow-up column, writer Ann Cottrell Free asked Raspberry why he believed "animal lover" really meant "people hater" and reminded him that Quaker abolitionist John Woolman wouldn't ride in stage coaches because the overworked horses distressed him too much. Newkirk was reminded of her mother's philosophy—it doesn't matter who suffers, but how.

Within a month, two more bills were introduced, in the House by Doug Walgren and the Senate by Bob Dole of Kansas. Both bills called for "animal care and use" committees that would have enough clout to turn down repetitive or poorly designed experiments.

Not surprisingly, the legislation was vigorously opposed by nearly every research institute in the land.

On the second day of the hearings, the 16 remaining monkeys were moved from IBR to the sprawling NIH breeding farm in the green hills of Poolesville, in rural Maryland. Of course, the monkeys couldn't see the grass or smell the fresh air, but at least the Poolesville facility was a lot cleaner than IBR.

Newkirk and Pacheco set about forging a relationship with the Poolesville staff so that they could see the primates, talk to them, and give them something to look forward to in their cramped lives. Newkirk spoke at length with Dave Rehnquist, the NIH veterinarian in charge of the Silver Spring Monkeys, who seemed to her to be startled by her request: who would want to visit macaques? Fortunately, Rehnquist was agreeable, and once a month Pacheco and Newkirk made the 40-minute drive to Poolesville, suited up in surgical gowns and masks, and headed into the sterile room that was now the monkeys' temporary home. They were greeted with excitement and welcoming coos, particularly from Billy, who wanted to be groomed, and Domitian, Sarah and Chester, who reached tiny black hands through the bars.

The monkeys were kept in a room separate from the thousands of primates, dogs and other animals who were imported, bred, bought or sold by NIH for experiments. Their cages, if not exactly spacious, were larger than those at IBR, and they had bowls for their food, watering mechanisms that worked and smooth metal perches half-way up the cages. The Poolesville staff also did in one week what Taub hadn't been able to do in his 24 years of deafferenting monkeys—they devised a simple method to keep them from mutilating their numb arms: they sprayed the limbs daily with an antibiotic yellow substance, nitrofurazone, so that the monkeys wouldn't see any lesions or irregularities to pick at or bite. The wounds finally healed.

Still, like most animals used in laboratories, the monkeys had nothing to do, nothing with which to occupy their minds. With some coaxing, Newkirk convinced Rehnquist to accept a television for the colony room, so they at least had their soap operas.

It took longer to convince the staff to provide objects for the macaques to play with. It was too difficult to sterilize toys, she was told, and they might choke or break the objects and injure themselves. With Michael Fox's help, Newkirk came up with heavy plastic angled pipes that could be fit together and manipulated in various ways. Eventually, Rehnquist agreed and before long the monkeys were twisting and turning, taking apart and putting together their new toys.

A poor substitute for a life swinging among the branches of the Philippine jungle, Newkirk thought, but better than nothing.

Before long, all the primates at the Poolesville facility were given objects to help relieve their boredom. The initially skeptical Rehnquist even wrote an article for a laboratory animal trade magazine about the use of nylon balls as toys for caged monkeys.

The Congressional hearings and the transfer to Poolesville, as important as these events were to both the monkeys and to PETA, were overshadowed by preparations for the first-ever criminal prosecution of an animal experimenter; Taub's trial was scheduled to begin October 27.

Roger Galvin was ticked off.

In his four years with the state's attorney's office, he had worked his way up to a coveted position in the Major Offenders Bureau. He was one of five attorneys who prosecuted the most violent criminals—convicted murderers and rapists accused of second felonies. His job was to "max 'em out"—put them away for as long as possible, with no plea bargaining, and no deals. (Galvin still holds the record for the longest sentence ever imposed in Maryland: three life sentences plus 1,080 years for the

1982 mass murder of employees at an IBM office building in Rockville.)

And now he was being asked to prosecute an animal experimenter charged with misdemeanor animal cruelty.

Galvin had seen the articles in the newspapers, but hadn't paid much attention. Then, one morning in early October, he arrived at his office and was handed a message to see Andrew Sonner, the state's attorney, immediately.

"I want you to take over the Taub case," Sonner said.

"What the fuck are you doing this to me for?" Galvin asked.

"We just want somebody who knows what they're doing to do it."

"Come on, Andy, I've got 30 or 40 felony cases in various stages of preparation."

"I'll spread some of them around," Sonner told him, "but I want you to do it."

Galvin felt like he was in the army, like he'd been "volunteered" for a particularly unpleasant task.

He never did find out exactly why he was chosen, and to this day, the people involved won't comment. There were rumors that prominent county officials were pressing the state's attorney's office to take the case seriously. The media coverage, which had steadily increased in the three weeks since the monkeys were seized, was a constant reminder that taxpayers and voters were watching. Whatever the reason, it was yet another deviation from the protocol; the Major Offenders Bureau just didn't do this kind of case.

Galvin, in his thirties, was confident and articulate, a rising star in the state's attorney's office. He was originally from the Midwest and a DePauw graduate when he came to Washington in 1973 to go to law school at American University. He describes himself then as a "blissfully ignorant meat-and-potatoes guy" who loved to spend his spare time with a fishing rod in his hands. He knew nothing of animal rights philosophy and next to nothing about the use of animals in laboratories. He certainly had never heard of Ingrid Newkirk and he didn't appreciate meeting her over the phone at his house, after hours.

Newkirk could hardly contain herself when Rick Swain told her one of the state's top prosecutors had been assigned to the case. With less than three weeks until the trial, she was beginning to panic about the amount of work that still needed to be done. She called information and got Galvin's number.

"I am not working now," Galvin said, with little effort to hide his irritation. He usually tried to leave his work at the office so that it didn't interfere with his family's time together. "Do not call me at home."

"Fair enough," Newkirk replied. "When can we meet?"

Galvin was not looking forward to this prosecution.

When his cases in progress had been parcelled out, Galvin went downstairs to Joe Fitzpatrick's cubicle and was handed a cardboard box with dozens of files and documents in disarray—obviously a blizzard of paperwork had been flying in court. Back at his desk, Galvin called Swain.

"What in the world is this all about?" he asked.

They arranged to meet the next afternoon.

Sitting across the table from each other, the cardboard box between them, Swain and Galvin sorted through the documents. The first thing to do was draft new charges to supersede the originals, which had been drawn up incorrectly. That was just the beginning. Galvin looked at Swain.

"Has the police department asked you to work the case?" he asked. He knew that once the evidence had been gathered Swain usually bowed out, leaving the rest of the work to the prosecutor, but he hoped Swain would be assigned to this one full time.

"I think I had the same conversation with the chief of investigations that you just had with Sonner," Swain answered.

Galvin was relieved. By the time Swain left his office, Galvin had given him a long list. He needed a couple dozen copies of papers that weren't in the box—the search warrant, the application for the warrant, the inventory of seized items, a property list, a floor plan of IBR, and so on. Then he asked Swain to arrange a meeting with PETA and the other animal groups involved.

At the appointed time, Newkirk, Pacheco, Jean Goldenberg, Patty Forkan from the Humane Society of the United States, Lori Lehner and several other activists were seated around a large table at HSUS's downtown office. Galvin was late and it was Newkirk's turn to be irritated.

"I won't call you at home," she told him when he showed up, "but you better give us the same respect by getting to our meetings on time."

Things went better after that.

Galvin repeated what Swain had already told them a few weeks earlier.

"The state's attorney is committed to this case," he said. "If they weren't I wouldn't be here. But if you want to do it right, you're going to have to have bucks. The only thing the state's going to pay for is me."

There would be travel expenses, he told them, to fly the experts in to testify. The photographs would have to be enlarged. He would use his graphics people to draft some diagrams of IBR, and that would cost. He also had a list of literature: he wanted copies of all the scientific papers Taub had authored, everything they could find on somatosensory deafferentation, books and articles on primate behavior in general and on crab-eating macaques in particular. He wanted to know who the experts were, what their backgrounds were; he'd heard that one of them, a fellow named Geza Teleki, might be in East Africa—somebody had to make sure he was in town by October 27. He would need to meet the others, too.

He closed the meeting by setting up an appointment with Pacheco to go over the evidence.

"How much time should I set aside?" Pacheco asked.

"All day," Galvin answered.

For the next week Galvin steeped himself in scientific papers and animal husbandry. He'd been impressed by Newkirk's resourcefulness. She'd dug out the literature he needed within 24 hours and put herself at his disposal after that. When he needed another book or journal article all he had to do was make a phone call and she had it on his desk the same day.

He found Pacheco straightforward and trusting in spite of his initial disillusionment with the District Court. They spent a long day together going over every photograph and viewing the film footage shot on several different nights at IBR. Pacheco explained the significance of each piece of evidence, each entry in his log. Midway through the day they broke for lunch and headed down to the cafeteria. Galvin ordered the fried chicken and sat down opposite Pacheco, who scrutinized the cooked bird.

"You don't eat meat?" Galvin asked.

"No."

"You really are a weird son of a bitch, aren't you?" Galvin muttered. But within months, Galvin would eliminate meat from his diet, too.

The scientific language of the case was foreign to Galvin and he worked late into the nights leading to the trial. He met with Michael Fox for a crash course on laboratories and veterinary care. John McArdle guided him through the intricacies of neurology and anatomy during lengthy telephone conferences. The veterinarians who examined the primates in Lehner's basement, Drs. Robinson and Ott, explained the physical condition of each animal. He met with Teleki several times to learn about diet and macaque behavior.

Galvin liked Teleki. He liked his irreverent sense of humor, his generosity with his time—he was willing to share as much about non-human primates as Galvin wanted to hear. Teleki seemed always to look just past the person he spoke to, but he didn't miss a thing, and Galvin respected his sharp mind.

Galvin like Dave Rehnquist, too, and sympathized with the Poolesville veterinarian. Galvin got the feeling that Rehnquist would have liked to ask, why me? Why have I been saddled with these 17 media celebrities? Galvin could identify.

The mountain of technical information Galvin had to read and grasp to do the case right might have intimidated less patient prosecutors, but he attacked it with the same energy he gave to a murder trial. He could deal with the hard work. It was the telephone that was driving him nuts. Ever since word got out that he was on the case, his staff had spent most of their time answering calls about the Silver Spring Monkeys.

"Yes," he heard his secretary say a dozen times an hour, "we're doing all we can to prosecute Dr. Taub." A pause. "No, we don't take it less seriously because it's a misdemeanor." Another pause. "No, you can't speak to Mr. Galvin."

Finally, Galvin pulled a witness coordinator from his regular duties and put him on the phone full time.

As the trial approached, the organizational flurry increased. Galvin got a list of witnesses for the defense and handed Newkirk a new task sheet. He needed to know who they were, what papers they had published, what professional contact they'd had with Taub, if any, whether or not they had served on any grant committees for Taub or if Taub had sent any funding in their direction. Newkirk again proved her energy was apparently limitless and gathered the information with speed.

One day in the last week of October, Galvin called Pacheco.

"The monkeys are my victims," he said. "I want to go out and see them."

Newkirk, loaded down with grapes, peanuts and other snacks, accompanied Galvin to the NIH farm. Galvin felt like a subject in a NASA experiment in his sterile gown and face mask as he followed Newkirk into the primates' room. Some of the macaques jumped up and down in excitement and screeched at the sight of a new visitor to their lair, while some tilted their heads and peered curiously at the stranger. When they calmed down they began reaching through the bars for pieces of fruit.

Sarah, who was often cross with people, took a liking to Galvin. She thrust her hand through the cage wires and as she grasped the grape Galvin offered her, something clicked in the tough, aggressive prosecutor. It's soft, he thought, velvety, an exact miniature of his own hand! The tiny fingernails and slender fingers reminded him of a baby's hand. For the first time since he'd taken over the case, he began to think of the monkeys as living beings who had suffered. As he looked at each of the macaques, he began to notice the differences. Nero circled his cage in boredom; Chester chattered loudly at the intruders; Billy, who physically couldn't do much of anything, gazed gently at Newkirk as she fed him treats. These were not just a lump, a mass of animals, he realized. These were individuals, each with his or her own feelings and moods and reactions.

Galvin's competitive juices had been flowing for some weeks, but that afternoon in Poolesville he began to feel the urgency of winning. If Taub was found not guilty, he thought, the monkeys would go right back to him. And that was something Galvin never wanted to see.

Another notable event occurred during this same week—the reinspection of IBR by the chief witness for the defense, Arthur Perry of the U.S. Department of Agriculture. Again, he found no problems in the facility, and again, he okayed IBR's feeding, watering, handling and veterinary care of its research animals, even though there weren't any monkeys in the laboratory.

Chapter Eight

The Trial

"Other scientists who perceive this case as a threat to the whole process of laboratory experimentation will not help the growing debate over ethical issues in animal research if they rush to defend the conditions at IBR. In the final analysis, the intentions or affiliation of Pacheco, the whistle blower, are irrelevant. Even without his testimony and his photographs, evidence given by the police and other witnesses clearly demonstrates that the care and sanitation were well below professionally accepted standards."
—Andrew Rowan, International Journal for the Study of Animal Problems, *1982*

Tuesday, October 27. The District Courtroom was packed and though it was a warm fall day, the heat was cranked high. Before the first witness was called, Judge Stanley Klavan told the attorneys to remove their suit jackets if they liked, as the maintenance staff couldn't get the furnace turned off.

Judge Klavan, strong-jawed, grey-haired and rotund, was used to presiding over several brief trials a day, but for the *State of Maryland v. Taub, Kunz*, with its long list of witnesses, he had cleared his schedule for the entire week. He was prepared to sit through the week and continue on Saturday, if necessary—something Roger Galvin had never seen in his half-decade with the state's attorney's office. Klavan would be deciding the case; misdemeanors with a maximum penalty of 90 days are not tried before juries. He was well aware that his actions and decisions would be scrutinized by the press, the public, the animal welfare activists and the scientific community, all of whom were now represented in his court.

Newkirk was startled by the number of people. She had expected the staff members from HSUS, the Animal Welfare Institute and the other organizations, and she knew the media would turn out—they'd even begun hanging about her house at odd hours. But there were people she didn't know, men and women from the community who had followed the story and wanted to know what would happen next or wanted to see Taub and Pacheco in person.

Sitting next to Shirley McGreal of the International Primate Protection League, who had flown up from South Carolina, Newkirk listened intently to the judge's opening remarks. Taub and Kunz had pled not guilty and their attorneys had requested a rule on witnesses, which meant, Klavan explained, that anyone scheduled to testify would have to leave the courtroom and was cautioned against discussing the case with anyone. When the witnesses, including Pacheco, had closed the heavy door behind them, Galvin stood.

"What the state is focusing on is the conditions of the facility, the conditions of the animals," he began, speaking clearly and deliberately. He was not challenging Taub's research or the use of animals for experiments. The state would attempt to prove that the defendants Edward Taub and John Kunz had violated state anti-cruelty statutes and caused unnecessary suffering of the 17 primates in their care. The animals did not have enough nutritious food, Galvin charged. They had no veterinary care, their cages were inadequate, the air they breathed was not conducive to good health. The state would call expert witnesses to testify on each of these points.

Taub and Kunz were flanked by their lawyers on the opposite side of the room. Jimmy Miller, who was well known in Rockville's halls of justice, quietly advised from his seat. Edgar Brenner, the downtown attorney from Arnold and Porter, the prominent high-priced firm, rose to his feet. Newkirk thought he looked a bit out of place in the small District Court, especially next to the forceful Galvin and the big, easy-going Miller.

Dr. Taub, Brenner began, was a "pioneer in his field," a respected scientist, and he unequivocally denied all charges. In fact, he explained, Taub's deafferentation studies required "gentle handling of research animals" and Taub was noted for his careful approach.

By whom, Newkirk wondered, the Marquis de Sade?

As for medical care, most veterinarians aren't capable of providing appropriate treatment, Brenner continued. Of course, there is no denying "monkeys indeed are messy animals" and no one can maintain pristine conditions at all times, but as the USDA site inspectors prove, the Institute for Behavioral Research is a well-maintained research facility. The animals' injuries as depicted in the photographs may be unpleasant to look at, but they are an inevitable consequence of Taub's specialized research. After all, Brenner pointed out, photos in medical textbooks are often graphic; it's no different. The people who brought this case don't have the technical background to understand what's really going on.

John Kunz's lawyer, William Wood, adopted Brenner's opening statement. He remained low-key, shadowing Taub's defense, throughout the trial.

The state called Alex Pacheco to the stand.

Pacheco was dressed neatly, his dark hair recently cut. Galvin had prepared him carefully for this day—he knew the defense would question his motives in blowing the whistle on IBR. But Galvin was convinced Pacheco had been straightforward and truthful in his journal and this was what needed to come through in his testimony. Pacheco may be opposed to all uses of animals in laboratories, but that had nothing to do with the hard evidence Galvin would introduce in the next few days.

In response to Galvin's questions, Pacheco described his background, when and where he went to school, what he studied. He talked about the *Sea Shepherd*, the anti-whaling ship upon which he had spent a hard, sweaty summer, and the animal rights organization he had started. When he told of his months at IBR, he spoke clearly, without hesitation, and the courtroom spectators listened intently. He described the "displacement" study, the wounds on the animals, and how he was told not to worry about them. As Galvin introduced the first set of the more than five dozen photos he had had enlarged and mounted, Pacheco explained what each portrayed—the excrement, the trash, the dirty, tattered bandages, the bloody finger stumps.

Galvin kept Pacheco on the stand throughout the morning and after an hour's break for lunch, continued in the afternoon. It was exhausting, but at last, under Galvin's detailed questioning, he could describe, for the record, the chaos and pain he had seen each day he worked.

But it was Pacheco's five-minute film that brought the monkeys alive to the courtroom. The color footage capped nearly five hours of testimony, and after a ten-minute recess to set up the projector, the judge, the defendants, the attorneys and the audience watched Billy repeatedly try to jerk his hand free of the wires where it was caught. They saw Domitian, sitting in the back of his cage, bow his head to lick a tear in the skin of his upper arm. There was a scan of a bank of cages with Charlie, Domitian, Allen and Paul huddled in their individual wire homes, trying to avoid the jagged wires that protruded through the floors. The only sound in the court was the click and whir of the projector.

Galvin returned to his seat behind the heavy table as Edgar Brenner rose to begin his cross-examination. As Galvin had predicted, Brenner questioned Pacheco's purpose in volunteering for Taub. He asked about PETA and the protests Pacheco had participated in, about the money donated to build cages and fly the veterinarians to Maryland. But Brenner's primary interest was the disappearance of the monkeys.

"You had advance notice, did you not," Brenner asked, his voice rising, "that the primates were going to be taken away from Beall Street without permission of Sergeant Swain?"

"Without permission of Sergeant Swain?" Pacheco repeated. "No."

"You had no idea that the animals would be taken away before they were removed." Brenner sounded disbelieving.

"No."

"After they were removed, you had a pretty good idea where they went," Brenner stated, more than asked.

Galvin rose abruptly.

"I object to this line of questioning," he said angrily. "It's out of the scope of the direct."

"Your honor," Brenner explained, "I believe it deals with the credibility of the witness and the bias of the witness."

"I'll allow it," Klavan said crisply. "You may proceed."

"Mr. Pacheco, you knew, did you not, where the monkeys had been taken after they were removed from Beall Street on or about September 22nd, 1981?"

"No," Pacheco answered evenly.

"Did you know who took them?"

"No, I didn't."

"Total surprise," Brenner countered, with some sarcasm. "Did you make efforts to try to secure the monkeys' return?"

"I didn't, no."

"At this point in time, Mr. Pacheco, do you know who took the monkeys?"

"No."

The questions were intended to show that Pacheco was duplicitous, but Galvin, at least, didn't think it worked. The five-and-a-half hours had revealed a young man whose beliefs were strong, but whose words were backed by physical proof.

The next line of questioning caught Galvin off guard. Brenner referred to two photographs introduced in evidence earlier that morning. Both depicted rusted, peeling cages and beneath them, trays loaded with mud-brown feces and monkey chow biscuits fat with soaked-up urine. Brenner asked how these shots were taken—had he moved any of the objects? Pacheco answered that he had pulled the trays out to show their conditions. Brenner's implication was clear. Pacheco had staged the photos.

To Newkirk and many of the spectators it was a ridiculous suggestion. How else could he have shown the sodden mess the monkeys sat above day after day? But if the charges of staging pictures had little effect in District Court in 1981, they would be more serious when they resurfaced unexpectedly nearly 10 years later, and became part of another lawsuit.

William Wood again followed Brenner, but his focus was money and profit. How much did PETA receive in donations? How much did the organization have as of this date? Pacheco responded without hesitation: they had raised $10,000, they now owed $11,000 and they had $8,000 currently in the bank. Nobody was getting rich. Wood's cross-examination didn't last long.

Geza Teleki was the first of the state's expert witnesses. He described his clandestine visit to Taub's lab, his shocked reaction, the poor conditions of the deafferented monkeys, who were thinner than the control primates. Monkeys use both hands to eat, he explained, but are subject to right- or left-handedness. If their dominant limbs are crippled, it would be difficult for them to feed themselves before the dry chow slipped through the wire floors.

"Can you tell us specifically what your observations were of the colony room itself?" Galvin asked.

Teleki sighed.

"That's the point where I hardly know where to start. Paint was peeling. Walls were crumbling. There were holes and fissures in the walls . . . There was fecal material all over the floors."

"Primate?"

"Primate as well as rodent," Teleki answered. "I think I might simply conclude by saying that I've never seen anything like that in any laboratory anywhere."

It was difficult for Brenner and Wood to dispute Teleki's expertise in primatology, so they attempted instead to cast doubt on Teleki's knowledge of deafferented monkeys. When asked about his lack of experience with this type of research, Teleki laughed softly, paused, and finally said, "I don't think you need to have experience with deafferented monkeys in order to know when something is suffering."

The audience, who had been sitting quietly for nearly seven hours, burst into applause.

"That was your first time," Judge Klavan said sternly. "That was your last time. You do that again, I'll clear the courtroom."

Rick Swain was the final witness for the day. He described, in the unemotional monotone of "police speak," the photographs taken by the police department at IBR: the putrified apples, the blood spattered on the restraint device, the corpses floating in formaldehyde. His detached, almost clinical narrative made the succession of pictures surreal to Newkirk. She had trouble connecting Swain's words to what she had seen in the laboratory.

At 6 o'clock, Klavan called Galvin and Brenner to the bench. He had planned to sit into the evening hours, but the furnace was still pounding away and it was too hot. He adjourned until 9 o'clock the next morning.

While Judge Klavan and the packed court heard the state open its case in the stuffy room, the veterinary staff at NIH's Poolesville center was making an uncomfortable decision. Another of the 16 remaining Silver Spring Monkeys was in trouble. Nero's exposed bone in his deafferented arm was infected, as Philip Robinson's report had indicated earlier, and to keep the infection from spreading they would need to amputate. The problem was that Taub refused to allow the surgery. Legally, the monkeys were still IBR's property and he wasn't about to be told how they should be treated.

Newkirk and Pacheco suspected another motive for Taub's objection to the diagnosis and treatment. Agreeing to the amputation would be tantamount to admitting that Nero hadn't received proper medical attention. Newkirk predicted Taub would delay his decision for as long as possible, or at least until the trial ended.

She was right. Two days after the testimony concluded, Taub agreed to the amputation.

John McArdle was Galvin's first witness on the second day of the trial. When he arrived in Maryland less than 48 hours earlier, he was startled to see one of his former professors listed as a witness for the defense. He was even more surprised when Galvin told him that Michael Goldberger, who had instructed McArdle in neuroanatomy at the University of Chicago, was Taub's co-investigator on his deafferentation study, and received a portion of the grant funds awarded to Taub by NIH. Goldberger was now at the University of Pennsylvania, where he conducted deafferentation experiments on cats.

Taub's attorneys were astonished by this unexpected coincidence. The connection between their witness and the state's didn't help their case. McArdle testified that he had known Goldberger for three years in Chicago until Goldberger was turned down for tenure and left the university. At that time Goldberger was performing cortical ablations—an operation in which the side of an animal's skull is cut and part of the cortex removed.

McArdle was followed by Don Barnes, Phillip Robinson and Michael Fox. Like Teleki before them, they were self-assured and authoritative on the stand, and as grave as their testimony was, it wasn't entirely humorless.

"I presume," Fox added, after describing the mouse feces in the corners of the colony room, "they were either studying free-range rodents or they had a rodent problem."

Fox was also concerned about the probability of phantom pain sensation in the monkeys. Impulses from the stumps of severed nerves can create the feeling that the deafferented limb needs grooming or itches, he explained. Such cases are common in humans whose arms or legs have been amputated, and Fox had treated dogs with similar problems.

By the close of the long second day, Galvin had only one witness remaining, but veterinarian Kenneth Cowell could not take the stand until he had a chance to examine radiographic evidence. The state rested until then. The next morning, Thursday, the defense would begin its presentation.

The District Court was just as crowded on the second day as it had been on the first, and because the media had turned out dozens of stories across the country, PETA's phones hadn't stopped ringing. After eight hours on the hard courtroom benches, Pacheco and Newkirk went to work returning calls and answering letters. Besides that, Galvin never stopped asking for more information, and that meant more trips to the library. Newkirk had taken a leave of absence from her job to deal with the endless tasks. Pacheco had missed the deadline for registration at George Washington University. They were fully committed to putting everything they had into winning the case. The thought of losing, of the monkeys going back to IBR—a vindication of the rotten system—was unbearable to them.

They were also reaching people. Every phone call, every letter tucked into the Washington post office box represented a potential animal rights activist. The public wanted to know what PETA was, what it stood for. Who was this young man who had dared to criticize Science with a capital S? Many of the new PETA supporters were relieved to find others who questioned animal experiments; they wanted to do the same, but lacked the confidence. Was it really possible, they asked, to challenge the powerful institutions responsible for killing so many millions of animals—the universities, the military, even the government?

When Dr. Arthur Perry took the stand for the defense Thursday morning, the fissures in the USDA's inspection program began to widen. During his nearly three hours before the court it was difficult to tell whether he was a witness for Taub or the prosecution.

He inspected nearly 60 laboratories a year, he explained under Brenner's questioning, and it was his responsibility to see that these facilities met the standards of the federal Animal Welfare Act. He normally looked over a lab once a year unless he found deficiencies. His July 13 inspection of IBR was unannounced—a follow-up to his April visit, when he had found loose floor tiles. Taub was out, so he talked with John Kunz.

What were the responsibilities of Dr. Paul Hildebrandt, the veterinarian on IBR's animal care and use committee? Brenner asked. Perry's response was typical of many he gave that morning—confused and nearly unintelligible. He stumbled over his words and repeated phrases as he appeared to search for the appropriate expression:

> Dr. Hildebrandt was their attending veterinarian for IBR and he, this responsibility as the attending veterinarian, uh, was delegated to him from IBR. Uh, it is their responsibility to carry out the attending veterinarian requirements at the facility. They have, they have, they have the responsibility. They delegate this to the attending veterinarian. The attending veterinarian then works out a program of veterinary care, that type of thing at the facility with the different researchers that may be involved with the research and, uh, they have consultation between themselves, how they're going to do it.

Galvin began to suspect he'd been handed a gift.

Line by line, Perry described the inspection form he filled out at IBR and the standards that must be met. Yes, he answered Brenner, the storage of food was adequate. Yes, the ventilation was fine. So were the sinks, the lighting, the drainage system and the watering devices, which Pacheco testified did not always work.

"You examined the watering system?" Brenner asked.

"We don't routinely examine the watering system in research," Perry answered. "We see it."

"You looked at it."

"We look at it but we don't open cages and that type of thing."

At the prosecutor's table, Galvin was scribbling notes as fast as he could.

Sanitation, cleaning, housekeeping and veterinary care? All adequate, Perry testified.

Galvin rose to begin cross-examination. The courtroom was silent. Galvin walked slowly back and forth in front of the witness stand, then began by asking Perry how many labs he'd visited that day and how many hours he'd worked. Perry was irritated—Galvin could check that information on his work sheets. After several vague answers, Judge Klavan interrupted.

"Doctor, I want to caution you that you're in a court, and when you're in a court and you're asked a question, you answer it. You're merely a witness in this case. You're starting to become argumentative. You're starting to become evasive. Please answer the question as simply and concisely as possible."

Perry was considerably more polite when Galvin asked him if he'd gone into every room in the facility on July 13. No, he said, he hadn't. He went into the colony room, the operating room and poked his head into the research room.

"Did you have an opportunity to notice what type of lighting existed in the colony room?"

"No, I didn't," Perry responded, "but the lighting is, the lighting is bright in the facility. It doesn't come to mind. It doesn't register."

"So would it be fair to say then that it did not register whether or not the lighting itself had any protective covering over it?"

Perry paused, as if trying to remember.

"It's possible," he said finally, "that the light itself may not have had any protective covering over it."

Galvin asked about the effects of excessive lighting. The Animal Welfare Act was clear on that, Perry stated firmly. Too much light could be injurious to animals. Galvin then asked if Perry noticed the light timer at IBR. Perry remembered a "little black box" by the switch, but he didn't really look at it. He just assumed it worked.

For Pacheco, the light was just beginning to dawn. Now he knew how IBR had passed inspections so consistently. As Galvin fired question after question at Perry, it became increasingly obvious that there hadn't been a real inspection at all. No, Perry answered again and again, he hadn't seen the capture nets or the ventilation system or the air conditioning unit. He didn't even know the janitorial closet, with its feces-loaded sink, existed on July 13. He'd never opened that door in the colony room.

Were all 17 monkeys listed on the form in the colony room?

"I did not take a count," Perry said with dignity. "We're not required to count monkeys."

Did he notice any wires sticking up into the cages?

"No, I didn't notice any, but you know, you can miss something like that. I may have missed something, but I didn't notice any." What kind of monkeys were in the colony? "Well, I don't know their real, the scientific names of 'em. I think that they were mostly long-tailed monkeys, to me. That's what they mean to me. I don't learn 'em by specific names."

No, he didn't look at the source of their drinking water. No, he didn't recall seeing any disinfectants on the premises, but there were brooms. Yes, there might have been rodent feces in the operating room, he might have missed them. Yes, it "seemed like" one of the monkeys had a wound in his upper arm, but no, he couldn't recall if it was bandaged.

Several times during the long morning session, Perry asked for a drink of water. He seemed confused by some of Galvin's questions and puzzled by Pacheco's photos, taken within days of his inspection. He didn't remember seeing those conditions, he said. If he had seen some of them, the feces caked on the wheels of the bank of cages for example, he would write it up as a deficiency.

Galvin paused for moment, emphasizing Perry's final statement with silence.

"No further questions," he said at last.

The afternoon session was anti-climactic; the rest of Brenner's defense witnesses were dull compared to Perry. He brought out a retired National Institutes of Mental Health (NIMH) employee who had conducted a site visit to IBR in early 1979. She called the facility "excellent" in her summary report, but, she told the court emphatically, she hadn't inspected the lab to see if it was adequate. "It was more or less taken for granted that that was the case," she said; her purpose was to question Taub about the emphasis of his research. She hadn't returned to IBR in more than two years.

Richard Wylie, a physiologist at the Walter Reed Army Institute of Research in Bethesda, worked with several deafferented monkeys and had collaborated with Taub on a study. He disputed the phantom limb phenomenon in deafferented primates, saying there was no evidence to support it. (Six years later, NIH would attempt to use phantom limb sensation as a reason to destroy the Silver Spring Monkeys.) Though he defended Taub's husbandry and bandaging methods, he admitted under cross-examination that he had only seen IBR twice in 1981—once in late

September, after the monkeys had been removed, and once in February.

Galvin asked how many times Wylie called in a veterinarian to his own lab the preceding year.

"I can't begin to give to you an answer," Wylie said, "but I would say a dozen times anyway."

Galvin's pause between this response and his next question allowed enough time for what was left unsaid to sink in—that this was 12 more times than Taub sought medical advice for his colony.

Georgette Yakalis, Taub's final witness for the day, had few compliments for Alex Pacheco. He didn't seem interested, she complained. She didn't think he was there much and he couldn't seem to sort out simple problems, like how to keep the two monkeys in his study from knocking the water bottles off their cage doors.

The hemostats, Pacheco thought as he listened to Yakalis. The judge will never hear how Yakalis clamped them on to Domitian's testicles.

Thursday evening was long and anxious for Newkirk, Pacheco and Galvin. The radiographs of Billy's and Paul's arms taken on September 30 had been sent to Phillip Robinson at the San Diego Zoo for analysis. Unfortunately, Robinson wasn't in California, but nobody knew it until this week. The X rays had to be found and sent back to Maryland in time for the trial.

They finally arrived at 10:30 p.m. and were rushed to Dr. Kenneth Cowell, a local veterinary orthopedic specialist. Cowell confirmed, and on Friday morning testified, that Billy's right arm was fractured and had been so for at least six to eight weeks, possibly much longer.

Cowell was Galvin's final witness, but the prosecutor didn't slow down. He cross-examined Taub's remaining witnesses longer than Brenner or Wood, carefully laying out his questions, going through the evidence piece by piece, steadily puncturing their defense.

Adrian Morrison and Peter Hand, both veterinarians, professors at the University of Pennsylvania and animal experimenters, had examined the photos of the monkeys and were confident that the macaques were in relatively good health for deafferented primates and did not require immediate medical attention. They weren't sure, they claimed, that mold in the cages, blood on the capture nets or feces on the food created any hazards.

Galvin asked Morrison how one could tell, on the basis of photographs, whether or not the monkeys were healthy. The hair coat, was Morrison's response, and the fact that the weight of the animals looked normal.

But when Galvin asked Morrison if he thought, looking at a photo, that the bandage on Paul's arm was soiled, Morrison replied, "I think one sees quite a bit of white on there. It's not very dirty. It's hard to tell."

"Because of the lighting?" Galvin asked.

"Yes," Morrison said, "right."

"Wouldn't the same thing apply then to your observations of these photographs of hair quality?"

Caught, Newkirk thought. Caught in his own trap.

"No, I don't think so," Morrison answered. "Looking here that the lighting is, uh, is very good on this particular monkey. It's a monkey with, I can see the hair very well there."

Even Klavan sounded irritated by Morrison's evasiveness on testimony that might damage Taub.

"In your professional opinion," the judge asked, "in a laboratory dealing with deafferented monkeys, if any showed lesions, what is the standard of veterinary care? Should a vet or should not a vet come in on a regular basis to look at your colony?"

"Well, I think a veterinarian should come to colonies periodically in a research institute," Morrison answered.

"How often?"

Morrison hesitated.

"I don't think that I could say that," he said.

"Can you give us some type of time frame?"

Again Morrison hesitated.

"Hmmm," he said, apparently trying to decide what to say.

"Isn't it true that these animals should be checked every three months for TB?" Klavan asked, trying to pin him down about tuberculosis, the dangerous disease shared by monkeys and humans that is often a problem in primate facilities.

"Well," said Morrison, who had been officially recognized by the court as an expert in veterinary science and care, "I don't feel that I'm qualified to talk about monkey TB. I have not worked with that."

Later in his testimony, Morrison told Galvin that he viewed the prosecution of Taub as an attack on scientists' right to use animals—a concern shared by many of his colleagues.

"Do you generally make your diagnosis by photograph?" Judge Klavan asked Hand later that morning, when the veterinarian repeated Morrison's opinion that the monkeys didn't need immediate medical attention.

Galvin asked both Morrison and Hand if they had ever visited IBR before September 11. They had not, they testified, ever been to Taub's laboratory before the monkeys were seized.

Taub's collaborator and John McArdle's former professor, Michael Goldberger testified that food bowls in monkey cages weren't a good idea, as the monkeys urinated in them. But when Galvin asked him to comment on the pieces of fiberglass insulation one of the monkeys had pulled into his cage from a hole in the ceiling, Goldberger didn't have an opinion.

"I'm not familiar with any danger posed by that material," he said, "so I wouldn't have been concerned."

Galvin, changing his tack, asked if the recovery of the deafferented limb was one aspect of the study. Goldberger agreed that it was. And reaching for raisins was one way to examine this? Goldberger agreed to that as well.

"If the monkey's got a broken forearm," Galvin continued, "that is going to affect the way in which he reaches for that raisin, is it not?"

"I've no experience with animals with broken forearms doing that," Goldberger answered.

"As a matter of common sense, if I've got a broken forearm, am I gonna be able to use it as efficiently and effectively as I would if I didn't have the forearm broken?"

"I would guess—the problem to me with common sense," Goldberger said, "is that I have to rely on what I observe, not on what I hope to observe."

Judge Klavan interrupted.

"Doctor, I've qualified you as an expert because of your background and I'm not asking you to—you're not being asked to give an absolute answer. You're being asked to use your background, your experience, your education to answer a—what I think—a rather simple question. There's nothing tricky about it and if you're gonna just say, 'If I haven't seen something I can't answer the question,' well, then I'd have to disregard a lot of your testimony . . . I think if you tried, you could answer it."

After this lecture, Goldberger admitted that broken bones could affect the use of the muscles.

Like Morrison and Hand before him, and psychology professor Sol Steiner after him, Goldberger testified that it was almost impossible to keep a monkey colony clean. Sanitation was a difficult problem because non-human primates are so messy. They toss their own feces through the bars of their cages and a freshly mopped floor can be dirty again in a matter of minutes.

For Pacheco, who cared deeply for each of the macaques as individuals rather than experimental tools, this characterization was simple-minded and unfair. What did they expect? They took a wild monkey from the Asian jungle, crammed him into a cage only 17-inches wide with nothing to touch but wires, and nothing to play with but his own surgically mutilated arm and his own shit. It was like forcing a human child to live in a closet. How was it, he wondered, that science allowed such convoluted logic?

Judge Klavan was curious about this, too.

"I don't understand why," he asked Taub later in the trial, "you can't hire someone to stay in that monkey room to keep it clean. I don't understand that. I mean, I've heard throughout the four, five days now we've been here, that these are dirty rooms . . . Why can't you hire somebody to stay in that room and keep it clean? Is it too expensive? Is it an economical problem? What is the problem?"

"It's not the standard practice in the industry," Taub answered.

Chapter Nine

The Verdict

"Edward Taub, 50, the principal researcher at the Institute of Behavioral Research in Silver Spring, testified that he used a technique called 'gentling' in working with the monkeys, because he believes a 'positive relationship between experimenter and subject' is necessary for good research results."
—The Washington Post, November 1, 1981

Edward Taub was the final defense witness to take the stand. It was Halloween, Saturday, October 31. For four long days he'd sat quietly in the District Court, listening to strangers, friends and employees discuss his experiments, his facility and his monkeys. He'd heard his two student caretakers, for whom he was responsible, testify that they didn't show up to work on six different occasions, and hadn't bothered to call in on five of those days because they were busy with school. He'd listened to the long list of medical problems afflicting the macaques. He'd endured Arthur Perry's embarrassing testimony.

How could he explain it? What would he say? The spectators who filled the courtroom to overflowing were about to find out he was far from apologetic. Not once did Taub acknowledge even the possibility that the Silver Spring Monkeys suffered physically or psychologically.

Taub was seated and sworn in. He sipped hot tea, with the judge's permission, to soothe his sore throat.

Under Brenner's gentle questioning, Taub spoke of his two and half decades of animal experimentation and how, in 1970, he had decided to put the results of his work "in service to mankind." From his work with deafferented monkeys, he wanted to develop ways to help people with central nervous system damage. He had already invented thermal biofeedback, he stated, and this stemmed directly from his work with primates.

As he talked, it became clear to those who had seen IBR that he was painting himself as a martyr. He was a scientist dedicated to curing the ills of humankind. His important work had been unfairly and destructively interrupted by ignorant lay people like Alex Pacheco and Rick Swain.

But Taub's initial depiction of his career did not address the central question of the trial—did he treat the 17 monkeys in his care in a humane manner? The state of Maryland was not attacking the goal of his experiments. The prosecution sought only to show that Taub hadn't provided the animals with proper food, water, shelter, air, veterinary care and protection from harm. For Taub, and for many in the scientific community, the two issues were irreversibly intertwined. They would not tolerate being told how to clean cages any more than they would accept criticism for the way in which they sliced the dorsal roots of a monkey's spine.

Taub dismissed not only the concerns of non-scientists like Pacheco, he questioned the competence of veterinarians who had no experience with deafferented monkeys. Their usual recommendation to bandage the wounds on the animals' arms was all wrong, he stated. The bandages actually made the situation worse because the highly dexterous macaques would simply attack the gauze.

As for the rust on cage wheels, the stains on the cages themselves, the insulation pulled from the roof, he wasn't sure why they were present. They weren't "characteristic of the lab," he assured the judge.

Certainly the monkeys didn't need food bowls, he said, they each had one perfectly good hand to pick up food with. He didn't mention the doubly deafferented Billy who had struggled to collect the biscuits with his mouth before they fell through the mesh floor. He agreed that some of the rooms were cluttered, but pointed out that they weren't all used for experiments. One of them hadn't been used for more than two years, he said.

"Alex Pacheco knew that as sure as night is day," he added, providing one of the few humorous moments in the trial. He laughed nervously, catching his error too late.

Again and again he tried to justify the conditions found in his laboratory. The drugs in the refrigerator were outdated because he needed them only for surgery, which hadn't been done in two years; the kitchen wasn't used as a kitchen anymore; the sink in the surgery room—which wasn't used as a surgery room—was used for employees to wash their hands after handling the animals; yes, the freezer, with its pounds of ice surrounding the bodies of two monkeys, did need to be defrosted.

"That's an understatement, isn't it?" Judge Klavan asked.

By the time Roger Galvin stood to cross examine the defendant, the prosecutor was annoyed. As far as he was concerned, the witnesses trotted out to defend Taub during the last two days cared no more about animal husbandry and good science than the man in the moon. They felt threatened, he believed, and they were trying to hustle the judge. He didn't think Klavan fell for it, but he was going to make damn sure he did everything he could to get a conviction. When he began questioning Taub, inconsistencies started to surface.

Only four monkeys in his colony had died during the last 11 years, Taub had earlier testified. How many monkeys did Taub have as of November, 1979? Galvin asked. Nineteen, Taub replied. Galvin handed him the November 13, 1979 report of IBR's animal care and use committee. According to the committee, there were 22 monkeys on the premises at that time, not 19.

And though Taub bragged that his colony was remarkably healthy, he admitted that no daily records on the monkeys were kept between May 11 and September 11. Blood hadn't been drawn for routine analysis in three years. Five years had passed since fecal samples were tested for parasites. In fact, Taub only visited the colony twice a week on average, for no more than 30 minutes. He relied on his one full-time employee, John Kunz, to tell him if a problem arose.

As for bandaging, Taub acknowledged that he had once believed and had written that frequent, even daily, bandaging was essential. But he had changed his mind.

"The point about this is," he said, looking at a photo of Paul's mutilated hand, "that if you tried to prevent a monkey from damaging its limb, you would have to keep the monkey bandaged for its entire life . . . then you would be unable to do any research with that monkey and it would be irrelevant to start the entire elaborate and extremely expensive procedure . . . "

Galvin asked how many times Paul was experimented on in the four months Pacheco worked in the lab. Only between May 11 and June 3, Taub answered, without explaining why Paul wasn't bandaged consistently during the remainder of the summer months.

With this, Galvin ended his cross-examination. He had backed Taub smack into his own excuses.

By the close of the trial, Judge Klavan had taken 207 pages of notes and listened to hours of contradictory testimony. To give himself time to review the evidence, as well as the dozens of photographs and documents entered as exhibits, he decided to delay his ruling. He gave Galvin and Brenner two weeks to submit post-trial briefs. At that time, he would set a date for closing arguments.

It would be three long weeks before Alex Pacheco knew whether or not his months in the laboratory were enough to convict Taub.

But tonight, the end of an historic trial, a first of its kind, was for celebration. Pacheco, Newkirk, Galvin and a small crowd of volunteers and supporters headed for Victoria Station, a local restaurant, for drinks, food—and more of the endless discussion on animal rights. Newkirk was determined to convince Galvin of the soundness of PETA's philosophy. She never missed a chance to razz him about vegetarianism, challenging him to give her a reasonable excuse for eating animals.

"We've always done it," he said emphatically during one of these discussions.

"You're a thinking man," Newkirk answered, "you understand philosophical arguments, and you're telling me the best you can come up with is: 'We've always done it'?"

Galvin wasn't easily convinced and after several beers at Victoria Station he happened to mention that his mother was disabled from multiple sclerosis.

"If it took a hundred thousand animals to relieve her of her pain," he said, "it would be worth it."

Galvin would remember his words later, when he studied animal rights philosophy and hammered out his own system of beliefs, when he came to believe more problems were created than solved by enslaving other beings.

Whatever the outcome of the trial for Taub, the overriding issue for Pacheco and Newkirk was how to keep the monkeys from going back to IBR. An acquittal would ensure their return to the tiny cages, Taub's experiment and their eventual destruction. But a guilty verdict was no guarantee of their safety. Taub could be convicted of animal cruelty and still have the macaques back within the week. The law just didn't provide for the deliverance of abused animals. This loophole led to the first in what was to be a chain of civil cases. A week after the testimony concluded, the Humane Society of the United States, with the Washington Humane Society and PETA, filed suit against representatives of the USDA and Secretary of Agriculture John Block, to mandate enforcement of the Animal Welfare Act.

Not long after, the Fund for Animals sued the directors of NIH, the USDA and IBR for custody of the Silver Spring Monkeys. Because government grant money had paid for the animals, they were technically research "equipment" that could be seized by NIH once the funds were cut off. Both cases were later dismissed.

Pacheco also turned to Capitol Hill. Although he had missed the fall college semester, Pacheco's earlier application for a Congressional internship was accepted. He had decided during the summer that it would be worthwhile to learn how to lobby for better laws to protect animals. He found a position with the tall, silver-haired Tom Lantos, a Representative from California.

Lantos and his wife, Annette, who works alongside her husband in his Rayburn Building office on Independence Avenue, knew nothing of the Silver Spring Monkeys case when Pacheco came to work for them. He was simply a personable young man, quite good looking, one of many interns in the office. They began to see something more when Pacheco asked them to help him keep the monkeys out of Taub's laboratory.

Tom and Annette Lantos were not animal rights activists. Annette liked animals, and she often took in stray dogs and found homes for them. When it came to experiments, though, she didn't really want to know what happened to the dogs and monkeys and rats. She probably wouldn't like it and there was nothing she could do about it anyway, so it was easier not to think about it. But she and her husband had a keen sense of justice and an intense dislike of exploitation of any sort.

They were Holocaust survivors, and they knew how it felt to be victimized simply because they weren't like others.

They still have one photograph, from 1939, when Annette was six, and Tom was 10, when they were happy in the playful days of their childhood in Budapest. But they were Jews, and not long after this picture was taken, Annette went into hiding, where she remained throughout the war. Tom was sent to a forced labor camp. Their families perished.

When they came to the United States in the late 1940s, scarred but anxious for a new life, they wanted to work for a world in which no one could be treated as an object rather than a living being. More than 30 years later, as Pacheco told them his story, Annette was reminded of their own experiences at the hands of the Nazis.

If the court ordered the monkeys back to IBR, she and her husband would try to help save them.

Judge Klavan looked out over the District Courtroom, once again crowded with animal rights activists and scientists, reporters and court artists, ready to go to work with sketch pads and pastels. Television cameras and crews lined the walk in front of the courthouse, waiting to record the first reactions to the ruling. It was November 23, more than three weeks since Edward Taub sat in the witness stand to defend his laboratory.

Roger Galvin argued for more than 90 minutes, Edgar Brenner for less than 30. Finally Judge Klavan cleared his throat and announced he was prepared to render a verdict—but he would tolerate no outburst of any kind from anyone in the room.

"I don't intend to make a hero or saint of anyone," he said. "On the other hand, I don't intend to tar anyone needlessly. But I do intend to follow my oath . . .

"I find that there has been no proof whatsoever that any of these animals were either suffering or in pain."

Newkirk leaned forward in her front row seat, clasping and unclasping her hands. Beside her, Alex Pacheco was still, listening to every word. Only the muscles in his jaw moved as he clenched his teeth.

"However, I am very deeply concerned about the final charge, and that is that he failed to provide for these primates necessary veterinary care . . . I accordingly find that he did not provide veterinary care to Paul."

The room was quiet, as Judge Klavan had demanded.

"I find also that Billy needed necessary veterinary care."

And Domitian, Nero, Big Boy, Titus.

"Accordingly, I find the doctor guilty of these six charges."

Newkirk let out a sigh of relief. Klavan had swallowed the defense testimony that the monkeys could not feel pain in their limbs, and he wasn't persuaded that they had suffered as a result of generalized infection, phantom pain or plain physical discomfort. But is was a clear victory for the prosecution. A respected member of the grant funded scientific elite had been convicted of animal abuse! Anyway you looked at it, it was a rude—an embarrassingly public—slap in the face.

John Kunz, who sat gaunt and silent, who had not taken the stand in his own defense, was acquitted of all charges. His job was to carry out Dr. Taub's instructions, Klavan explained. How could he have forced his employer to call in a veterinarian?

Taub's attorney requested immediate sentencing to clear the way for a prompt appeal. Five hundred dollars for each count, Klavan said, a total of 3,000 dollars plus 15 dollars court costs, with payment deferred pending appeal.

Galvin's concern was the disposition of the monkeys. Legally, he could only dispute the return to Taub of the six animals involved in the decision. Fortunately, Rehnquist and the Poolesville staff had had time to evaluate the animals and Galvin hoped his report would weigh against Taub. Paul's fracture wasn't healing properly and Billy needed veterinary attention at least every other day for his fractures, which were prone to infection.

But Klavan was making no more decisions on this day. He would hold a hearing later to decide the matter.

The trial left few of those involved untouched, and for many, the five days in court had a profound effect on their lives.

John McArdle became convinced that the burgeoning animal rights movement lacked scientific expertise. The activists could dig up the research protocols and experimental results, but they couldn't interpret them. He knew that he could make a contribution in this way, and despite his lifelong dream of being a research scientist, he began to think about a career change. Soon after he returned to his disapproving supervisors at Illinois Wesleyan, he was fired—a liberating event, as it turned out. McArdle eventually came to work for the Humane Society of the United States and has worked for animal rights ever since.

Don Barnes's early stirrings of sympathy for the monkeys used in laboratories evolved into a full-fledged animal rights philosophy during the course of the trial. He was already doing some consulting work for an animal protection organization. Now he, too, began to wonder what else he could do, how he could help animals who were shocked, irradiated (as his own experimental monkeys had been), shot, or just warehoused in cages their entire lives. Before long, he became the director of the Washington office of the National Anti-Vivisection Society, for whom he still works today.

Geza Teleki returned to Africa as planned to set up the national park and has continued to work on primate conservation issues, but the Silver Spring Monkeys incident left an indelible mark. "You can't go through an experience like that," he says today, "and not be influenced down to the very core of your beliefs." A few years later, he and Jane Goodall would work with PETA to improve conditions for chimpanzees in another Maryland laboratory.

For Roger Galvin, the regular meat-and-potatoes guy, the trial began a journey that would eventually lead him away from prosecution to a new field, animal rights law, and to a new way of life. He took the first step when he touched Sarah's hand that October afternoon in Poolesville, and was shoved along a little farther when he cross-examined the witnesses who spoke for Taub. Soon after the close of Taub's appeal trial in 1982, Galvin became vegan—he gave up meat, eggs and dairy products which came from animals who were cruelly confined and used as tools for profit—and stopped wearing leather.

"Justice is justice for all," he told a reporter at that time. "It is not just for one species, or one age group, or one sex."

Two years later, he left his coveted position at the Major Offenders Bureau and took a job with the public defenders office to work on cases involving the death penalty, which he now opposed. In 1986, he and two partners set up a firm dedicated to animal rights law.

Adrian Morrison and Michael Goldberger, two of the experimenters who testified for Taub, began to defend and promote the use of animals in laboratories. A decade later, Morrison became director of the Office of Animal Research Issues created by the National Institutes of Mental Health (NIMH) to fight animal rights. Goldberger joined the board of directors of Americans for Medical Progress (AMP), an organization formed in 1992 to convince the public that animals must be used in experiments. Not long after AMP took out ads in prominent newspapers, the *Wall Street Journal* reported that much of the group's funding came from corporations that test commercial products on animals.

By the close of the trial, Edward Taub's life had begun to unravel, and although he was appealing both the court's ruling and NIH's suspension of his grant, he had no funds and, temporarily at least, no research subjects. The *Washington Post* reported that four IBR employees had been laid off and that Taub himself had drawn no salary since the beginning of October. He sought help from the professional associations he belonged to and eventually found it at the American Psychological Association (APA), which later gave IBR $10,000 toward legal fees. Michael Fox promptly resigned his membership from APA in protest.

APA's response typified the growing polarization between animal experimenters and animal rights supporters. Out of fear that they, too, would become targets, or that their livelihoods might be threatened, many researchers defended any and all uses of animals. To concede Taub's guilt would be to acknowledge flaws in their world, and they weren't willing to risk the consequences of that. Instead, they tried to turn Taub into an icon, a symbol of scientific inquiry triumphing over misguided zealotry.

Of course, the damage had already been done. A rift had opened between the scientific community and the public because Pacheco, Newkirk and PETA, with the state of Maryland's help, had managed to accomplish the one thing that no opponent of animal experimentation had been able to do in the last 100 years—they had proven, in a court of law, that animal abuse occurred in a laboratory. No other animal protection organization had so effectively challenged the scientific elite. Before the Silver Spring Monkeys case, critics of experimentation could be written off as "bunny-hugging softies"; now, with the legitimacy conferred on them by a judge's decision, animal activists had the attention of the public as never before.

Pacheco and Newkirk didn't waste the opportunity. The rift between scientists and taxpayers would continue to widen during the next decade as PETA uncovered case after case of abuse.

Chapter Ten

Back in Court

" . . . [S]ometimes it takes 12 people such as we have here to say:
'You've gone too far and we don't want you to go any farther.' "
—Judge Calvin Sanders to Edward Taub at his sentencing,
September 1, 1982

Congressman Tom Lantos was as good as his word. A week after
Taub was convicted and fined, Lantos sent a letter signed by 20
of his colleagues to NIH's acting director, Thomas Malone, urging
him to hang on to the 16 remaining animals rather than send them
back to IBR. It was the first Congressional action on behalf of the
Silver Spring Monkeys. Little did Lantos know, within a few
years several resolutions and bills would be introduced to wrest
the macaques from NIH.

Pacheco hoped the influence from Congress would be the
deciding factor for NIH and, at the hearing Judge Klavan had
scheduled for early December, the agency would argue to keep
the animals rather than return them to Taub. But he wasn't quite
so trusting of people's motives as he had once been. He and
Newkirk sat up late in the evenings following the trial, formulat-
ing and rejecting plan after plan to protect the monkeys. Finally
they decided to speak to Edward Genn, the attorney who repre-

sented Newkirk when the monkeys were taken from Lori Lehner's basement.

Newkirk liked Genn. She respected him for one thing—he had been involved in civil rights cases since the 1950s and eventually chaired the ACLU. He also seemed to be sensible and meticulous, yet kind and fatherly as well. When Newkirk needed to make calls from a public phone after her release from the Montgomery County police in September, Genn handed her a roll of quarters. It was a small act, but to Newkirk it seemed proof that she had discovered a generous and resourceful attorney.

Genn believed that Pacheco and Newkirk and some of their supporters had a constitutional right to have some say in the disposition of the animals. The monkeys could not speak for themselves and the state was in a position, for legal reasons, to help only six of them. It seemed there was no one who represented the monkeys' own best interests but the animal rights activists. Clearly they had established personal relationships with the macaques. They had also spent a good deal of their own money to care for them while they were in Lehner's basement sanctuary. And they were taxpayers, whose taxes supported NIH's grant recipients. Genn felt these were grounds to file a class action suit against the animals' owners and custodians.

Genn's approach was unique and set yet another precedent in a case already filled with first of a kind actions. He likened the monkeys to battered children, who, because they cannot protect themselves in court, are represented by "next friends"—guardians who can bring legal actions on behalf of the abused children. If the suit were successful, it would mean that animal protection organizations could have the right to serve as next friends to animals used in laboratories. It would also show that the court recognized that these animals have the legal right to exist as something other than experimental tools.

To Newkirk and Pacheco, it meant simply that there was some chance the Silver Spring Monkeys might not have to go back to IBR. On December 3, International Primate Protection League (IPPL), the Animal Law Enforcement Association (a group of humane officers), PETA and seven individuals filed suit in the Montgomery County Circuit Court against IBR and the monkeys' custodians, Rick Swain, James Stunkard and the NIH Poolesville facility. Although PETA had catapulted to front page headlines in the last six months, it was still a new and small organization.

Newkirk and Pacheco turned to Shirley McGreal, who agreed to the established IPPL being listed as chief plaintiff. *IPPL, PETA, et al. v. IBR, et al.* would wend its way slowly through the court system for the next five years, each side gathering steam for a final battle in the Fourth Circuit Court of Appeals—the last stop before the Supreme Court.

Taub, who by now had hired a public relations firm in addition to two law firms, was also writing to NIH's Thomas Malone. Although his grant had been suspended, he wanted the monkeys returned immediately. But he also appeared to recognize that NIH was being scrutinized by both the public and by Congress, and was likely to be cautious.

"If return of the monkeys to this laboratory would create a situation that was potentially undesirable," he suggested in a December 30 letter to Malone, "other solutions might be possible . . . the monkeys could be kept somewhere else and brought into this laboratory, one or two at a time, for the terminal experimental work."

As Newkirk and Pacheco had guessed, Taub wouldn't keep the monkeys around for long if he ever got them back.

In the last days of 1981, the PETA volunteers began preparing for the second trial. Newkirk had returned to her job with the D.C. government, but continued to spend every free moment on the case. On the day before Christmas, she and Pacheco visited the monkeys at Poolesville and brought 1,000 oranges as gifts to the 1,000 primates who lived at the center. NIH, irritated by the publicity, cut off their visiting privileges.

Pacheco continued his work for Lantos and began a period of lobbying for the monkeys that lasted through the decade. With the filing of the suit and Congressional support he had received, he began to hope the monkeys might be released to a sanctuary, where they could be rehabilitated to some extent and live out their days in decent, spacious surroundings in the company of other macaques. The thought was always present, though, that they might be snatched from NIH any day and killed, and his periods of optimism were interspersed with long dark days of doubt. "Have I done all I could?" he asked himself repeatedly. By now he knew that the trial could have a huge impact on the lives of other animals imprisoned in laboratories. Still, he couldn't help but wonder if it would have been better for the monkeys if they had never returned from their secret sojourn in September. He tried to concentrate on Taub's second trial and the role he would play in telling the story to a jury.

Roger Galvin was back on the case, and after his first run-in with the scientific community, was eager to get started. This time, because the appeal was from the District Court, they would be starting essentially from scratch, and the jury could hear only that evidence involving the six monkeys listed in the original guilty verdict. This was frustrating for the state's chief witness. Pacheco had painstakingly gathered the information from IBR and now the jury would never hear about the barrels of dead monkeys or see many of the photos of accumulated filth.

But there would be some advantages, too. They would have more complete health records, thanks to Dave Rehnquist, and therefore more conclusive evidence that the six monkeys were desperately in need of veterinary care when they were seized from IBR. There was also much more time to prepare. The trial, originally scheduled for January of 1982, was delayed until June.

Then, in February, while Pacheco and Newkirk were trying to have their visitation rights reinstated, they got word that another one of the monkeys was in trouble. Hard Times, the monkey whose pain was so severe that he shifted constantly from one leg to the other, trying unsuccessfully to find a position he could tolerate for longer than a few seconds, was paralyzed from the neck down. The NIH veterinarians recommended euthanasia and Hard Times was destroyed, with PETA's blessing, but over objections from Taub and IBR.

There were now 15 Silver Spring Monkeys left.

The list of expert witnesses was long and once again Galvin immersed himself in the scientific literature gathered for him by Newkirk. He would have to lead the jury through the intricacies of dorsal rhizotomies, afferent roots and simian hematology. Once again, flights for Don Barnes and John McArdle had to be arranged, witnesses prepared and the exhibits sorted.

Through it all, the media interest never let up. Taub's conviction had sparked another round of newspaper editorials and television debates. The *New Republic* ran a cover story entitled "It's You or Fido," with a photo of a long-faced basset hound puppy under the masthead. "Taub has become a national scapegoat for the anti-vivisection movement" the article bemoaned. But not to worry, it concluded, "anti-vivisection may never amount to much . . . "

"Nightline" examined the issue on July 19, just after the second trial ended. One of the correspondents was Roger Caras, who had arrived before the police and hidden in the bushes outside IBR to cover the seizure of the monkeys. (Ten years later, Caras left ABC to become the president of the ASPCA in New York.)

The media worried Jimmy Miller, who was handling Taub's defense this time, rather than Edgar Brenner. In his 30 years practicing law in Montgomery County, he had never seen so much publicity.

"And if you are lucky enough to swear some 12 people, your honor," he complained to Judge McAuliffe at a pre-trial hearing, "I suspect you are going to have a combination of illiterate people or liars who said they did not read anything or know about this case in order to get on that jury."

To avoid a contaminated jury, he suggested moving the trial to Garrett County, Md., which received Pittsburgh rather than Washington news stations.

Taub and his attorneys had granted numerous interviews themselves, Galvin argued, and had added to the media interest they now claimed to be a problem. Taub had even done television debates.

" . . . Society is coming to grips with some very difficult decisions that are going to have to be made now and in the future," McAuliffe responded. "And maybe that is one of the reasons why there is publicity and has been publicity."

Ultimately, the judge declined to move the trial. He also denied another of Miller's motions—to sequester the jury.

The jury commissioner's office brought in 180 prospective jurors, more than Galvin had ever seen for any of the cases he had prosecuted, including death penalty cases. It was clear county officials were responding to public pressure—they didn't want any accusations of bias from either side. To everyone's surprise, more than 30 people were excused when they stated their belief that animals should not be used in any research. This wasn't thought to be a common view in 1982. Certainly Newkirk wouldn't have expected one-sixth of a randomly chosen group to oppose all animal experimentation. Once again she felt sure the time was right for an organization like PETA.

The trial began June 15 and lasted three weeks under Calvin Sanders, a round-figured, pink-skinned judge. He had presided over some of Newkirk's animal abuse cases in District Court and she liked the kind way he treated the people in his courtroom. Galvin knew Sanders as a conservative Republican who had been a very good trial lawyer before becoming a judge.

The *State of Maryland v. Taub* appeal set the county record for the greatest number of expert witnesses ever to testify in a single trial. Day after day, the testimony continued, until Newkirk began to lose track of time—it seemed to be an endless procession of experts for one side or the other. Pacheco's testimony alone took the entire opening day. The 12 regular members of the jury, seven women and five men, and the three alternates took notes throughout each of the long sessions. Each evening, Judge Sanders warned them not to speak to anyone about the case, not to watch news programs that might cover the trial, and not to read any newspapers that hadn't had the Silver Spring Monkeys articles clipped from them.

Many of the same witnesses returned and many new ones were brought into the County Circuit Courtroom. Taub's were even more laudatory than they had been the previous fall, and this time he had lined up representatives of the professional organizations of which he was a member to speak for him.

Galvin had carefully prepared for the witnesses from the American Psychological Association, the Society for Neuroscience, the Psychonomic Society, the Biofeedback Society and the Pavlovian Society. He figured these longtime colleagues of Taub's would have studied the case carefully and he was ready to delve into their scientific realm. As it turned out, he needn't have bothered.

"Has the Psychonomic Society done any investigation into this case?" he asked Michael D'Amato, who represented the group of research psychologists.

"The chairman of the governing board . . . contacted the other members of the board," D'Amato explained, "and it was agreed by the board that a representative be sent here to testify on behalf of Dr. Taub's scientific standing. In fact, a statement was drawn up to that effect."

"But in essence, there was no investigation by the board into the facts of this case?"

"No."

"I have no further questions, your honor," Galvin concluded.

The Society for Neuroscience did claim to have conducted a thorough investigation. Adrian Morrison, who had testified for Taub in the first trial, served on the investigating committee.

"Did you contact Dr. Hildebrandt?" Galvin asked him.

"No," Morrison testified.

"Did you know that Dr. Hildebrandt was listed with NIH as the attending veterinarian for IBR?"

"I don't remember the names of the veterinarians, to be honest," Morrison said.

"Did you talk to Dr. Stunkard?"

"No."

"Did you know that IBR had proposed him as a court custodian of the monkeys?" Galvin asked.

"Yes."

"But you didn't talk to him?"

"No."

"He had examined some of these monkeys, hadn't he? Or do you know?"

"No," Morrison answered, then said, "and I know that he had, yes."

"Did you talk to Dr. David Rehnquist at NIH, Poolesville, in the course of this investigation?"

"No, I did not."

Galvin glanced at the jury to see their reaction. He was pleased to see that they had stopped taking notes.

Galvin was also prepared to challenge Taub's assertion that the monkeys, without question, felt absolutely no pain in their deafferented limbs. They wouldn't mutilate their own arms if they felt pain, the defense claimed. This wasn't enough evidence for the prosecution. After all, some had lost fingers on their normal, feeling hands, and Sarah, who hadn't undergone surgery at all, had repeatedly attacked her own foot, apparently out of boredom and frustration.

Newkirk had even unearthed studies involving humans who had undergone deafferentation in an attempt to alleviate chronic pain. But some of the patients did not lose all feeling to their limbs; they complained of a burning sensation or the feeling of a pin prick. When Galvin questioned the defense witnesses, they seemed unsure of what to make of it.

"I'm aware of that," said psychology professor and animal experimenter Sol Steiner, "and I'm also aware, by the way this is not all patients, this is a small percentage of patients . . . I'm also aware of several other factors. Okay? Because the question is how do you interpret that? What does that mean?"

It seemed to Pacheco another example of convoluted scientific logic. Taub and his witnesses testified they knew beyond any doubt that the Silver Spring Monkeys, who could not explain what they experienced, had absolutely no feeling in their deafferented arms. But the views of deafferented human beings, who could describe exactly what they felt in their affected limbs, were somehow open to question.

The jury exited the courtroom on Wednesday afternoon, June 30, to begin deliberation, and for Pacheco, Newkirk and Galvin, a tense period of waiting began.

"When you have arrived upon a verdict," Judge Sanders instructed, "please knock on the door."

Several hours passed and no knock came. Sanders interrupted and sent the fatigued jury members to dinner at a nearby restaurant. They disappeared once more behind closed doors after the meal.

At 11 o'clock Sanders interrupted again.

"You have now been deliberating for some six hours or six and half hours . . . I would like to know, do you feel a verdict is imminent at this time?"

"No, I don't," the jury forewoman answered.

By the end of the second day of deliberation, the jury despaired of reaching a decision. Sanders encouraged them to be open to each other's arguments, but by late in the evening, when no verdict came in, he sent them home again.

It wasn't until Friday afternoon, the third day of deliberation, that the jury members filed back into the courtroom. They were obviously tired and some seemed agitated.

"Ladies and gentlemen of the jury," the clerk began, "look upon the accused. What say you? Is Edward Taub guilty or not guilty of cruelty to animals?"

For Big Boy, Billy, Domitian, Paul, and Titus—not guilty. For Nero—guilty as charged.

Though only the 12 jurors know exactly what was said during their three days of deliberation, several of them called Galvin after the trial. The verdict, they told him, was a compromise. The vote was 11 to one to convict on all six counts, and the lone dissenting juror wouldn't budge.

A few weeks later, on August 24, three of the jurors met with representatives of NIH to urge them not to return the monkeys to Taub.

The guilty verdict was another victory for PETA and the fledgling animal rights movement, and it capped a year of violent emotions and hard work for Pacheco and Newkirk. Their organization was now established, and with its success came an increasing number of demands on their time and financial resources. Dozens of people called each day with stories of animals suffering in their communities; letters were stuffed in their post office box by the hundreds. The requests usually followed a pattern: "Please investigate the (laboratory, ranch, slaughterhouse, zoo, animal shelter) in my town. The (dogs, horses, cats, goats, pigs, rats, sheep) are being (tortured, starved, killed). Only PETA can save the animals."

The impossibility of responding to each call for help prompted Newkirk to set up a network of activists around the country, and to write and distribute "how to" activist packs. Pacheco began a public speaking tour, traveling by car or by plane to dozens of cities and telling people how they could investigate abuse and begin their own campaigns.

With little time for anything but work, Newkirk's and Pacheco's personal relationship began to suffer. When the man Newkirk had been seeing before she met Pacheco began calling, she was startled to find that she still cared for him, and she began to question the depth of her feelings for Pacheco. But it was when Newkirk discovered that Pacheco had been spending time with a young research assistant from another animal protection organization that the romance in their relationship came to an abrupt end. After a round of verbal fireworks, Newkirk threw him out of her house.

Pacheco moved in with some PETA volunteers who lived nearby, but again, his and Newkirk's animal rights work came first. The two continued to spend so many hours together that before long Pacheco moved back in—this time as a housemate.

The new relationship worked well for both. Although Newkirk was irritated by Pacheco's occasional impracticality, and he was frustrated by her obstinacy about campaign tactics, they developed a friendship—and partnership—that would remain solid for many years.

Throughout the late summer and fall months of 1982, the battle raged over who owned the monkeys and what should happen to them after Taub's second conviction. NIH said the monkeys belonged to IBR, but they weren't planning on returning them until PETA's civil case was either heard in court or dismissed. Taub wanted them back—but not until his grant was reinstated. To be on the safe side, Edward Genn and PETA filed for a restraining order to prevent NIH from moving the monkeys.

Interest was growing in Congress, too, thanks to Tom and Annette Lantos's support and Pacheco's lobbying. In late August, 47 Representatives and six Senators, including Joe Biden of Delaware and Alan Cranston from California, wrote to NIH director James Wyngaarden and asked him to terminate Taub's grant and release the monkeys to a sanctuary.

A week later, Wyngaarden notified Taub that the suspension of his grant had been made permanent. Wyngaarden also warned "that either IBR or Dr. Taub, or both, may be made subject to additional sanctions. In particular, senior staff . . . now are considering whether there should be restrictions on future funding opportunities . . . "

Taub was fined $500 by Judge Sanders the next day. Jimmy Miller asked for a one to two month delay on any discussion of the monkeys' future because Taub was appealing NIH's decision, and of course, he would appeal the court's decision, too.

Once again, the monkeys were in limbo.

Dr. Edward Taub leaving the District Courtroom on the day of his sentencing, November 23, 1981. He was convicted on six counts of cruelty toward animals.

Alex Pacheco and friend.

Ingrid Newkirk and friend.

Faces of pain: two of the monkeys at IBR.

Dr. Taub's office at IBR. Items include a monkey's skull and hand.

The monkey's hand, displayed on Dr. Taub's desk, was evidently used as a paperweight.

This half-size refrigerator served as the monkeys' "medicine cabinet" at IBR. Note the bag of rotted apples mingling with the medicine on the floor.

Pacheco was shocked to discover two dead monkeys in this formaldehyde-filled vat.

A monkey huddles in his 18-inch-wide cage. He has bitten all the fingers off his left, deafferented hand. Note the wires jutting from the walls.

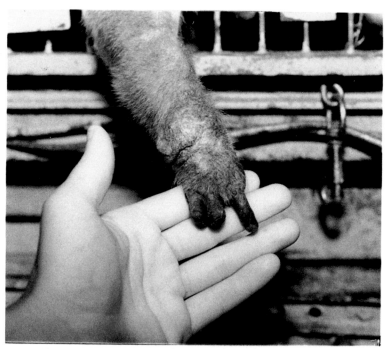

A monkey's mutilated, deafferented hand grasps at a healthy, human one. Despite the fact that nearly all of the monkey's fingers are gone, his hand has not been treated.

Naturally social animals, two monkeys make a pathetic attempt at contact.

A monkey is strapped into a restraint chair used for "acute noxious stimuli" tests. The term means purposely inflicted pain.

Alex Pacheco at the Congressional hearing on the use of animals for experimentation in October, 1981.

A monkey enjoys fresh water and sunshine after years of captivity.

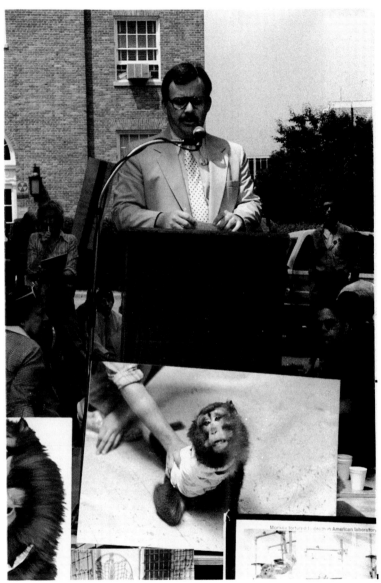

Roger Galvin, Taub's prosecutor, addresses the press outside the District Courtroom.

This photograph, perhaps more than any of the others, brought home to the public the degree of suffering that the animals endured.

The 15 candles, one for each surviving monkey, placed outside NIH director James Wyngaarden's home by Newkirk and Pacheco.

Pacheco surrounded by thousands of letters from supporters.

Congressman Bob Smith, an animal research supporter, became one of the monkeys' most vigorous champions.

Congressman Tom Lantos and his wife, Annette, as children in Budapest, Hungary, in 1939. Not long after this picture was taken Lantos was sent to a forced labor camp. The couple's suffering during the Holocaust may account for their compassion for the plight of the animals.

Congressman and Mrs. Lantos today. Both proved immensely helpful in the fight to save the Silver Spring Monkeys.

Ingrid Newkirk and Alex Pacheco.
all photographs except Congressman and Mrs. Lantos courtesy PETA

Chapter Eleven

Monkeys in Limbo

"It's not that humans and non-humans are identical . . . but the lack of understanding that led to the slave trade is the same lack of understanding many people have about animals today. When slaves were brought over from Africa, many people believed they were not human, that they didn't have feelings. Many people believe that primates and other animals don't have feelings, too, and they do."
—Jane Goodall, the Miami Herald, *May 11, 1993*

Nero's furry coat became glossy after the amputation of his deafferented limb, and his health improved rapidly. Not long after the surgery, he began to move easily around his small quarters, climbing up to his perch, feeding himself fresh fruit with his remaining hand. Dave Rehnquist, the Poolesville veterinarian, was pleased with Nero's recovery. In fact, he felt the treatment had worked so well that he recommended amputation for some of the other monkeys whose arms had been repeatedly battered and traumatized over the years. To his increasing frustration, he was not permitted to treat the 15 macaques as he thought best for them; they did not belong to NIH, and Rehnquist was to do only what was necessary to maintain them for their temporary stay.

But the "temporary" arrangement stretched on and on. Rehnquist, along with his caretakers and technicians, took care of the monkeys for nearly five years while PETA and its attorneys fought their way through the courts and negotiated with NIH officials.

Ultimately, Pacheco's and Newkirk's countless hours in legal libraries, plotting strategies with Edward Genn, writing to NIH's William Raub, who handled the case, and James Wyngaarden, were to no avail. It became clear in the following years that the Silver Spring Monkeys case was a political hot potato. While PETA's suit sat mired in the court system, NIH officials continued to claim that they were not free to release the animals, and wouldn't be, as long as Taub and IBR claimed ownership. This was expedient for the government agency, which was under increasing pressure from the scientific community. NIH's investigation of Taub and termination of his grant (because he was not in compliance with NIH policy on the care of laboratory animals) triggered a backlash from scientific organizations whose members regularly used primates and other animals in their studies. NIH was accused of pandering to a group of "animal lunatics," of selling out one of their own. It didn't seem to matter that Taub had been convicted in two courts of law and that the NIH investigating committee hadn't even talked to Pacheco. Animal experimenters perceived the proverbial thin end of the wedge—if they gave in now, they argued, if they didn't stand united against their enemy, the animal protectionists, science as they knew it would come crashing down around them. They were already creating lobbying and public relations organizations like the Foundation for Biomedical Research to spread the gospel of animal experimentation.

NIH was as sensitive to criticism from within their ranks as from without, so for five years, agency officials did the one thing that angered just about everybody—nothing. They refused to vindicate Taub, who was working his way through the Department of Health and Human Service's grant appeal system, and they refused to release the monkeys from their bondage.

Pacheco and Newkirk, whose visiting privileges were reinstated soon after Taub's second conviction, continued to drive to Poolesville to see Sarah, Augustus, Sisyphus, Brooks and the other monkeys. Adidas, one of Newkirk's favorites, remained playful, eager to be groomed, and made friendly smacking noises when visitors approached. It was encouraging to see the animals in relatively good physical health, but for Pacheco particularly, it was heartbreaking to watch them spend month after month in such confined, if clean, quarters. Monkeys are naturally social animals, and for these macaques, torn away from their family groups in the wild, it seemed to Pacheco cruel and pointless to deny them the small comfort they would have if they were allowed to live as a group. He and Newkirk began to push for resocialization and group living arrangements.

Eventually, Pacheco felt compelled to ask for a more permanent solution for one of the monkeys. Domitian, Pacheco's favorite of all the animals, who was so like Chi Chi, was slowly losing his mind. His bizarre actions were described by Rehnquist as "behavioral abnormalities," but to Pacheco, who had forged a bond with Domitian, the monkey had clearly lost his connection to reality. Initially he became more aggressive with the people who entered the colony room. He no longer puckered his lips or offered himself for grooming. Then he began to circle, around and around, inside the steel walls of his cold home. Eventually, he sat motionless, unresponsive to anyone, staring up at the gray ceiling of his cage. Pacheco couldn't bear to see him like this when he had been so friendly, so ready to grasp Pacheco's hand, to have a relationship with someone who didn't hurt him. Rather than see Domitian suffer the madness of his imprisonment, Pacheco wanted him destroyed.

Rehnquist was inclined to agree. He didn't see the point in keeping the animals year after year. But it would be years before Rehnquist's supervisors at NIH agreed with him, and when they did, it was on their terms.

In the meantime, PETA continued to grow. Though the scientific community was successful in keeping the Silver Spring Monkeys out of the hands of the activists, the animal rights movement nevertheless gathered steam in the form of members, contributions and public support. By 1985, PETA's membership list had grown to more than 95,000 and would double in the next year.

Newkirk quit her job as poundmaster in 1984 to devote herself full-time to PETA's work. She took no salary (and still doesn't), choosing instead to funnel every penny directly into the campaigns. She drew from a pension fund to meet her expenses, and she began to live even more frugally than before. She remembered the thousands of people in India who lived without the luxuries that had become necessities to the Western world, and felt fortunate that she could choose to live inexpensively, that she wasn't forced into poverty. She began to arrange her priorities. For one thing, she stopped buying clothes and became the willing recipient of "hand-me-downs" from her friends. She sold the book collection she had been saving for her retirement, her small collection of antique furniture and her jewelry.

Newkirk covered Pacheco's living expenses in those early years before she left the D.C. government, so that he could run PETA's campaigns. Their recently cooled romance had developed into a comfortable working relationship, with only occasional clashes regarding campaigns and similar matters. During one such confrontation Newkirk dumped the entire contents of Pacheco's briefcase on the floor; but both agreed that these heated arguments were the result of their shared concern about choosing the most effective course of action, and not from an inability to work together.

Pacheco remembers those early years as ones of non-stop work, seven days a week. There was no money for clothes or record albums, hair cuts or any of the things most college students deem indispensable. His car was ancient, rusting and battered. He and Newkirk survived on a few hours sleep each night, sometimes napping in their clothes for a few hours after a late strategy meeting, then up early for a hot shower, coffee and more work.

The Silver Spring Monkeys case gave a boost to the animal protection movement, and long-established organizations enjoyed increased media attention and burgeoning membership. At the radical edge and growing fast was PETA, which by 1984 was bringing in enough in donations to pay Pacheco and a few employees the whopping salary of four dollars an hour. (Since then, Pacheco has never drawn more than $20,000 a year.)

PETA employees and volunteers followed in the tradition of the civil rights movement and organized acts of civil disobedience—a tactic seldom before used in the fight to protect animals. Newkirk and Pacheco racked up more than two dozen arrests between them; their hours behind the bars of various city jails were a reminder of what monkeys, rabbits and other animals endured for their entire lives.

Pacheco's work at IBR was the forerunner of what was to become PETA's hallmark—undercover investigations. In the next decade, PETA employees would work as laboratory technicians, slaughterhouse workers and animal caretakers, documenting and releasing information that would change the way people perceived the meat and medical industries in this country.

PETA began to send newsletters to its members and in each issue listed simple actions for supporters to protest the use of animals for food, clothing and experimentation. Everything from letter writing to demonstrating was encouraged, and stories about new animal rights groups began to pop up in newspapers across the country. PETA also offered complete confidentiality to anyone reporting abuses in laboratories, and in the summer of 1983 received a tip that the Department of Defense was shooting dogs, pigs and goats in two "wound study" labs and was planning to open a third.

PETA sought opinions from medical doctors who served in Korea and Vietnam. They agreed that shooting a goat in a laboratory did not accurately simulate the conditions of a battlefield, and further, that treating these artificially induced wounds did not prepare surgeons to help soldiers shot in combat. Seven hundred physicians signed PETA's petition denouncing the wound labs.

When PETA went public with its information, Secretary of Defense Caspar Weinberger suspended all military funds for shooting animals. It was the second time in U.S. history—Taub's case was the first—that federal funding was pulled from an animal research project exposed by animal rights activists. Experimenters who had thought that the Silver Spring Monkeys case was a one-of-a-kind occurrence were rapidly learning otherwise.

But there was little time to celebrate. Hard on the heels of this success came another devastating setback in the Silver Spring Monkeys case. On August 10, 1983, nearly two years after the monkeys were seized from IBR, the Maryland Court of Appeals overturned Taub's conviction.

Pacheco was shocked to learn their decision had nothing to do with the evidence he and the Montgomery County police collected. The dozens of photographs introduced in the trials, the experts' testimony, the conditions of the monkeys themselves were not relevant because the court, under Judge James Couch, found that Maryland's anti-cruelty statute did not apply to research facilities funded by the federal government. The law exempted hunting and pest control and therefore, the court decided, in a rather broad leap of logic, the legislature meant to exclude animal experimentation under a federal program, too.

Pacheco, Newkirk and the PETA supporters were not about to sit quietly while Taub won on what they believed was a misinterpretation of the law. Within hours, phone calls were pouring into Maryland Attorney General Steve Sachs's office, asking him to urge the court to reconsider its ruling as there was nothing in the statute that exempted federally funded laboratories. When Sachs didn't respond, the activists picketed his office. But the ruling stood.

Although Sachs could do little to change the decision, Maryland legislators didn't hesitate to show their displeasure— they rewrote the law. Within a year, the language of the statute was changed to read: "It is the intention of the General Assembly that all animals, whether they be privately owned, strays, domesticated, feral [domestic animals turned wild], farm, corporately or institutionally owned, under private, State or *federally funded scientific or medical activities* . . . shall be protected from intentional cruelty . . . " (emphasis added). The legislature hadn't thought there was a loophole in the law in the first place, but they wasted no time in closing the one created by the Court of Appeals.

It came as no surprise to Pacheco, Newkirk, Roger Galvin, Rick Swain and those who had worked with the state on the prosecution, that Taub trumpeted the ruling as a vindication of all charges. The decision was also heralded as a victory by the organizations that had attempted to shield him behind the cloak of scientific inquiry. Within weeks, Taub was speaking before a convention of the American Psychological Association in Anaheim, Calif.

During his hour long speech, he told the audience he had been charged with 119 counts of animal abuse, although the actual number was 17, one for each monkey seized (he added all the subsections of each of the single counts to come up with the higher number); that he had been acquitted of 118 counts (he was acquitted of 16); and the Appeals Court had found him innocent. He again claimed that Pacheco had admitted to staging two of the photographs, apparently referring to the pictures of the fecal trays Pacheco had pulled out in order to show the thick layer of urine and excrement. But his real message could be summarized in one word: beware.

"What is happening to me is beginning to happen to other scientists," he is quoted as saying in the *San Francisco Chronicle*. "We can anticipate more incidents, and it is important to know what to do."

While Taub spoke inside the convention center, his effigy was burned outside by more than 100 members of recently formed grassroots animal rights groups who carried signs with such slogans as "Research Means Animal Torture" and "Experiments Repeated Again & Again for Fat Government Grants." For these activists Taub had come to represent all that was wrong with animal experimentation: his work had been funded by tax dollars, "policed" by a USDA inspector who didn't even bother to verify the number of animals in the facility, and no matter what he did to the monkeys in his care, he was defended by many of his fellow animal experimenters.

Even NIH officials grew impatient with the claims of some researchers that Taub had provided optimum care for the Silver Spring Monkeys. William Raub and NIH veterinarian Joe Held wrote to the *Neuroscience Newsletter* in April, 1983, to dispute several points in an article by Taub's trial witnesses Adrian Morrison and Peter Hand.

"Hand and Morrison suggest that a 'repugnant appearance of the limbs' is an inevitable sequel to deafferentation. However," Raub and Held wrote, "monkeys subjected to the same surgical procedure and maintained at [NIH] since May 1981 have not developed lesions comparable to those in five of the nine deaf-ferented monkeys from IBR . . . Based on these observations it would appear that fractures, dislocations, lacerations, punctures, contusions, and abrasions with accompanying infection, acute and chronic inflammation, and necrosis are not the inevitable consequences of deafferentation."

As if to prove the point, the NIH ruling to terminate Taub's grant was upheld in June of 1984 by the Department of Health and Human Services despite the Appeals Court decision. Although sanctions were never brought against Taub, as NIH had earlier threatened, he would not have his funding reinstated.

This appeared to be the end of the line for Taub's experiments with the Silver Spring Monkeys. He had resigned from IBR, which by now had changed its name from the Institute for Behavioral Research to the Institute for Behavioral Resources. Though he had recently received a Guggenheim fellowship, he told a local reporter, "My career's been destroyed. I haven't worked in three years."

The HHS decision to cut Taub's grant once and for all seemed to remove the final obstacle to the release of the monkeys to a sanctuary. Neither Taub nor IBR had requested the return of the animals, and even if they did, it was doubtful NIH would comply; *IPPL, PETA et al. v. IBR, NIH et al.* was still pending and the growing animal rights movement was becoming increasingly vocal.

Just two weeks before HHS upheld the grant termination, the Animal Liberation Front broke into a head wound laboratory at the University of Pennsylvania, where many of Taub's supporters taught and conducted their own experiments. More than 70 hours of videotape were removed, copied and left on PETA's doorstep. The footage, which had been taken by the experimenter, showed inadequately anesthetized baboons strapped into a hydraulic device that pummeled their heads. Lab workers laughed at the brain-damaged primates. "You better hope the antivivisection people don't get a hold of this film," one worker joked, as another held a wounded baboon in front of the camera, waving the animal's hand—a parody of a human mother helping her baby wave goodbye.

PETA soon organized a campaign and within weeks, another embarrassing example of federally funded animal studies hit the media.

Throughout this time, Pacheco and Newkirk tried to push NIH along by simplifying the process of releasing the Silver Spring Monkeys. For one thing, they located three possible homes for the macaques. One was Primarily Primates in San Antonio, Texas, which specialized in rehabilitating monkeys and chimpanzees used in experimentation. The director, Wallace Swett, provided the primates with enormous indoor/outdoor enclosures, and worked to resocialize animals who had been isolated during their years in laboratories. The facility was licensed by the state of

Texas and the U.S. Department of the Interior, and had two veterinarians on call 24 hours a day.

But NIH wasn't budging. The letters from Lantos and other members of Congress, the letters and editorials in newspapers urging NIH to retire the monkeys didn't move the agency. Pacheco and Newkirk were furious that NIH seemed to care less about the animals than about remaining politically safe. NIH officials and their attorneys seemed to be speaking out of both sides of their mouths. They couldn't release the monkeys, they said, because they were named in PETA's lawsuit—even though PETA's attorneys had made it clear that the suit would be dropped if the animals were released. The Justice Department attorney handling the case for NIH had even filed a brief which stated that "perpetual care of the primates at NIH, an agency authorized to conduct and fund biomedical and behavioral research, would not be an appropriate expenditure of taxpayer dollars."

Yet the monkeys were still in NIH's custody three years later and the bill for their housing, food and veterinary care was being footed by the taxpayers.

By 1985, NIH's political fence-sitting had become intolerable to Pacheco and Newkirk. Though the monkeys were in relatively good physical health, they remained caged individually at NIH's animal center, with few of their psychological needs met. Domitian's mental state continued to deteriorate, and to Pacheco, all of the monkeys appeared depressed. They were paying dearly for their "crimes" of being members of a species abundant in number, easy to capture for experimental tools, and most of all, for being symbols of the ever-growing animal rights movement.

It seemed so little to ask that 15 unwanted monkeys be allowed to sit in the sun, to groom each other, to breathe fresh air, Pacheco thought. He had been visiting the animals in Poolesville for four years, while document after document was filed by an endless succession of attorneys from all sides. He began to suspect that NIH was playing a waiting game; maybe they were hoping he would get tired of the whole exhausting mess and go home. If so, they underestimated him. Pacheco could never turn his back on the monkeys. He was committed to this battle, no matter how long it took or how much it cost.

Congressman Lantos's wife Annette believed NIH's resistance to releasing the primates was personal, as well as political. It was obvious Raub and the other NIH officials were sensitive to the complaints of the scientific community. But they also knew Pacheco cared deeply about each of the monkeys. Keeping these animals in their steel cells, she believed, was the worst punishment they could inflict on Pacheco, short of returning them to Taub, for interference in their "private" world.

By now, PETA's lawsuit had been transferred from the Montgomery County Circuit Court to the U.S. District Court, at NIH's request. To argue the case, Edward Genn first had to prove that his clients had a legitimate interest in what happened to the monkeys, that they had standing to sue. NIH's attorneys believed the District Court was less likely to grant standing.

As it turned out, they were right. In April, Judge John Hargrove dismissed *IPPl et al. v. IBR et al.* without hearing any oral arguments.

Chapter Twelve

Congress is Watching

"Now the scientific community is seeing a need to account for itself—and that's uncomfortable for a lot of scientists. It's gone from the notion that 'if it's good for science, it must be good' to 'if it's science, we'd better be able to account for it.' "
—Charles R. McCarthy, NIH, the Washington Times, *August 4, 1986*

It was raining when Newkirk learned that Judge Hargrove had dismissed the suit. Great drops of rain pelted the window of her Takoma Park house that now served as PETA's headquarters. The bird feeders hanging from several tree branches in the leafy backyard swung back and forth in the wet gusts of wind. It was the right sort of day to be depressed, but she didn't have the energy to spare on feeling bad. If she had learned anything in the last four years, it was that tenacity and good hard work were the most useful reactions to bad news. It would have been easy to give in to gloom, but what good would that do? The one trait she had always disliked about the animal welfare movement was its short attention span. Some organizations donned new campaigns each spring, and by fall, shoved them into storage like worn-out clothes. She and Pacheco decided early on that they wouldn't drop a project; once they started something, they'd finish it. Animals needed more than five-minute friends.

The thing to do now was to sit down, take a look at the situation and come up with the right course of action. This couldn't have come at a worse time. They were working 18 hours a day to stop the head bashing at the University of Pennsylvania and had several other cases in progress. Nevertheless, they were in Genn's office within hours.

Edward Genn hated injustice. Although he was a quiet, meticulous man, not given to outbursts of rage, it seemed to Newkirk on this day that his eyes glittered with anger. He always worked with intensity, but now his carefully controlled energy was rising to the surface. His clients had a right to voice their concerns, and their rights were being trampled on by the court. To make matters worse, this was the second time it had happened.

Judge Hargrove inherited PETA's lawsuit, along with 450 other cases, when he was appointed to the U.S. District Court in 1984. In the fall of the same year, he requested a brief letter describing the relevant points of the lawsuit from the attorneys representing both sides. By this time, it was clear that a resolution could not be reached without going to court. For this reason, the case was referred to U.S. Magistrate Frederic Smalkin, who was to review the file and give the lawyers a chance to argue their points in person, then make a recommendation to Hargrove. Since NIH and IBR had filed for a dismissal of the case, Smalkin would examine this issue first. After this they would go on to depositions, pre-trial and trial.

But Smalkin never called Genn or the other attorneys. He never heard their arguments, never asked for an update on what had occurred since the suit was filed several years before. In January, 1985, he simply issued his recommendation to Hargrove that the case be dismissed because the plaintiffs didn't have the power to assert the rights of animals.

"Federal case law simply does not confer standing upon animals, at this juncture," Smalkin wrote in his report.

Genn was furious. He filed a 30-page objection in which he accused Smalkin of failing to address the relevant issues. The magistrate didn't appear to know the law had been changed to specify protection for animals in laboratories. He'd ignored the relationship between the PETA volunteers and the primates— they had visited the animals far more than Taub had in the last three years—as well as the expense they'd incurred caring for the monkeys.

Most troubling, the magistrate seemed to think the monkeys faced no threat, even though Taub had stated they would be experimented on and killed if he ever got them back.

"While it may not seem a harm to the Magistrate," Genn wrote, "most people would consider that the inflicted death of something living is a real harm, not only to them but also for those bonded to them."

Genn asked that the recommendation be set aside, at least until he had a chance to argue his case in court. For years, his clients had negotiated and waited for the court, hoping against all logic that an agreement could be reached. Genn wasn't going to let Smalkin's version of the suit go unchallenged.

Despite Genn's impassioned objection, Judge Hargrove accepted Smalkin's report and refused to hear oral arguments. Now, on this rainy afternoon in April, Genn fumed as he explained the next step to Pacheco and Newkirk. The first thing to do was file a motion to set aside the dismissal.

Pacheco asked what would happen if the motion failed.

If it failed, Genn answered, Pacheco's constitutional rights to due process would have been denied, and Genn would appeal to the next higher court.

This time, Genn's motion to set aside the dismissal ran 17 pages.

"We are candid to say," Genn wrote, "that, while we most appreciate the fact that this Court is burdened, as are all courts, these litigants have a constitutional right that cannot be dismissed in this manner."

Seven months passed before Judge Hargrove responded.

In the meantime, the enmity between NIH and PETA grew.

In July, Newkirk and Pacheco led 100 activists up to the eighth floor of Building 31-B on the NIH campus in Bethesda. Here, in the offices where research grants were denied or approved, the activists sat down and refused to leave until funding for the University of Pennsylvania head injury experiments was cut.

Pandemonium followed. Campus police cleared the employees from the floor, shut off the water and cranked up the air-conditioning in an attempt to freeze the activists out. But the siege continued for three days and nights. While the police tried to figure out what to do next, reporters broadcast live from the scene, showing segments of the head bashing videotapes.

On Day Two of the takeover, a beleaguered NIH asked to meet with PETA's legal counsel to try to hash out a compromise that would bring an end to its embarrassing loss of control. Pacheco put together a list of demands to be met before he would leave Building 31-B, the most urgent of which was the termination of the head wound grant. Among other conditions he called for was the release of the 15 monkeys. Then he handed the list to PETA's attorney for the sit-in, Gary Francione.

This was the first time Francione had represented PETA, though he'd known Pacheco and Newkirk since 1982. At that time, not long out of University of Virginia Law School, Francione was clerking for Supreme Court Justice Sandra Day O'Connor—and picking up stray dogs. For some reason D.C.'s homeless dogs seemed to lurk in the shrubbery around the Court and Francione found it difficult to ignore their lean ribs and hungry eyes. So he did what he thought was the only logical thing to do—he brought them into his office (which didn't please the occupant of the next room, Justice William Rehnquist) and called animal control.

Newkirk answered the call herself, curious to see what kind of person would bring a stray animal into the marbled mausoleum where the country's most important decisions were made. She like what she found—a young, energetic, dark-haired lawyer whose words couldn't keep up with his thoughts. And he was a vegetarian.

Like Pacheco, Francione happened to tour a slaughterhouse when he was younger. He walked into the plant a normal college student and came out vowing not to participate, even as a consumer, in such a bloody business. Later he read *Animal Liberation* and followed the newspaper accounts of the student who exposed abuse in a laboratory in Silver Spring, but it wasn't until he met Newkirk and heard the story from Pacheco's own lips that Francione began to change the direction of his life. Later, Francione and his wife, Anna Charleton, also an attorney, started the Animal Rights Law Clinic at Rutgers University.

At the time of the sit-in, Francione was teaching law at the University of Pennsylvania, across campus from the head wound laboratory.

Roger Galvin, now working for the public defenders office, accompanied Francione to the meeting with William Raub, NIH attorney Robert Lanman and Murray Goldstein, whose office was occupied by the activists. It was Francione's first meeting with Lanman and the others. He didn't know then that he would be spending the following summer negotiating with them on a daily basis for PETA's right to protest NIH's handling of the primates.

On this day, Lanman was placating. He assured Francione and Galvin that NIH was investigating the Penn experiments, would examine the evidence and would decide what to do in a couple of months. They were acting in good faith; they weren't trying to hide anything, he said.

"If you're acting in good faith," Francione asked, "why are you fighting PETA on the Silver Spring Monkeys case?"

This was the turning point in the meeting, as Francione remembers it. The cordial expressions on the faces of the three men sitting opposite vanished. Goldstein leaned forward and shouted, "You want the fucking monkeys? You can have the fucking monkeys!"

A calmer Lanman explained that it was NIH's position that the primates belonged to IBR. Raub, the middle-aged scientist who had spent his career pushing NIH policy, nodded his head in agreement.

Francione argued that NIH could take legal ownership at any time under the provisions of its own grant program or under the USDA guidelines. Lanman disagreed. They argued for the next half hour, neither side willing to concede.

Francione and Galvin should get IBR to relinquish ownership to NIH, Lanman finally said, exasperated, and Lanman would agree to transfer the monkeys to a sanctuary.

Realizing it was the best they were going to get out of the meeting, Francione and Galvin agreed to approach IBR. They reached no compromise on ending the takeover of the NIH offices.

On Day Four, soon after the "Today" show interviewed Newkirk and aired footage of the sit-in, Health and Human Services Secretary Margaret Heckler ordered NIH to cut the funds to the University of Pennsylvania. She had watched PETA's video the night before and was shocked by the treatment of the baboons. Pacheco, Newkirk and the activists emerged, cold, hungry, exhausted from lack of sleep, but victorious.

Newkirk and Pacheco headed home for hot showers after the press release was typed and distributed, and the interviews were over. The intervention of a cabinet-level official was an unexpected conclusion to four difficult days, and later there would be drinks and celebration, but each had a stack of correspondence and phone messages to deal with first.

Their triumph rankled NIH officials and embarrassed director James Wyngaarden, who had defended the experiments when PETA first released the videotape. But worse than that, from the standpoint of NIH and the scientists they financed, PETA's campaigns had shown that the conditions at IBR were not the exception. The Silver Spring Monkeys had turned out to be just one example of flaws within the federally funded research system. NIH officials, still under pressure from grant recipients, Congress and animal rights supporters, had begun to deny any problems. PETA may have invaded their territory and won a few skirmishes, but they weren't giving up any more ground without a fight.

By fall, without ever speaking directly to anyone from IBR, Francione and Galvin succeeded in persuading Taub's former employers to give up the monkeys. They spent hours on the phone with Jimmy Miller, Taub's defense attorney, now representing IBR. Francione found Miller's straightforward "good ol' boy" approach refreshing after circling the fire with Lanman. Miller seemed to have a genuine desire to work out an arrangement. There was no way, he said, that IBR would give those monkeys to PETA or any other animal group, but they just might let NIH have them.

Two months after the siege, a letter was sent that should have solved everyone's problem.

On September 24, IBR chief executive officer, Joseph Vasapoli, wrote to William Raub at NIH. In his brief letter, he cleared the way for release of the monkeys.

"At a recent meeting," Vasapoli wrote, "of the Board of Trustees of the Institute for Behavior Resources, Inc., it was resolved that IBR relinquish ownership to NIH of the fifteen primates presently under NIH care."

Although IBR's "objective is to relinquish ownership of the primates without publicity," Vasapoli explained, it "appears that NIH is the sole entity in a position to determine what use or disposition of the primates should be made in public interest."

With his signature at the bottom of the page, Vasapoli eliminated the only impediment to releasing the animals that NIH publicly acknowledged. The primates didn't belong to them, NIH officials had stated again and again, so they couldn't turn them over to a sanctuary. Now the monkeys *did* belong to NIH. There was no longer any legal reason to keep them confined within their steel prisons. Nor should there have been any other obstacle. PETA had already offered to pay all costs for relocating the monkeys and to shoulder the expense of lifetime care. To alleviate NIH's worry about negative publicity, Pacheco also agreed not to distribute photographs of the animals in their spacious new homes.

But NIH suddenly forgot its promise to turn the animals over. Pacheco and Newkirk had no idea that while they were working with Genn to change Hargrove's decision, and persuading IBR to give up ownership, NIH was plotting to get rid of the monkeys in a way that suited its own political goals. Rather than quietly accepting custody and negotiating the terms of a transfer to a sanctuary, NIH refused to take the animals.

"The NIH does not accept the proposal that we take ownership of [the monkeys]," NIH's William Raub wrote to Vasapoli on October 2. "We have no research protocols, either ongoing or planned, for which these animals are appropriate."

Then, as though he was unaware of PETA's lawsuit, as though he had never discussed transferring the macaques to a sanctuary, Raub added, "we wish to discontinue our temporary custody of the IBR monkeys as soon as possible. We are prepared to release the animals immediately to an IBR official or an IBR designee."

Raub undoubtedly knew that IBR would never turn the primates over to the people who had exposed Taub's laboratory. His letter was proof that NIH had no intention of letting the monkeys slip out of the hands of the animal experimenters, or more to the point, into the hands of the animal rights activists. NIH officials seemed to be taking the coward's course. As long as they refused ownership of the monkeys, they could avoid saying no to PETA; if they gave the appearance of being powerless to make a decision about the animals, Congress and the public couldn't accuse them of being heartless and manipulative. Rather than accept the animals, retire them and close the case, they chose to keep the monkeys in limbo and fight PETA's lawsuit—at taxpayer expense.

It would be months before Pacheco and Newkirk discovered how close they came. When Francione found out, he called Lanman and demanded an explanation. Lanman had none, and that, Francione remembers, was when he lost the little composure he had left and began call Lanman every name he could think of.

"But Lanman wasn't an evil man," Francione says today. "He just worked for evil people."

It didn't take long for NIH officials to cook up a more acceptable version of the facts: Vasapoli had agreed to relinquish ownership without consulting the other members of IBR's board. When they learned what he had done, they rescinded the offer.

It was a transparent lie as far as Francione was concerned, and the letter from Raub proved it. If the board forced Vasapoli to retract, why did Raub write to refuse ownership of the monkeys?

Although NIH tried to abdicate responsibility to IBR, the agency's motives were clear: they were willing to go to great lengths to protect their castle walls, which thanks to PETA and an increasingly indignant public, were beginning to crack.

In the next few years, NIH's battle against the animal rights movement would escalate, and the agency would organize and fund, with tax dollars, its own campaign to sway the public's perception of animal experimentation.

Judge Hargrove didn't make up his mind about Genn's lengthy objection until nearly Thanksgiving of that year. By this time Pacheco was used to the agonizingly slow pace of the legal system, and even though his better sense told him not to expect too much, he still pinned some hope on Hargrove's upcoming ruling. He felt that if he could argue his case in court, he could show how important this was. He could describe the monkeys as the living, breathing, suffering beings they were. If he could just make the court understand that he didn't care about the publicity anymore—PETA had enough to deal with as it was; if NIH would let the macaques go to a sanctuary, he would never again utter the words "Silver Spring Monkeys" in public.

But it was not to be. On November 19, Judge Hargrove denied Genn's motion, again without a hearing, and upheld his earlier decision to dismiss the case.

Genn filed an appeal with the Fourth Circuit Court.

Although PETA made little progress in the Silver Spring Monkeys case in 1985, NIH was powerless to stop the inevitable changes brought about by the animal rights movement. In April, the Animal Liberation Front broke into a laboratory at the University of California at Riverside and drove away with more than 1,000 animals. One of them was an infant monkey reared in complete isolation for use in a vision study.

PETA later received a copy of a videotape showing Britches, as the tiny primate was called, at the time of his rescue. A heavy, cube-shaped, metal apparatus connected to an electrical wire was taped to his head. Beneath layers of surgical tape and two grimy pads, his eyes were sewn shut with thick black suture. After hearing about the experiment, the president of the American Council of the Blind, Dr. Grant Mack, condemned both the treatment of Britches and the waste of research funds it represented. NIH again defended the experimenters.

But Congress was watching. In 1985, amendments to the inadequate Animal Welfare Act were passed that required federally funded animal laboratories to set up an animal care and use committee to review every research protocol. At least one member of the committee had to be a member of the community and unaffiliated with the institution. Experimenters using primates were also required to provide for the animals' psychological welfare. Many scientists tried to poke fun at this, claiming it was an impossible task, that no one really knew what would make monkeys and chimpanzees happier in the laboratories. They accused the supporters of the bill of shameless, unscientific anthropomorphism and began a long battle with Congress over implementation of the new regulations.

But they could not ignore the changing sentiment in the United States over the use of animals, and it frightened them.

Chapter Thirteen

Conscience Camp

"The relationship between NIH and the research community is incestuous."
—*Gary Francione, attorney for PETA, the* Montgomery Journal, *April 29, 1986*

Congressman Bob Smith had heard little of PETA when Alex Pacheco walked into his office one day in early 1986. Pacheco seemed no different from the dozens of others who visited Smith's office each month. He had a story to tell and a favor to ask. But his story was unusual and compelling, and before long Smith found himself wondering if he could help straighten things out.

The Republican from New Hampshire had no idea he was about to become tangled in what he would later describe as "the most frustrating thing I've ever done."

Smith was a tall, imposing figure, with dark hair and big bones. In 1986, he was still this side of middle age but carried himself with a confidence it took most people much longer to acquire. He prided himself on being straightforward and clear thinking; he liked to get things done.

Although he liked animals, he was by no means an animal rights activist, and was far better known for championing the rights of POWs and MIAs than non-human primates. Still, he felt that a resolution could be reached in the Silver Spring Monkeys case, and in spite of warnings from the scientific community that PETA was anti-science and anti-human, he began negotiating with both sides.

Smith wanted to be fair in whatever he did. After all, he served on the House Science and Technology Committee and he wasn't opposed to all uses of animals for experimentation. He understood that NIH officials didn't want to give in to PETA and would have to be appeased in order to get the primates released. But the bottom line was that the experiments were over and that neither NIH nor IBR had any use for the monkeys.

Smith was also bothered by the money being spent to keep the monkeys at the Poolesville animal center. Every cent came from taxpayers and since there wasn't any benefit for the people footing the bill, it seemed an inexcusable expenditure. With a little digging he found that housing alone for the animals cost $30,000 a year. Add to this veterinary care, staff hours for NIH executives and attorneys, and Justice Department lawyers, and in Smith's view, you came up with "an unjustifiable waste of taxpayers' dollars."

It seemed to him that NIH director James Wyngaarden could simply say, "We believe wholeheartedly in the need for animal experimentation, but the Silver Spring Monkeys have served humanity, and we're letting them live out the remainder of their lives in a peaceful, natural setting."

It was such an easy solution, Smith thought, but perhaps another little nudge from Congress would help.

On April 21st, he wrote to Wyngaarden: "NIH not only has an obligation but a duty to reclaim these animals and facilitate their transfer to the sanctuary." He spelled out his concerns about fiscal mismanagement, but he also wrote of his concerns for the monkeys themselves: "There is also no doubt that the continued confinement of these highly intelligent and social primates in small steel cages, for no reasonable purpose, is . . . inhumane."

His co-signers included Democrat Charlie Rose from North Carolina and 54 other House members.

Again Pacheco hoped. Lantos hadn't yet been able to shift NIH, but maybe Smith, a Republican who supported the Administration that appointed Wyngaarden, would make a difference. It was also encouraging that Smith wasn't going to let go of the case after he sent the letter, but had promised to gather even more Congressional support.

Still, Pacheco couldn't count on any one thing. He and Newkirk were convinced that public pressure and press coverage were essential components of successful campaigns and they knew, after all that had happened, that this case was only going to get tougher. They still had the lawsuit, which would be heard in early May, and they had growing support on Capitol Hill. Now they needed a way to stir up the public and the media.

Through the early weeks of 1986, they tossed ideas back and forth, drawing up lists of the strong and weak points of each proposed plan. NIH's growing list of excuses upped the stakes and served as a warning not to trust its officials too far. Whatever they did had to expose the agency, make its representatives accountable for their statements.

It was NIH's indifference to the suffering of the monkeys that most angered Pacheco and Newkirk. NIH was willing to sell out the animals in order to remain at the top of the animal experimentation heap. Maintaining Control, with a capital C, was their goal. If they had to keep pathetically maimed and emotionally frazzled monkeys in steel crates to maintain Control, they were willing to do it—apparently without troubling dreams or twinges of conscience.

Newkirk hadn't been so fortunate. Bloody finger stumps and monkeys gone mad from confinement were nightly images in her dreams. She began fantasizing, just before sleep, that the macaques were healthy and whole and back in their native jungle. She imagined them chattering in their family groups, resting in the branches of the lush treetops.

"If only we could force NIH to develop a conscience," Pacheco muttered one evening.

"We have to be their conscience," Newkirk said. "The public has to be NIH's conscience."

This late night exchange sprouted the seeds for the Conscience Camp. PETA would set up camp right in NIH's lap, literally in their front yard, on the gently sloped, carefully tended lawns of the National Institutes of Health campus. And they would stay there until the Silver Spring Monkeys were released.

The negotiations for permits, handled by Gary Francione, dragged and sputtered through the month of April. Francione sent letter after letter to NIH's administrative review board arguing that PETA had a First Amendment right to speak publicly on government property. He answered dozens of questions about who would camp out, what literature they could distribute, what equipment they would be allowed to have.

NIH dallied with the permit application, refusing to give a definite response until three days before the vigil was scheduled to begin. The answer was no.

Furious, Francione drafted a preliminary injunction to prevent the agency from blocking the vigil, and Newkirk decided to set up camp whether NIH approved or not. But when Francione phoned Robert Lanman to invite him to federal court, Lanman said the NIH review board had changed its mind.

Francione spent the day with NIH attorneys, hammering out innumerable details. Thirty days only and no cooking, NIH insisted, no sleeping and definitely no tent. An unreasonable rule, in Newkirk's opinion—what was a vigil without a tent? Besides, they had video equipment and displays that needed protection from rain. They could come and take it down themselves if they wanted to, she thought.

On Monday morning, April 28, 10 days before the hearing at which Edward Genn would argue for the right to have their case considered in court, Pacheco and 50 PETA volunteers and staffers pitched a large white tent, strung banners and set up a podium and sound system.

Pacheco, dressed in a dark suit and white shirt, stood close to the microphone. Behind him was a banner stretched between two poles and hoisted above his head by PETA employees. "Save the Silver Spring Monkeys!" it read. To Pacheco's left was a four-foot square oil painting of one of the deafferented monkeys, one arm bound with gauze to his body, a grimace of fear on his face.

Before Pacheco were reporters from the *Washington Post, Washington Times,* Associated Press and several television stations.

"We're here to begin the Conscience Camp," Pacheco said. "They want to kill these animals just to spite the humane community. The monkeys are political footballs in a boondoggle that NIH is responsible for!"

"These are people," said Newkirk of the NIH officials, "who see monkeys as test tubes with tails."

The press conference was the beginning of a four month long battle for Francione, on summer break from the University of

Pennsylvania. He was at the camp daily, arguing with NIH security officers, negotiating with Lanman. The Institutes may have agreed to PETA's presence on their campus, but they were going to make them fight for every move they made. There were skirmishes over the size of the banners, how close to the street the protesters could stand, how many people would be allowed at the camp at one time, what size bullhorn they used. It was the most trying summer of Francione's life. He was angry and frustrated, and because he was too busy to bother with food, and followed Pacheco's example of living on cold vegetarian hot dogs straight from the can, he was hungry nearly all of the time.

PETA was busy in other areas, too. Before the year was out, consumers nationwide would be shocked by a graphic videotape shot undercover in a Gillette product testing laboratory. In one scene, white rats shuddered with convulsions after being forced to inhale massive amounts of aerosol sprays. The investigator reported that laboratory technicians laughed as they dripped test substances into the eyes of screaming rabbits.

Although several other animal protection organizations had protested consumer product tests on animals, the public had never seen what actually happened inside the walls of those commercial laboratories. The Gillette footage and a subsequent videotape shot at a New Jersey laboratory called Biosearch, which was hired by cosmetics manufacturers to perform animal tests, became the visual foundation for what would soon become one of PETA's most successful efforts—its Compassion Campaign, as it was dubbed in 1987.

The guinea pigs whose skins were eaten away by caustic chemicals and the rabbits with chunks of red lipstick shoved beneath their eyelids weren't suffering to cure human disease; they were literally dying for a new hair color or shampoo or floor cleaner. But the companies that conducted such tests were more vulnerable to public opinion than NIH, and consumer pressure would eventually knock over the first domino when the Avon and Benetton companies, both Biosearch customers, became the first mainstream cosmetics companies to eliminate all animal tests. (Benneton later became a supporter of PETA's and incorporated its cruelty-free policy into its advertising and packaging.)

When PETA added the Gillette and Compassion Campaigns to its agenda, NIH and its federally funded experimenters gained a new ally. It didn't take them long to pull corporate scientists into their folds.

As their date in court grew close, Raub and NIH, who just a few months before "had no research protocols, either ongoing or planned, for which these animals are appropriate," suddenly decided that they had 15 valuable research subjects. Raub began telling reporters that the monkeys should be used in the experiments Taub planned for them. He didn't explain why NIH hadn't suggested completing the studies during the last four years. Besides, NIH didn't own the primates, he claimed yet again, flouting the facts.

NIH's motive wasn't difficult to grasp. If the case went to trial and PETA won, what was to keep animal rights groups from coming back again and again, tying up their time, gumming up their experiments? More and more organizations were springing up every year; PETA was just the beginning. NIH would have to spend its budgets on attorneys and justify its protocols to the scientifically ignorant public.

Just four days after PETA's Conscience Camp launched its "Vigil till Victory," Raub wrote to Smith expressing his worry that the suit "could become a precedent for hundreds of such suits throughout the nation." He added an ominous warning about the "adverse effect this could have on the progress of biomedical research."

Behind Raub were members of dozens of scientific organizations who feared the loss of their former freedom and desperately wished for a return to their "good old days," when they could do practically anything they wanted to the animals in their laboratories without giving a thought to the political fallout of their actions. Twenty-nine of these organizations signed a letter to the Senate dated two days before Raub's. Their message was remarkably similar to his:

> The precedent that would be established by acceding to their demands would have a disruptive effect on both the research and academic communities.

Pacheco and Newkirk wondered who exactly was organizing this sudden push. Raub? Wyngaarden? Or was it someone from the American Psychiatric Association, the Shock Society, the

American Diabetes Association or one of the other groups? Whoever was behind the letters was probably responsible for the amici curiae—the statements supporting NIH and IBR—filed with the Fourth Circuit Court. Nearly 70 scientific front groups, fearful of ending up in court themselves some day, tripped over each other to defend animal experimentation to the judges.

At least one person besides Pacheco and Newkirk, who were busy by day at the Conscience Camp, and by night preparing for the hearing, wanted to find out who was behind the transparent interest in completing Taub's experiments. A psychiatrist named Neal Barnard, who had himself been trained by the scientific establishment, decided to see just how much a group like the National Foundation for Infectious Diseases or the American Council on Education even knew about dorsal rhizotomies.

Barnard, tall, slender and dark-haired, was a 1980 graduate of George Washington University Medical School in the District of Columbia. When the Silver Spring Monkeys were seized from IBR, Barnard was beginning his internship at GW, and by the time Taub's conviction was overturned, Barnard was Chief Resident in Psychiatry at the university's medical center. He followed the ins and outs of the case with some curiosity because his own experiences with experimental animals as an undergraduate eventually led him into research reform.

He'd done the usual psychology experiments—deprive a rat of water until the animal was so terribly thirsty a drink could be used to compel him to perform certain actions. Later he'd drilled holes in rats' skulls and implanted electrodes to see how shocks to different parts of the brain affected behavior. The principles were elementary, the kind of things that could be, and were, explained in textbooks.

But the lessons they taught Barnard weren't limited to scientific theory and procedure.

"I began to discover," Barnard said years later, "that even animals who might considered to be homely or unpopular, like rats or pigeons, suffered so obviously that I became very concerned about all use of animals in experimentation."

In medical school, Barnard matter-of-factly refused to participate in the mandatory dog lab, the only part of his curriculum that required the use of other-than-human animals. He didn't see the point in drugging some pathetic animal shelter reject with human medications and then killing him when data more relevant to his future patients could be compiled from other, less painful sources.

"I'm going to the medical library," he told his instructor. "I'm going to write up the effects these drugs have in human beings. I'm going to draw a graph showing their effect over time."

Because the fear of animal rights hadn't yet penetrated the medical school faculty, and perhaps because it never occurred to Barnard there could be any negative consequences to his pronouncement, his alternative project was accepted without question. His advisor simply thought he was overly soft-hearted—not a negative quality for a physician to have, Barnard thought.

Another student joined Barnard in the library rather than kill an unlucky canine, and within a couple of years the dog lab was made optional. Later it was done away with altogether.

Barnard worked at St. Vincent's Hospital in New York for a year after his residency, but he couldn't escape his feeling that something could be done, that *he* could do something about the incredible suffering of animals in research laboratories. In medical schools and universities particularly, students were encouraged to think up projects involving animals that may not advance science in the least. He was certain that initiative and creativity could be fostered without so much misery and loss of life, and he knew that there were thousands of students and MDs who agreed.

By 1985 he was back in D.C. with a faculty appointment at GW that left him enough time to begin the Physicians Committee for Responsible Medicine.

Not long after, while driving down the congested Wisconsin Avenue in Bethesda, Md., Barnard saw a few demonstrators waving anti-fur posters in front of a department store. How pitiful, he thought. How could so few activists hope to influence anybody? He swerved his car into an open space; at least he could lend a hand.

This was how, quite unexpectedly, Barnard met PETA's national director, Ingrid Newkirk, and how he found out about the government's shenanigans in the Silver Spring Monkeys case.

Over a number of days, Barnard sat at his desk and called most of the groups that filed amicus briefs. Most, he found, had been contacted by Raub, Wyngaarden or someone at NIH. None of the representatives he questioned knew much about Taub's work. They'd been told the deafferentation studies were significant, but the real reason for shooting a brief at the court was fear.

Barnard remembers being told by the Association of American Medical Colleges: "If PETA is able through the political process to establish the ability to influence the outcome of something of this nature, we're in for some real trouble."

The Association of Academic Health Centers was "in support of the general issue and the need for animals in research. We have no specific interest in the animals."

It was obvious to Barnard after his hours on the telephone that the hasty proposal to finish Taub's work had nothing to do with good science. There was no genuine interest in the results of the experiment. It was merely an effective weapon to use in court. Barnard was staggered by the open admissions of the people he spoke to; they seemed to see nothing wrong with killing animals in a trumped-up experiment solely to influence the judges' decision.

The Congressional support for PETA's position probably had something to do with the frenzied mobilization of scientific troops, too. In the final days before the hearing, Bob Smith sent an additional 79 signatures from the House of Representatives, bringing the total to 135 members urging a transfer of the monkeys to Primarily Primates.

The Senate got into the act again, too. Charles Mathias from Maryland wrote to Wyngaarden on May 5 complaining that "continued inaction by NIH will perpetuate an unacceptable, costly, and useless situation." Fifty-three of his colleagues signed the letter, among them Jesse Helms, Barry Goldwater, Arlen Specter, Lloyd Bentson, Sam Nunn and Alan Cranston. In both the House and Senate buildings, the Silver Spring Monkeys case was a bipartisan issue.

The scientific community had been trying to fend off stronger legislation for the protection of laboratory animals since 1981, with only mixed success. Congress was working its way into their sphere, mandating larger cages, exercise for dogs, toys for monkeys, committees to review protocols and more. The line had to drawn somewhere or, it was feared, Congress would legislate the animal experimenters right out of business. They chose to draw the line right in front of the monkeys from IBR, the most famous victims of modern science.

Raub and his colleagues in the universities and research laboratories across the country probably didn't realize that their inflexibility on this issue would drive such a thick wedge between NIH and Congress. To representatives like Bob Smith, their stubbornness, and worse, their duplicity, was profoundly disappointing. Though in his heart Smith felt PETA was right, he was trying hard to be fair and objective. But it was becoming more and more difficult.

When the sun had completely disappeared, it was still warm enough for those who had driven to NIH to leave their jackets in their cars. Dozens arrived directly from work, exiting the subway at the Medical Center stop on the edge of the campus, briefcases in hand.

It was the evening of the third day of the Conscience Camp. There had been no arrests—so far NIH had tolerated the tent—but it wasn't Pacheco's intention to maintain a silent presence on the Institutes' grounds for the next month. He wanted to be the fly in their ointment; he wanted Raub, Wyngaarden and the NIH employees to think about PETA and the Silver Spring Monkeys day and night. A conscience is not to be easily escaped.

As the activists gathered at the camp, a PETA staff member handed each a thick white candle. In all, more than 100 candles were distributed, and after each was lit, the crowd began its march to James Wyngaarden's home. As director of NIH, Wyngaarden lived in a picturesque stone house set among the grassy knolls of the campus. Though the home was pretty, surrounded by towering leafy trees, and certainly convenient for the director, it struck Newkirk as odd that anyone would choose to live there ... its windows overlooked the NIH buildings in which animals were confined, experimented on, killed and cut up for analysis. What would it be like, she wondered, to sit in the sunny dining room each morning, lingering over coffee, orange juice and the *Washington Post*, while just a few hundred yards away a monkey deliberately addicted to cocaine retched and shivered through withdrawal?

Each of the activists risked arrest on this warm Thursday evening just by being there. The NIH permit prohibited PETA from remaining past sundown. They marched across the campus, keeping to the wide sidewalks, holding the burning candles in front of them.

One by one, the candles were placed on Wyngaarden's broad, semi-circular stone doorstep, behind two front white columns. The activists stood quietly before the house until a hundred tiny yellow flames lit the entranceway, then quietly dispersed, returning to their cars or riding the long escalator down to the subway. There were no arrests.

Newkirk and Pacheco hoped that Wyngaarden would, quite literally, see the light. Just to be sure, they returned each Thursday night for the remainder of the month and placed 15 candles, one for each of the Silver Spring Monkeys, on his step.

The Fourth U.S. Circuit Court of Appeals, on 10th and Main Streets in Richmond, Va., is just over an hour's drive southwest of Washington, D.C. It was here, at 11 o'clock a.m. on May 8, 1986, that the most celebrated and potentially far-reaching animal protection case in American history would be argued.

Edward Genn had prepared carefully. His goal was to secure his clients' right to bring their case into a court of law. He had to convince the court's three judges that PETA had established enough interest in the monkeys to be given the chance to challenge IBR's ownership. If Genn was successful, he would be back in court later to state their case in full.

Gary Francione, who had helped Genn put his argument together, was with the older attorney early that morning, and he knew that Genn was upset. For one thing, Genn had opposed the Conscience Camp from the beginning, and he told Francione, Newkirk and Pacheco that he felt it was a mistake, that it would bring the wrong kind of publicity. Even more annoying was the bombardment of amicus briefs from the scientific groups claiming that this was a case about the use of animals for research. Genn saw this argument as a red herring. As far as he was concerned, the case was only about the fate of 15 primates. He had no desire to put animal experimentation on trial.

Cleveland Amory flew down from New York for the hearing and joined Pacheco, his protégé, on the steps of the courthouse for a brief press conference at 10 a.m. Reporters and dozens of representatives of animal protection organizations gathered around Pacheco and Amory, and when the questions had been answered, followed them into the courtroom.

Robert Lanman represented the National Institutes of Health and Edgar Brenner returned to court once more for IBR; Jimmy

Miller and two attorneys from the Justice Department supplied briefs supporting their position.

In the end, the three judges, Sam Ervin III, J. Harvey Wilkinson and H. Emory Widener, seemed confused about what, exactly, they were deciding. Genn contended it was the right of his clients to sue for guardianship of 15 specific primates.

Lanman suggested it was up to the three-member panel to protect the future of biomedical research. This was merely the beginning of something that would set the precedent for much worse, he claimed. To allow PETA and its supporters to become "next friends" of the monkeys could lead to a myriad of problems. A rancher's neighbor could even try to stop the slaughter of cattle for food, he said.

The judges weren't being asked to decide the case at that very point, Genn countered, but only to give PETA its day in court; his clients' interest in the monkeys was legitimate and should not be denied because NIH was frightened of some mythical floodgate busting wide open.

The judges appeared to listen attentively. They asked questions frequently. But there would be no immediate resolution. They would consider the arguments, review the briefs—while the monkeys sat in their cages in Poolesville—and render a decision in some weeks.

Pacheco and Newkirk, somewhat depressed, immediately went back to the matters at hand. After a quick supper with Amory and Francione, they headed back to the Conscience Camp for a second trip to Wyngaarden's front door.

The hearing had been a disappointment to them, not because of Genn, who they both felt did an exceptional job, but because they had begun to see just how shut out of the legal system they were. The judges, Lanman, the representatives of the scientific groups seemed like part of some judicial landed gentry, more concerned with protecting each other's interests than hearing the whole story.

No wonder people broke into labs, Pacheco thought.

Early next morning, Newkirk was jarred from her sleep by the telephone.

"Have you seen it?" a friend from the Midwest asked excitedly.

"Seen what?" Newkirk asked, snapping awake.

"James Kilpatrick wants the monkeys freed!"

The nationally syndicated columnist, known for his conservative jabs at Shana Alexander in their confrontation on CBS's "60 Minutes," had written a piece on the Silver Spring Monkeys.

Newkirk reached for the pencil and pad next to the phone as her friend read it to her.

"You would have to travel a long way," the column began, "to find an uglier or more depressing story than the story of the 15 monkeys of Silver Spring, MD. The primates are now living out what is left of their tormented lives in cages at the National Institutes of Health. The government's conduct in this case is both appalling and indefensible."

Kilpatrick went on to describe the frustrating events of the last five years and finally concluded, "For legal reasons that baffle understanding, the NIH has refused to cooperate . . . The situation is infuriating—but when one is dealing with the obstinacy of bureaucracy and the law's delays, what else is new?"

During the next few days, Kilpatrick's column turned up in newspapers across the country. The *Washington Post* titled it "Caged in Poolesville," while the *Chicago Sun-Times* labeled it more directly "Federal Monkey Business." It launched a new volley of letters at Congress from the public, and from PETA's point of view was timed perfectly for their next event, scheduled for just two weeks later.

"We send you a message loud and clear," Cleveland Amory said into the microphone on the NIH campus. "You give us back those monkeys, or you, damn it, will pay and pay dearly!"

Shouts and applause rose up from the crowd gathered in front of the speakers, not far from the Institutes' administration building, in which James Wyngaarden's office was located. Nearly 1,000 people had traveled from surrounding states to this rally during the third week of the Conscience Camp.

"This is an army out here," Amory said, his voice booming, his already imposing height made even greater by the platform beneath him. His wild hair gave him the look of fierce warrior.

"We try to be kind and decent and fair, but when we find that the other side is neither kind nor decent nor fair, then we will fight with other weapons. They have seen our polite side today. We want them to know that our patience is at an end!"

Above the crowd was a 10-foot banner: "SANCTUARY for the Silver Spring Monkeys!" It was a warm, sunny Saturday, and many of the supporters were dressed in T-shirts with logos from animal rights organizations on them. More than a few in the crowd could trace their own involvement in the animal rights movement back to the raid in 1981. Some had gone on to form their own grassroots community groups and still looked to PETA for direction and fresh campaign materials. They were the letter writers, the protesters, the local organizers who keep any social movement alive, and if they depended on PETA, PETA likewise relied on them to supply the groundswell of support needed to spread the word about animal rights.

To many, Alex Pacheco had become a hero, a symbol of the animals rights movement, in his fight to free the monkeys. His dark good looks, his intensity and his passion for his work were as appealing as his message, and when he unabashedly equated animal experimentation with torture and slaughtering animals for food with murder, he made as many friends as he did enemies. To his great embarrassment, he frequently received marriage proposals—or other personal offers—through the mail.

Despite the attention, he had changed little since 1981. He considered himself less naive, less trusting than he had once been, and perhaps more experienced at television interviews and public speeches. But he still put his work—his calling—above everything else in his life. He sometimes forgot even to eat and friends had taken to sending him baskets of fruit and packets of vegetarian soup mix, which he ate because they sat on his desk in front of him.

Today, as Pacheco stepped up to the microphone, the applause was loud and welcoming.

"NIH," he warned, "if you try to touch those animals, we'll show you fireworks like you've never seen!"

The day before, William Raub stated publicly that NIH was not going to comply with the wishes of either PETA or Congress. IBR's board of directors now wanted Taub's work completed by another laboratory, he claimed.

Pacheco could hardly contain his outrage. Until they'd set up the tent for the Conscience Camp, NIH had barely spoken to them. When they did open their mouths, it seemed to Pacheco that it was only to break promises.

He wanted the hundreds of people at the rally to inspire taxpayers to flex their muscle—to write to their federal representatives, to their local newspaper editors, to James Wyngaarden. Whatever the Fourth Circuit Court decided, he and Newkirk were going to expose NIH's underhanded tactics and, they hoped, bring so much pressure that releasing the monkeys would look easy compared to dealing with an angry Congress and even angrier public.

By the end of May, Representative Smith was really ticked off. He'd finally received an answer to his April 21 letter to Wyngaarden, not from the director himself, but from Raub. Raub chose to respond only to Smith's questions concerning the cost of caring for the macaques and didn't even comment on the request to release the primates. He defended the expenditure of tens of thousands of dollars easily: ". . . because NIH recognized that the litigation constraining it from returning the animals to IBR also had potentially significant import for the entire national biomedical effort, we elected to continue bearing the cost of the primates' care."

Smith immediately fired off another letter to Wyngaarden. He was furious that NIH would try to use "national interest" as an excuse to keep the monkeys.

"Must NIH be reminded," Smith demanded, "that its constituency is the American people, whose tax dollars NIH is wasting on senseless litigation involving 15 primates whose research was terminated five years ago?"

Smith enclosed even more signatures from the House of Representatives, bringing the total to 253—enough to carry a bill if he introduced one. Since 59 Senators had signed, both houses had the majority needed. Smith would do this only as a last resort; he still believed a compromise could be reached between PETA and NIH. But he did warn Wyngaarden that he would not hesitate to introduce a resolution in Congress and would also "press for hearings to air the facts" if NIH "continues to refuse to take responsibility in this matter."

Although a sense of Congress resolution would not mandate NIH to give the monkeys to Primarily Primates, it would show Wyngaarden just how irritated the legislators were with his refusal to cooperate. Politically, it could have a negative impact on NIH, which depended on Congressional votes for it funding.

Wyngaarden was going to have to choose between two unappealing choices—displeasing Congress or incurring the wrath of the scientific community by "giving in" to PETA and its supporters.

Chapter Fourteen

Bureaucratic Bullheadedness

"No one with any decency can defend everything that happens to animals in laboratories. To do so is to take a truly extremist position . . . The strident apologists for anything and everything in the laboratories are so determined to keep the public out of their sacred arenas that they actually defend even severe and well-documented abuses."
—*letter from Ingrid Newkirk,* Washingtonian, *October, 1986*

When Congressman Smith threw down the gauntlet at Wyngaarden's feet, Newkirk made sure the press knew about it. PETA's media department sent information packs to newspapers, magazines and radio and television reporters and was rewarded with a spate of editorials calling for release of the primates.

James Kilpatrick wrote a second column on the case which appeared in the *Washington Post* under the headline, "Why Can't They Just Let Those Monkeys Go?" After his first piece, he received a volley of angry letters from pro-experimentation groups like the National Association for Biomedical Research. Kilpatrick spelled out his view in response: he was not opposed to all animal research, but, he reminded his readers, the purpose of PETA's lawsuit "is to let these crippled monkeys, having served their medical purpose, live in peace."

United Press International interviewed Smith and the story that ran on their wire service called the controversy a "showdown" between Congress and NIH's overseer, the Department of Health and Human Services. Smith gave his ultimatum: if HHS and NIH did not make a decision by the first week in June, he and a counterpart in the Senate would introduce concurrent resolutions.

Wyngaarden's response was loaded with what Smith had come to expect—excuses. The NIH chief had the same ones, that the monkeys belonged to IBR and that Taub's work should be completed, and a new one as well: the primates' deafferented limbs made it impossible to keep them in anything but individual cages, and since they could not be placed together, they could not be resocialized. Wyngaarden and his advisors apparently believed that monkeys with crippled limbs were at risk of injuring each other in fights.

Pacheco was astonished. He thought he couldn't be surprised by anything printed on NIH letterhead, but this was a new one. Raub seemed to ignore Wally Swett's expertise in resocializing primates with a wide range of disabilities from many different backgrounds. Besides, seven of the monkeys had never undergone surgery and physically, were completely normal!

But by now, all the publicity, added to the pressure from Congress, was making life difficult for Otis Bowen, who had replaced Margaret Heckler as Secretary of HHS. In spite of Raub's excuses, he agreed to send a representative, HHS Undersecretary Donald Newman, to meet with Smith during the critical deadline period in the first week of June.

Several heated meetings took place during this time, and miraculously, a rough agreement was hammered out. Smith knew PETA would never agree to NIH's original plan to kill the monkeys and finish the deafferentation studies; he also knew that NIH wouldn't simply let go of the primates after all they had done to keep them. He listened carefully to the concerns of both sides and searched for a solution, a compromise that would give the animals a chance at decent lives, while allowing NIH to save face.

It was a tense period for Newkirk and Pacheco. While Newkirk concentrated on PETA's current campaigns and running the growing organization, Pacheco stayed on Capitol Hill, in close contact with Smith and his staff. In fact, Pacheco was spending an increasing amount of time away from the PETA office for a variety of reasons. In addition to his lobbying efforts for the monkeys, he had begun to enlist the help of celebrities like Candace Bergen and Bea Arthur for PETA's campaigns. He often shuttled between Washington and Hollywood, where he and PETA staffer Dan Mathews, a striking six-foot, six-inch former model, were organizing PETA's first record album, "Animal Liberation."

Pacheco was also a favorite with PETA members and he frequently visited long-time supporters and spoke to their local groups, returning to D.C. for critical periods like this one. As it turned out, the present negotiations were particularly complicated, and it wasn't long before he was asked to make a decision that he didn't want to make.

NIH was willing to give up the plan to kill the monkeys immediately, Smith told him, but weren't ready to say the monkeys had no scientific value. They wanted to study the resocialization process in order to gain a "better understanding of primate behavior in group situations."

Suddenly, resocialization was possible again! Still, the study did not seem credible to Pacheco. Didn't they already have enough primates in captivity to monitor? He might be willing to agree, he told Smith, as long as the researchers merely observed the monkeys; the problem was, how could he trust NIH? They hadn't been exactly straightforward in the past.

After discussing the proposal with Newkirk, he finally said he was prepared to accept it under the condition that the monkeys be sent to Primarily Primates and that the study be conducted there.

On June 9, Wyngaarden wrote to Smith outlining the key elements of the arrangement as he saw them: the monkeys would be allowed to live out their lives in a facility that met the requirements of the Animal Welfare Act; they would *not* (Wyngaarden underlined the word) undergo invasive experimental procedures; an autopsy would be carried out on each primate after the animal died of natural causes; private funds would be raised to cover the cost of care; and finally, "every reasonable effort" would be made to resocialize all of the monkeys except Billy, whose double deafferentation made it, Wyngaarden felt, more difficult to place him in a group environment.

Wyngaarden also recommended amputation for the monkeys with only one disabled limb.

"This surgery should be done in the animals' best interest, irrespective of where or why they are relocated," he wrote, without explaining why he hadn't agreed to NIH veterinarian Dave Rehnquist's recommendation to amputate several years before.

It wasn't a perfect proposal, but Smith was relieved that NIH was at last ready to inch forward on the case. He met with Pacheco and between them they fine-tuned the plan and outlined it in a letter sent the next day to Donald Newman at HHS.

"I must emphasize that the conduct of NIH over this matter in recent weeks has caused me and my colleagues considerable concern," Smith wrote. "In my judgment, my proposals in our previous discussions incorporated sufficient concessions in light of NIH inaction over the past five years."

He would agree to the behavioral study, and to the autopsy upon the natural death of each primate. Naturally, he would agree to the amputations, which, he added, should have been done a long time ago. But he insisted that the facility be Primarily Primates; it had been agreed in one of the meetings in Smith's office that the monkeys would go to a sanctuary. The only appropriate place was Wally Swett's.

Finally, Smith could not accept the plan to keep Billy housed separately in a laboratory.

"Billy is very passive," he explained, "Special arrangements have been made with Primarily Primates so that Billy may live in a special facility that will meet all federal requirements."

The completion of the letter brought an enormous feeling of relief to Pacheco. Smith seemed confident that the disagreements could be worked out and once that happened, they could get on with the arrangements for relocating the monkeys. For the first time in many months he relaxed just a bit, thinking, hoping the end of the five-year battle was in sight.

He returned to Capitol Hill early the next morning, the day after the letter was sent from the Congressional office building to the Department of Health and Human Services. Smith planned to call Newman, who had promised a response, in the late morning and work out the remaining details. Pacheco had to be there to give his consent to unexpected offers, in case there were any.

He drank more coffee, remembering briefly that he hadn't had breakfast. He talked with Smith's staff. He called Newkirk to fill her in. It was Day 45 of the Conscience Camp—they had renewed their permit after a month—and Newkirk was busier than usual at the office since several PETA staffers were out at the NIH campus. He hoped it would be the last day of the vigil.

Then the bomb dropped. NIH rejected Smith's counterproposal. They would allow the monkeys to go only to a primate laboratory.

Smith was angrier than he had been in a long time. As far as he was concerned they had a firm agreement with only one or two points to work out. Now NIH was rejecting the whole plan.

Within minutes his staff was working on a press release: "Negotiations On 'Silver Spring Monkeys Case' Break Down." Before the day was over he had introduced House Concurrent Resolution 351, calling on the director of NIH to transfer the monkeys to Primarily Primates. The resolutions was cosponsored by 70 of his colleagues, including Tom Lantos, Charlie Rose, Rod Chandler of Washington, Bob Dornan and Barbara Boxer from California.

At the same time, Alan Cranston, the tall liberal Senator from California, introduced an identical resolution on his side of the capitol.

"NIH has stated," Cranston explained to his colleagues in the Senate, "that it has no further research requirements for the monkeys, yet resolution of the custody issue continues to go unresolved in the face of growing public—and Congressional—opinion in favor of transferring the Silver Spring monkeys to the Texas facility."

Smith, Charlie Rose and Rod Chandler then sent a "Dear Colleague" letter, looking for more co-sponsors. Two hundred fifty-three members had signed the original letter to Wyngaarden; Smith was confident he would find plenty of support from both parties for the resolution.

If the resolution didn't work, he would introduce a bill. He would legislate the monkeys from NIH's grasp if he had to.

The collapse of the negotiations was a blow to Pacheco and to Newkirk—another bitter disappointment in a case already full of them. Just a few days before, through the Freedom of Information Act, they got copies of some of the earlier correspondence between NIH and IBR. When they read Raub's letter refusing custody of the monkeys from IBR, they realized they would never be able to get the primates out on their own. It sickened them to find out they had been so close, that NIH officials had deliberately lied to them.

Now Pacheco felt foolish for hoping that Congress would be treated with any more respect than PETA. It had been a long, messy fight and it was obviously going to get worse.

To complicate matters further, an activist in Delaware named Stas Kaczorowski was slowly starving himself to death to show "solidarity with the monkeys." He stopped eating when the Conscience Camp tent went up and had been existing on fruit juice and water for more than 40 days. Now 25 pounds down, he was still at it.

Newkirk respected his commitment to freeing the monkeys, but his fast was distracting other activists from work that needed to be done. She was getting calls from supporters wanting her to do something about Stas.

"I've got my hands full trying to help the Silver Spring Monkeys," she answered, trying to keep the irritation out of her voice. Between sending out press materials, organizing more protests and contacting grassroots groups nationwide, there was, as usual, little time left for dealing with anything that wasn't essential to their fight.

Pacheco spent the 48 hours following NIH's rejection going from office to office on Capitol Hill. It was a blur of meetings with impeccably suited, neatly manicured staffers. Some of them, he knew, spent as many hours on their jobs for Senators and Representatives as he spent working for animal rights. They knew of the case, they told him, and most were supportive. They would do what they could, as soon as they could.

Smith and his colleagues did act fast. On Friday the thirteenth, just two days after the resolutions were introduced, James Wyngaarden was before Congress trying to explain why he was party to what Smith called "bureaucratic bullheadedness."

The plan to continue Taub's experiment, which NIH and nearly 70 scientific organizations had sworn to Congress and the Fourth Circuit Court was absolutely essential, had been inexplicably dropped. What NIH really wanted to do, Wyngaarden told the legislators, was to study the resocialization of the monkeys and then attempt to incorporate them into breeding colonies. To do this, he explained with some gravity, the animals must go to a recognized primate laboratory.

Smith took exception to Wyngaarden's account at a press conference the same day.

"It has already cost the taxpayers $120,000 to house these monkeys," Smith said. "For humanitarian and economic reasons, the primates should be released to a sanctuary to live out their lives in peace and at no cost to the federal taxpayers."

Not surprisingly, NIH officials countered with the excuse that they had been trying to work out a plan, but PETA was unreasonable in its demand that valuable experimental animals be released from the scientific community. NIH had the animals' best interest at heart, they claimed.

"We are trying to ensure that the animals will live out their lives in first-class facilities," Raub is quoted as saying in the *Montgomery Journal.*

For nearly two weeks, NIH and Congress argued and discussed, flinging barbs back and forth, while over on the Institutes' campus the vigillers, worked up to fever pitch, chanted and held up "Honk to Free the Silver Spring Monkeys" signs for the traffic on four-lane Wisconsin Avenue. Smith and Cranston racked up more names for their resolutions; Pacheco and Newkirk called reporters and columnists, pushing newspaper editors to take a stand.

Then, without warning, on June 23, in the dusk of the summer evening, the week before Congress was to recess for the Fourth of July holiday, the 15 monkeys were quietly loaded into an unmarked van and driven away from the animal center in Poolesville.

Newkirk was working late at the office on that warm Monday night. When the phone rang, she picked up the receiver immediately, expecting to hear a PETA staffer or volunteer.

"It's happening," a voice said, "I'm calling from the animal center."

Then the caller hung up.

Newkirk knew immediately what it meant. It was what she and Pacheco had worried about for several years—the monkeys were being shipped to another laboratory, perhaps to be experimented on and killed.

She dialled the center's public number.

"It's done," she was told. "There's nobody to talk to you."

After visiting the Poolesville facility at regular intervals for nearly five years, Newkirk and Pacheco were now completely shut out. No one would speak to them by telephone; they were never again allowed inside the buildings. It was obvious that the staff members who had been friendly to the activists were under orders to remain silent. They would never know the details of the move. Had the monkeys been sedated? Did they have something soft to lie on to cushion them against the jarring of the vehicle? Where did they go?

Newkirk heard later that the plan to remove the macaques was so secret that the plain van didn't even have a license plate. Dave Rehnquist was on vacation that week, and though he'd cared for the monkeys for five years, he was not asked to help with the transfer. He had no warning either. He didn't even know the monkeys were gone until he returned to work several days later.

Representative Smith didn't find out what had happened to the animals until the afternoon of the 24th, and it was what Pacheco and Newkirk most feared. They had been taken to the Delta Regional Primate Research Center in Covington, La., outside New Orleans. It was one of seven federally funded primate laboratories in the United States—and therefore in tight with the National Institutes of Health.

Congress erupted in anger. Charlie Rose was the first to speak on the floor: "One hundred Members of Congress—and more are signing every day—have signed a sense of Congress resolution ...[N]ot knowing how to count, Dr. Wyngaarden, is a serious mistake."

Barbara Boxer's words were even stronger: "In this most recent move by NIH, it seems the Federal agency has justified what the animal community has felt all along. Compassion and humane treatment of these living creatures has somewhere, somehow been overlooked and ignored by an entire research community."

It became clear in the next few days that NIH never intended to follow through on its agreement with Smith to move the primates to a sanctuary, that the discussions were little more than a public relations ploy. In fact, the decision to relocate the monkeys to a primate laboratory had been made several weeks earlier.

Smith angrily demanded an explanation for the back door tactics. In response, the Department of Health and Human Services circulated a form letter, addressed to "Dear Representative" and signed not by Wyngaarden, Raub, Otis Bowen or even the HHS negotiator, Donald Newman, but by the Acting Assistant Secretary for Legislation.

The action taken, the letter claimed, "assures that an important investment in the terms of biomedical research and the health of the public has not been lost."

Smith knew that whatever scientific value the monkeys had now they would still have at Primarily Primates under the terms of his original proposal. He'd prodded Pacheco to agree to the behavioral study and spelled out the terms carefully. It was clear to Smith that the HHS letter was masquerading as the truth. The real reason behind the nighttime move was much more underhanded and self-serving. NIH wanted the monkeys safely deposited far away from PETA, from Congress and out of the spotlight. They would be, for all practical purposes, inaccessible to the people who really cared about them.

Accessibility was one of Edward Genn's concerns. He, Roger Galvin and Gary Francione were on a conference line to NIH's legal counsel, Robert Lanman, as soon as they could reach him on the 24th.

Lanman informed him that a letter of explanation would be on its way to the Court of Appeals that day. NIH was well aware that the suit was still pending.

Genn pointed out that his clients would need to see the monkeys upon arrival at Delta in order to respond to that letter.

Lanman assured him that his clients would have the same visitation privileges that they had had in the past.

The way it worked out was somewhat different. As soon as the Silver Spring Monkeys were carted through Delta's front door they were placed under a 90-day quarantine. No one could see them for three months. It was soon made clear that PETA representatives would not be welcome at any time.

Lanman later claimed he had simply made an incorrect assumption about visitation, but Genn was convinced that NIH was stonewalling. Throughout July the agency's attorneys continued to submit briefs to the court based on written evaluations of the monkeys before, during and after the transfer to Louisiana. But they not only refused to allow PETA representatives to see the monkeys for themselves, they refused to provide Genn with copies of the examination reports. It was impossible for Genn to respond fully to NIH's filings.

As soon as she heard the monkeys' destination was Delta, Newkirk put a PETA researcher in charge of digging up everything she could find on the facility—USDA reports, mortality rates, newspaper clippings, research reports, grants from NIH and anything else that would give them some idea of what they were dealing with.

Then she rounded up the phone numbers of the animal protection groups in the southern Louisiana area. It was blind calling—she didn't know any of the activists in New Orleans. In fact they weren't really activists at all, and as far as she knew, they hadn't sponsored even a single direct action event. But there wasn't much choice.

She asked if they could be at the Delta entrance when the monkeys arrived, and if they would be willing to protest, or better, block the driveway to keep the van out. Roseanne Tarantolo, the president of Animal Peace of New Orleans agreed, as did the directors of the Capital Area Animal Welfare Society, the Jefferson SPCA and the Louisiana Coalition of Animal Activists.

It didn't take long for R & I to put the Delta factsheet together. Pacheco spent hours poring over the material, studying the research projects conducted at the facility. This was one of his strengths. As Newkirk had early learned, Pacheco may not know how to knot his necktie, but he could find the weak point, the one that would crack the case, in the most difficult scientific data. Delta's statistics, as it turned out, were grim. Its mortality rates were higher than any of the other primate centers, according to the 1985 annual progress reports for six of the seven facilities (statistics for Yerkes center in Georgia weren't available).

Although more than 90 percent of the center's four million dollar budget came from taxpayers via the federal government, Delta was associated with and administered by Tulane University. It was a big place, taking up nearly five hundred rural, pine-covered acres next to a swamp and housing more than three thousand monkeys. Experiments were conducted in laboratories on the premises. Delta's two breeding colonies provided most of the live subjects.

Delta's director was Peter Gerone, a middle-aged man with a Doctor of Science degree from Johns Hopkins University. Though he'd been at Delta since 1971, Gerone referred to himself as a virologist rather than a primatologist. He'd worked for the government for 17 years before moving to Louisiana and during that time had lived just 30 miles northwest of Silver Spring in Frederick, Md. He was the father of seven, a former PTA president and a firm believer in the use of animals for experimentation.

Newkirk guessed Gerone wouldn't take kindly to the visit, just hours away, from local animal rights activists.

Twenty men and women, some from New Orleans, some from farther away, were waiting for the van on Tuesday evening, June 24. They were neatly dressed in suits or skirts and blouses, which stuck to their bodies in the warm and humid air. They weren't sure when the monkeys would arrive, and they weren't convinced they could keep the vehicle from running right over them if the driver got irritated with the delay. But they weren't going to watch the primates hauled into yet another prison without protest. They were joined by a reporter and photographer from the *New Orleans Times-Picayune*, and by several crews from nearby TV newsrooms.

At 9:15 p.m. they saw headlights and quickly formed a human chain in front of Delta's entrance, their hands clasped. The van stopped just short of the protesters. A security guard appeared. There was a short scuffle and a few angry words before the activists cleared the road.

Peter Gerone put in an appearance for the media. The monkeys were valuable animals, he told reporters, but they would not be used in invasive experiments. Delta staff would try to resocialize them, help them learn to live with other primates. Then, when they came to the end of their natural lives, their bodies would be useful to science and their tissue would be studied.

Gerone's statements were outlined by NIH and HHS in several letters sent to Congress and in statements released to the press. Over and over again the agencies promised to resocialize the primates, to amputate their deafferented limbs, and most importantly, they vowed that no experimental procedures would be performed on any of the monkeys.

Nobody knew then, in the furor surrounding the clandestine transfer, that the National Institutes of Health, with Delta's assistance, would break every one of these promises.

Chapter Fifteen

Maintaining Control

"*Animal protectors, including world famous primate rehabilitators who specialize in cases of gross cruelty, were refused custody of the abused animals. Instead, custody was granted to NIH... That was like asking Jack the Ripper to protect a woman's dormitory.*"
—*Karen L. T. Iacobbo*, Providence Journal-Bulletin, *December 28, 1990*

Congress wasn't the only governing body NIH tried to placate in June of 1986. Reportedly, IBR's board of trustees wasn't too happy about the move to Delta, either. It was the ultimate in hypocrisy, as Pacheco saw it. After years of using IBR's ownership of the monkeys as the excuse to keep them out of Primarily Primates, NIH suddenly moves them to another laboratory without IBR's permission!

"The transfer has been initiated," William Raub wrote to IBR chairman Joseph Brady on June 23, "and may be completed by the time you receive this letter."

Raub then outlined the conditions of the transfer, including the financial arrangements: "Delta will charge the NIH for the care of the primates, and NIH will in turn charge those costs to IBR."

Finally, Raub added, "We hope that after further consideration you will agree to endorse our plan fully."

By the time the monkeys arrived at the Delta facility, Raub was telling reporters that IBR had agreed to the transfer and would assume the costs.

NIH then set about convincing Stas Kaczorowski, whose fast was in its eighth week, to begin eating again. The agency succeeded, according to Gary Francione, because they completely misrepresented the truth. Kaczorowski was shown photos of the plantation-like setting of the Delta center, nestled in a grove of pines. On the strength of these pictures, the activist put down his juice glass and picked up his fork.

But the true picture of the monkeys' new living quarters that emerged later was not so idyllic. The primates were placed in steel boxes, solid on three sides with a barred door, and measuring just 24 inches by 26 inches by 34 inches. They could not see or touch each other any more than they could gaze up into the branches of the trees outside or smell the fresh air. The temperature inside their sterile room was controlled and lights timed to go on and off at intervals provided artificial days and nights.

Most of the monkeys would spend the rest of their lives in this room banked with cages, oblivious to the legislation and lawsuits filed on their behalf.

Newkirk and Pacheco learned of the macaques' new dwelling from others. Even though they had visited the primates regularly for years, Delta's new director soon made it clear that they weren't welcome at his facility.

Newkirk phoned Peter Gerone on the morning after the monkeys arrived at Delta and asked if she could make arrangements to see them some time soon. She took detailed notes of the conversation that followed.

Gerone's reply, as she remembers it, was, "You can't visit them now or any day."

Anyone who wanted to see the monkeys, she was told, must have the permission of the president of the university, the chancellor, NIH, IBR and the university's attorneys.

Newkirk asked for the names of the attorneys.

"I'm not going to tell you. That's for you to find out," Gerone replied, according to her notes.

Frustrated, Newkirk pressed on, but says the conversation wound up with this annoying exchange:

"Could a representative of PETA or any other animal protection group visit the monkeys today?" she asked.

"No," Gerone answered.

"Could we visit them tomorrow?"

"No."

"Could we visit them next week, on Monday?" she asked.

"Do you want to discuss the whole year?" Gerone asked.

"I do," Newkirk said. "Could we visit them at any time in the coming year?"

Newkirk was to find all her conversations with Gerone just as pointless.

For Pacheco it was like losing a piece of his heart. The monkeys whose rescue he had engineered, whose future he had fought for, who seemed, in human terms, like his own children, were now completely cut off from him. He could not imagine how he was going to cope with the loss. It had been difficult seeing the primates in their narrow room at Poolesville, encased in the packing crate-sized cages, but at least he could see for himself that they weren't being used in experiments; he could see for himself what their conditions were.

Now, if he wanted to know how the monkeys were faring, if Adidas and Sisyphus still chattered to each other, if any were ill, he was forced to rely on the statements of people with a track record for deception.

Representative Smith was one person who understood the impact this had on Pacheco and it only added to his anger. He thought, not for the first time, how ironic it was that he had been cast in the role of PETA's champion on Capitol Hill. He wasn't even opposed to the use of animals for experimentation.

He wrote to Gerone at Delta to ask about seeing the primates. Gerone's response was defensive. He was still stinging from PETA's distribution of Delta's mortality rates, which he claimed were inaccurate, though they had been taken from the primate center's own reports.

" . . . [I]f you *personally* are interested in seeing the monkeys," he wrote to Smith, "I would suggest you send us a written request . . . I can tell you that animal rights activists will not be allowed to visit them. We have no intention of cooperating with organizations and their members who persist on making unfounded, scurrilous statements and charges against this Center."

William Raub backed Gerone up, and by August, when Raub was promoted to deputy director of NIH, it was obvious to Pacheco and Newkirk that their protests at the agency were getting them nowhere.

They turned instead to the Department of Health and Human Services, the agency NIH is responsible to, and asked to meet with Secretary Otis Bowen. He had been moderately responsive to Congressman Smith, Pacheco remembered. Maybe he was getting a trumped up version of the facts from NIH. Maybe he would at least listen to a different source. It wouldn't be the first time a cabinet official acknowledged PETA's interest in a case. Margaret Heckler, Bowen's predecessor, swiftly concluded the University of Pennsylvania head bashing campaign after reviewing the videotape of the experiments. Perhaps Bowen could be open to both sides of the issue—if he heard both sides.

But Bowen was not going to make himself available to Pacheco, Newkirk or anyone else from PETA. His office staff made it clear that Bowen was hearing all he needed to know from NIH.

Pacheco followed his polite invitation to meet with a more dramatic demand to be heard. On Tuesday morning, August 5, 15 activists dressed in striped prison shirts and monkey-face masks locked themselves in a specially constructed lightweight cage directly in front of the broad glass front doors of the HHS offices on Independence Avenue. Somewhere inside the great stone slabs of the Hubert Humphrey Building sat Otis Bowen. The activists, chanting "Save us from the death camps!" refused to leave until Bowen agreed to hear them out.

None of the activists expected that he would; that wasn't the point anymore. What they wanted was Bowen's refusal to help 15 abused animals splashed across the pages of the next day's morning newspapers. If he was going to close his doors to evidence of underhanded tactics and misrepresentation at NIH, the public was going to know about it.

Three hours after locking themselves in the symbolic cell, the activists were arrested and put behind the real bars of the D.C. jail—and the Associated Press and United Press International had several rolls of film in the can. The next morning, photos of the human "monkeys" flanked by husky Washington cops were scattered in papers throughout the states.

To reach even more people, Pacheco and Newkirk decided in August to pull up stakes at the Conscience Camp and move it to the National Mall. They'd kept it going in the rain and steamy East Coast summer heat for four months. It had served its publicity purpose, sparking dozens of news stories on the monkeys, including one on the "NBC Nightly News" with Tom Brokaw, but NIH was as firmly entrenched as ever. If Raub and his colleagues were willing to withstand the censure of Congress, they weren't going to be uprooted by a vigil.

The Mall, on the other hand, with its hundreds of thousands of tourists, presented a ready-made grassroots opportunity. Vacationers who cared enough about free speech and equal justice to travel to the nation's capital to sit at Abraham Lincoln's feet might just write a letter to their Representatives asking them to sign on to the Silver Spring Monkeys Congressional resolution.

By Labor Day Weekend, the camp, enlarged and improved with additional audio-visual displays and artwork, was in place on the wide lawn between the museums and monuments of Capitol Hill. Extra staff were hired to hand out literature and answer questions about the monkeys, vegetarianism, the fur trade and consumer product tests on animals.

The extra support drummed up on those hot fall days on the Mall was going to be needed more than Pacheco and Newkirk knew when they applied for the exhibition permit. The same week the display went up, the Fourth Circuit Court of Appeals dismissed PETA's case.

To allow individuals to sue, wrote Judges Ervin, Widener and Wilkinson, "might entail serious consequences. It might open the use of animals in biomedical research to the hazards and vicissitudes of courtroom litigation . . . It might unleash a spate of private lawsuits that would impede advances made by medical science in the alleviation of human suffering."

Pacheco couldn't believe it. He was being denied the chance to state his case in court because the court was worried about future hassles. It had less to do with the Silver Spring Monkeys than with protecting political territory. Why were animal experimenters considered so far above the law that they could be protected even from the *possibility* of litigation? Pacheco's father, a medical doctor, was given no such legal shield. Physicians are frequently sued and the courts have no hesitation about deciding the scientific dilemmas of these cases.

Many attorneys shared Pacheco's reaction. One such attorney, Bridget Klauber, later wrote in an article published by the University of Colorado Law Review that the Fourth Circuit "entered into the discussion surrounding the use of animals in biomedical research and took a side. The decision by the court . . . contained value laden statements that were not based on legal reasoning or analysis, but rather ethical and political opinions."

Moreover, she wrote, the court was wrong to rely so heavily on the amicus briefs submitted by scientific organizations: "Medical researchers are not simply concerned bystanders. They are professionals who will gain or lose by decisions involving the use of animals."

Most infuriating for Pacheco was the judges' statement that they could not risk the possibility of future lawsuits "in the absence of clear direction from the Congress."

Congress could not have made its wishes more obvious. In fact, if the "clear direction" NIH got from the House and Senate had been respected, there would have been no need for PETA's lawsuit in the first place.

Pacheco, Newkirk and Edward Genn had little recourse. They filed yet another appeal with the only court left—the U.S. Supreme Court.

Congressman Bob Smith, along with Representatives Charlie Rose and Rod Chandler also appealed to a higher office. On September 25th they wrote to President Ronald Reagan and asked him to intervene. Smith knew a phone call from Reagan to Secretary Bowen at HHS was all it would take to get the monkeys on a flight to San Antonio, and he was confident the President would help. It was such a simple action. And Smith had worked hard to help Reagan get elected.

"We have personally investigated every aspect of this case," Smith explained in his letter, "and can assure you that on scientific, monetary, and moral grounds there is no justification for keeping these animals in a federally-funded research facility for the next fifteen years, which is how long they are expected to live.

"NIH has been less than straightforward," Smith added. "We, and many of our colleagues, regret the unprofessional and sometime deceptive treatment we have received from this federal agency."

Despite his allegiance to the President and his support of Reagan policy, Smith received no help from the White House. A low-level aide from the executive staff did call the Congressman, but he made it plain the Silver Spring Monkeys case was a hot potato Reagan didn't want to handle.

Smith, already angry at NIH and fed up with their games, was bitterly disappointed by the Presidential door slam. It wouldn't have hurt Reagan to shove NIH along the right path and give some abused animals a break, he thought. The Reagan brush-off would still rankle years later, when Smith was a Senator, after another Republican President refused to intervene in the case.

Since it would be months before the Supreme Court decided if it would hear the case, Pacheco and Newkirk focused on building grassroots support for the resolutions and on getting into the Delta fortress to see the monkeys. They were frustrated by Peter Gerone's dismissal of their requests—it seemed to Newkirk that he saw the primates as political prisoners who were to be denied any contact with outside radicals. Genn complained in a letter to NIH attorney Robert Lanman of "Dr. Gerone's seemingly condescending, patronizing, and excessively partisan attitude" and suggested that it would be helpful to everyone if he were a bit more professional in dealing with representatives of the animal protection organizations.

Gerone's refusal even to pretend to be civil was a red flag to Pacheco and Newkirk. They had had a cordial, if not terribly friendly, relationship with the veterinarians and technicians at the NIH animal center, and consequently followed the moneys' ups and downs with some regularity. They saw Domitian slowly losing touch with his physical world of stainless steel. They had watched Billy, in his helplessness, forfeit more and more of his natural wildness and become more trusting as the months passed.

It hadn't been particularly easy or enjoyable to see the way the monkeys adapted to their lives in Poolesville, but at least nothing was hidden. Their worry now was what they weren't told about and couldn't witness for themselves. Decisions about medical treatment, housing, reintroducing the monkeys to group colony life would be made without their input, and without their permission.

Pacheco still refused to accept his loss of control over the monkeys. He had little illusion that anyone at Delta, NIH or HHS cared about the primates as the individuals he knew them to be. If he were shut out of their lives entirely, who would take his place? He brooded over the events of the last five years, rereading the hundreds of pages of notes he had typed detailing each new turn in the case. Had he overlooked something, or not acted fast enough at some point? But he could find nothing he would have done differently, except perhaps refuse to trust the NIH officials. The endless negotiations yielded nothing but broken promises.

Ironically, as the Silver Spring Monkeys slipped farther and farther from Pacheco's reach, PETA's membership and donations sky-rocketed. The organization moved from the Takoma Park house to a warehouse tucked among auto repair garages in the more suburban Kensington, Md., and converted the cavernous brick building into a huge common office divided by partitions. The furniture was mismatched and makeshift, either donated or built by hand to accommodate the staff, which had grown to more than 30.

Under Newkirk's direction, the organization was formally divided into separate departments: research and investigations, to document abuse on fur farms and in laboratories; media and campaigns, to take the proof to the public and organize grassroots actions; publications, to produce *PETA News* and assorted brochures on dozens of animal protection issues; correspondence and mail departments, to open and respond to the thousands of letters received every month; finance and membership.

Kim Stallwood, an experienced British activist Pacheco and Newkirk met several years earlier, was lured from his job as head of the leading anti-vivisection organization in England to become PETA's first executive director.

The warehouse was a hum of activity from 7:30 in the morning, when the first employees arrived, until well into the evening, often past midnight when events were being planned. The phone rang several hundred times each day with calls from members, out-of-state activists and reporters.

To the scientific community, PETA loomed threateningly, ever-present, a menace from which no animal experimenter was safe. Researchers complained that promising students were moving away from careers in animal laboratories. Their fear was evident in the newly implemented security precautions in some facilities—extra lighting, alarms, electronic locks and additional staff. The Delta primate center had spent more than $10,000 on increased security since the monkeys arrived.

In April of 1986, just a few months before the monkeys were moved, several of the scientific trade groups—fresh from their victory in the Fourth Circuit Court—organized a press conference to tout medical advances they claimed resulted from animal experimentation. The public defense of their profession was a new approach for Ph.D.s more accustomed to the laboratory than the microphone, and was indicative of their heightened concern about how they were perceived by people whose opinions had never before mattered.

Soon after, as if to underscore their new found solidarity, the American Association for the Advancement of Sciences elected Edward Taub a Special Fellow—an honor reserved for scientists whose work is deemed exceptional by their colleagues.

To Newkirk and Pacheco, all this scrambling proved PETA had succeeded in calling into question at least some experimental procedures. But it added to their difficulty in the Silver Spring Monkeys case. This was one case—the case that jump-started the animal rights movement—the scientific world still had control over, and apparently they weren't above holding the primates hostage to win a point against a rapidly growing army of opponents.

While Pacheco lobbied and worried, busier than ever with his duties as president of PETA, the monkeys' fates were being discussed and decided in Louisiana. On October 1, the eight deafferented primates were anesthetized and examined by two physicians with expertise in the rehabilitation of humans with spinal cord injuries. Drs. Joseph Biundo and Douglas Koltun watched the macaques move a few inches in the tiny cages first, noting particularly how well Nero, whose deafferented limb had been amputated by NIH veterinarians, managed to reach for food with his one remaining arm. They also scrutinized X rays that showed the abnormalities in the primates' hands and wrists.

Their conclusion should have cemented the plans NIH had already laid before Congress. They saw no evidence of pain and felt the best course of action was to amputate the deafferented arms of all the monkeys except Billy. Once the surgeries were complete and the animals completely recovered, they could probably be resocialized safely. The doctors did not recommend euthanasia for any of the primates.

But for some reason, Gerone did not act on his own experts' recommendations and NIH did not insist that he keep their promises. Even worse, in a fact sheet on the case later circulated by NIH, Koltun's and Biundo's findings were reduced to a single sentence: "Their report indicated that prognosis for rehabilitation and functional recovery of the deafferented limb is poor." It wasn't untrue, exactly, it was just half true. There was no mention of their conclusion, based on this prognosis, that amputation and resocialization would give the monkeys a chance to lead decent lives.

Newkirk knew nothing of this examination when later she was invited to New Orleans to appear on a television program.

She suspected, before she and PETA supporter Loretta Hirsh boarded the plane at Washington's National Airport, that there was little point in calling Gerone to arrange a visit. He'd made his views on that subject apparent in their less than cordial June telephone conversation.

She would simply show up on his doorstep and see how far she could get.

Dressed conservatively in sweater and slacks, and joined in the car by Hirsh and a local activist named Stephanie Stevenson, Newkirk headed toward Covington and the primate research center.

The area looked like a swamp, she thought as they drove toward the secluded facility, and she remembered that in Louisiana bodies had to be buried above the saturated ground. The mosquitoes must have been incredible. She wondered if there was a problem with infections and wound healing in the indoor/outdoor enclosures of the breeding colonies.

To Newkirk's great surprise, Gerone allowed them inside the offices and after a short time agreed to a brief meeting. He brought with him one of Delta's veterinarians, Robert Wolf, and Dr. Margaret Clarke, who was reportedly working on a resocialization plan for the primates.

Gerone asked Newkirk if she would mind if the meeting was tape recorded.

Newkirk agreed on the condition that she be given a copy of the tape.

It was an unsatisfactory exchange. As far as Newkirk could tell, nothing that had been promised had yet happened and Gerone's answers to most of her questions were vague or negative. No, she would not be allowed to see the monkeys that day, even though the quarantine period had ended. No, he didn't know what the visitation policy would be.

Gerone was definite about one thing—all the monkeys were in good health. Newkirk asked about each of the macaques and was somewhat reassured by Gerone's responses. She remembers asking specifically about her favorites, Adidas, Chester and Brooks.

Newkirk and Hirsh flew back to Washington and waited for the audiotape, the record of their discussion, to arrive by mail. Newkirk was anxious to share it with Pacheco, who would copy it for Senator Smith. But the tape never came.

Two weeks later Brooks was dead.

Chapter Sixteen

Broken Promises

"Disgruntled employees and employees who may be sympathetic to the cause of the more radical elements of the animal rights movement are the basic weakness in most well-planned state-of-the-art security systems. No matter how expensive the security equipment and how large and well-trained the security staff, these employees can and will expose the institution, its personnel, its projects, its animals, and its records to theft and vandalism."
—*"Security in the Research Laboratory,"* Lab Animal magazine, April, 1986

Brooks's death was a shock to Newkirk and Pacheco. Because he was a control monkey he didn't have the medical problems or disabilities of the deafferented primates. During his five years at the Poolesville facility he had suffered no significant illnesses. He'd been healthy and playful just a few months before. Suddenly he was dead.

The circumstances surrounding his death were never fully explained. The death wasn't even reported until 24 hours after it occurred, and then only because Newkirk received an anonymous tip and immediately called the facility. The first words out of her mouth were, "We want the body to be examined."

But within 72 hours, after Delta veterinarians had removed tissue samples, his body was incinerated—eliminating all possibility of an independent necropsy.

The story of the monkey's sudden demise kept changing.

Brooks was found dead in his cage, Gerone told reporters initially, and an examination showed that he had had pneumonia.

Gary Francione spoke to Gerone by telephone on November 17, three days after Brooks died. According to Francione's notes, Gerone claimed that Brooks hadn't eaten properly since he arrived at Delta and had suffered "substantial weight loss" for "two or three weeks" before his death. And even though Delta had performed an X ray exam of Brooks on November 12 that showed no evidence of bacterial pneumonia, it appeared that the cause of death was in fact bacterial pneumonia.

HHS later claimed that Brooks had been in "failing health for several months" and "had been under close medical surveillance since arrival at the Delta facility." The cause of death, according to HHS, was aspiration pneumonia complicated by bacterial infection. This version of the Brooks's last days lent credence to the letter from a PETA member who said she called Delta and was told by Peter Gerone that Brooks was force-fed while under anesthesia and had inhaled food particles during the procedure.

Still another story surfaced in a January, 1987, letter by Tulane president Eamon Kelly: " . . . [Brooks] developed a spontaneous kidney infection while in quarantine" and "subsequently developed feeding problems. This history of poor health culminated in the case of acute bacterial pneumonia from which he died . . . "

For Pacheco, the entire case had begun to take on a surrealistic quality. After so many years and so many successes in other campaigns, he was still battling for the animals who had led the way. It was as though the Silver Spring Monkeys were being punished for opening the door on a world of abuse—in laboratories, in slaughterhouses, on fur farms. They had to carry the burden for the "sins" of PETA, In Defense of Animals, Last Chance for Animals and dozens of other animal rights organizations formed in the wake of the Taub conviction. Pacheco was sure that the monkeys were still suffering because the lives of the people who exploited and abused animals had not been the same since Domitian's picture proved there was a need for a new social movement.

What NIH and the scientific community did not understand was that the movement would continue to grow, regardless of whether the monkeys lived or died.

Now Brooks was gone, and Pacheco would probably never know the whole story.

Either Gerone lied when he told Newkirk Brooks was in good health in October, or he, HHS and Tulane's president were lying about the way he died. Somebody wasn't being honest and Delta's refusal to release treatment records immediately smacked of a cover-up. It was difficult to avoid the conclusion that the monkeys weren't being cared for properly.

Gerone may have been angry at PETA for circulating Delta's mortality rates, but Brooks's death didn't bolster his argument that his facility had been unfairly maligned.

Fourteen Silver Spring Monkeys remained.

Brooks's death pushed Bob Smith a little closer to chucking the resolution and introducing a bill. Like Pacheco he was tired of the case and angry that it seemed to go on and on for no good reason. His letter to HHS Assistant Secretary Robert Windom showed his frustration with the agency's bob and weave on the case.

"Were undue stress or poor physical conditions contributing factors in the death of the primate?" he demanded. " . . . why was an independent necropsy not performed? . . . Was a specialist consulted? . . . Please provide me with . . . x-rays and the pathology report(s) . . . Please specify what condition each remaining individual Silver Spring Monkey is in . . . What efforts are underway and/or planned to resocialize the Silver Spring Monkeys?"

More than a month later, he received a reply from William Raub:

> . . . this animal had been in failing health for several months. Weeks before his death from natural causes, the animal had undergone extensive therapy for a spontaneous kidney infection . . . the animal followed a downhill course . . . It is not uncommon for an animal in poor health to aspirate its stomach contents during the debilitated phase of illness.

Raub's letter did not explain why neither Congress nor PETA's legal counsel were told of Brooks's medical condition until after his death. Nor did it explain why the clinical and pathological report, which was eventually sent to Smith, detailing Brooks's treatment, made no mention of an X ray exam the day before the monkey died.

Raub also assured Smith that Gerone was working on a plan for the remaining monkeys. In December, four more experts were consulted. Their conclusion—the eight deafferented primates should be destroyed.

Smith couldn't believe it. First no one in the scientific community wanted the monkeys, then everyone did. First they were not appropriate for further studies, then they were valuable research tools. At last they were going to be retired and resocialized, now they were slated to die.

Over the course of several days in February, 1987, Pacheco and Barnard, now firm friends and colleagues, pieced together a partial sequence of events at Delta following Brooks's death. The official reason, they found, was that the primates were supposedly in pain.

Two weeks after Brooks's body was incinerated, Gerone, with Raub's knowledge, convened a meeting of what he call the "Ad Hoc Committee for the Resocialization Plan of the Silver Spring Monkeys." There were four people on the committee, later described by HHS as "specialists in veterinary care and primate behavior." Despite their veterinary expertise, the panel did not conduct examinations of the primates; they merely observed the animals in their cages. They also read Biundo's and Koltun's report and were briefed by two Delta veterinarians. One of the vets was Robert Wolf, who sat in on Newkirk's October meeting with Gerone and did not dispute Gerone's statement that Brooks was fine.

Even though the committee didn't see any behavioral problems indicating pain, and even though Koltun and Biundo believed the monkeys did not suffer physically, the Ad Hoc Committee concluded that euthanasia would be the best solution.

Failing that, the committee suggested amputating the deafferented limbs and housing the primates in pairs. Other options, in descending order of preference, included amputation and housing individually, leaving the monkeys as they were; or attempting resocialization without amputation.

On February 16, 1987, two months after the Ad Hoc Committee issued its report, Gerone called a special meeting of Delta's Committee on Care and Use of Laboratory Animals to consider the recommendations. Wolf discussed the need for amputation of the deafferented limbs. Behaviorist Margaret Clarke then presented her plan for resocializing the monkeys by housing them in pairs.

The committee then voted to endorse the Ad Hoc Committee's recommendations in the order listed, which meant that Delta's first choice was death. It would be up to NIH to make the decision.

Pacheco didn't understand how HHS, NIH and Delta could act as though they hadn't already formulated a plan for the monkeys. All three agencies had repeatedly stated that the primates would be resocialized after undergoing the surgical removal of the limbs. They had promised to allow them to live out their natural lives. They had given their word to Congress and the public and had acted aggrieved at any suggestion that they might not keep their word.

Before Brooks died, Pacheco couldn't imagine they would get away with it. Now, the only thing standing between the monkeys and their execution was the lawsuit pending before the Supreme Court. The Court's refusal to hear the case would be the death warrant for Domitian, Nero, Allen, Titus, Big Boy, Paul, Augustus and Billy.

Smith demanded to see the primates. He had visited them at the Poolesville center when they were in good health and he wanted to see for himself whether or not they were in pain. The monkeys' medical reports said nothing of treatments for their supposed suffering—no painkillers, no rehabilitation therapy.

Despite Smith's repeated requests, it would be a long time before he stood looking down at any of the monkeys. In the meantime, Raub assured Smith that "we remain willing to consider alternative arrangements for the primates."

By early 1987, Pacheco had begun to cast a wider net in his search for allies. Taking a leap of faith, he tried an unlikely source—the scientific community. He knew there were researchers who might disagree with PETA's general philosophy, but who would not be willing to sacrifice the Silver Spring Monkeys simply to protect their territory. Two unexpected events early in the year eventually resulted in an unlikely friendship with one such scientist.

In January, much to the surprise of animal rights activists, the U.S. Department of Agriculture deemed unfit the primate facility at the State University College at New Paltz, New York. The university was suddenly faced with emptying its cages of several dozen stump-tailed macaques. New Paltz officials approached the nearby New York University Laboratory for Experimental Medicine and surgery in Primates (LEMSIP), a large, well established laboratory that conducted hepatitis and AIDS studies on chimpanzees. LEMSIP was already at full capacity, but Jan Moor-Jankowski, a physician and LEMSIP's director since 1965, watched with interest when PETA's upstate contact Ed Ashton offered to help relocate the animals.

Because there were so many monkeys, an immediate transfer was impossible; there were very few facilities that could handle an additional 50 primates. After months of searching, followed by months of working out complicated travel and funding arrangements, the macaques were flown to a tropical island primate sanctuary in Mexico. New Paltz officials were grateful to PETA and didn't hesitate to express their appreciation publicly in several press accounts.

Moor-Jankowski was impressed, but it was in connection with yet another incident involving PETA, primates and a federally funded laboratory that brought Pacheco and the LEMSIP director together.

In late 1986, not long after Brooks died, an Animal Liberation Front-like group calling itself True Friends broke into a chimpanzee laboratory called SEMA, located near Washington, and took four infant chimps not yet infected with any of the viruses being studied at the facility. The video footage taken during the raid and later sent to PETA showed adult chimpanzees encased in chambers called isolettes—refrigerator-sized glass boxes with inner metal frame cages. The primates could do nothing more than sit or stand. They had nothing to look at but the wall opposite their coffin-like containers. They rocked back and forth in boredom-induced madness, oblivious to the masked invaders.

PETA sent copies of the video to Geza Teleki, the primatologist who five years before had visited IBR with Pacheco and subsequently testified against Taub, and to Teleki's friend and colleague Jane Goodall, the world's most famous chimpanzee expert. Goodall later asked to see SEMA and was appalled by the sight of these primates, some of whom had been warehoused for years, existing in a kind of living death. She wrote hauntingly of this experience in articles and books, and undertook the difficult project of trying to change the way chimpanzees were treated in experimental laboratories.

A few months after the break-in, Pacheco wrote to Moor-Jankowski and asked him to comment on the videotape and the written reports on SEMA. Rather than pass judgment on a facility he wasn't familiar with, Moor-Jankowski instead invited Pacheco to visit LEMSIP!

Pacheco was astonished. He knew his reputation among animal experimenters—he was a member of the enemy camp, not to be trusted, certainly not to be treated as though he had any valuable advice to offer. He was even more amazed when LEMSIP agreed to his taking photographs or video.

"As a result of the visit," Moor-Jankowski later wrote in a letter to a colleague, "Mr. Pecheco [sic] made some suggestions which were helpful towards improving the psychological well-being of our chimpanzees, but which did not occur to us previously."

One was to give each of the chimps a coconut—a strange-sounding suggestion to the LEMSIP staff, who knew very well that chimpanzees in their natural habitat would never come in contact with this large seed. They tried it anyway and were surprised to find that such a simple thing could provide the primates with so many hours of delight. The chimps "groomed" the coconuts, rubbed them against their bodies, and eventually picked the coarse hair off. They shook them and listened to the milk slosh around inside. Eventually, when they grew tired of the coconuts, the caretakers sliced them open for the primates to eat.

There were others in the scientific world, physicians, experimenters, professors, who endured the censure of their community to support PETA's position on the Silver Spring Monkeys case: Roger Fouts, a professor at Central Washington University's Chimpanzee Research Laboratory; Donald Doll, chief of hematology and oncology at the Harry S. Truman Memorial Veterans Hospital in Missouri, and a professor of medicine; Peter Wood, the associate director of the Stanford Center for Research in Disease Prevention; Alfred Cohen of the Memorial Sloan Kettering Cancer Center in New York. These and eventually more than 200 others risked offending the nation's largest funder of biomedical experiments and studies, NIH, by openly endorsing the transfer of the monkeys to a sanctuary.

Pacheco also began working with California Congressman Bob Dornan, who had followed the case from the beginning. His interest in the monkeys was inspired at least in part by his daughter Kate, a young actress who had become concerned about the treatment of animals in laboratories and had watched the tangled events of the Silver Spring Monkeys case unfold. Dornan himself was a fiery, red-headed conservative whose views were for the most part far to the right of Pacheco's, and as Pacheco came to know and like the Congressman, he was struck once again by the unlikely allies he found on Capitol Hill. None of the Representatives or Senators he knew liked to be called animal rights activists; they didn't oppose all uses of animals for experimentation, but their support for PETA on this issue was strong.

Because Dornan's district lay in southern California, he approached Douglas Myers, the executive director of the San Diego Zoo, and asked him if the zoo would provide a home for the 14 monkeys. Even though the National Zoo in Washington, D.C., had already refused to take them, Dornan thought NIH might consider the San Diego Zoological Park scientific enough to agree with his proposal, so he was pleased when Myers's response was cautiously positive. Myers felt they could resocialize and house the control monkeys with little difficulty, and at least one zoo employee was enthusiastic about taking the deafferented macaques as well.

Donald Lindburg, Ph.D., a behaviorist, had served on Delta's Ad Hoc Committee. He'd seen the monkeys and read their medical reports. Contrary to his fellow committee members, he was optimistic about attempting to resocialize them—if NIH would let them go.

Throughout the negotiations in the early months of 1987, Pacheco and Newkirk wondered what they weren't being told by NIH and Delta officials. They knew by now not to accept what they were told, not to trust the promises, but they couldn't be sure when the next punch to the gut would come or where if would come from.

In the middle of March they received a warning.

One afternoon, an employee of the American Physiological Society (APS) left the downtown office, got in a car and drove north for 40 minutes to PETA's suburban headquarters. In the car was a copy of a memo for Newkirk and Pacheco.

The two-page memo, marked "confidential," outlined a plan concocted by the American Psychological Association, the Society for Neuroscience, IBR and NIH to get rid of the embarrassing problem of the Silver Spring Monkeys:

> PROPOSED AGREEMENT—IBR gives title to the monkeys to Tulane University, thus freeing NIH from any responsibility as to the future of these animals . . . After gaining title to the monkeys Tulane could euthanize the treated primates and complete the research . . . Because animal rights advocates have been gaining public and congressional support by telling how tax dollars are being used to maintain these monkeys when they (the advocates) would pay for their keep, Tulane wants an endowment so neither state nor federal funds are involved.

Two prominent people had already volunteered to solicit donations for an endowment from scientific organizations and universities—Fred King, the director of the Yerkes Regional Primate Center in Atlanta, Ga., and William Danforth, the president of the prestigious Washington University in St. Louis, Mo.

It took Newkirk a moment to comprehend the significance of the document in her hands. It represented months of plotting in secret meetings behind closed doors, trying to figure out how to kill the deafferented monkeys with the least amount of controversy. It proved that NIH's negotiations with Congress were just as meaningless as they had always been.

The memo was also filled with fear. The eminence of the fundraisers showed how high the stakes were for the scientific community. If a university president was willing to beg money to gain custody of 14 animals with no practical use to science, he obviously felt he had a lot to lose if they didn't succeed. Another memo Newkirk wouldn't see until years later revealed even darker motives. In it, Peter Gerone tried to sell the APS plan to John J. Walsh, chancellor of Tulane University. He wrote:

> In some ways, ownership [of the primates] simplifies our task and gives us greater control . . . We would not have to report our activities in regard to these animals to NIH and therefore the animal rights groups would not have access to such information through the Freedom of Information

Act . . . The worst thing that can happen at this point is to have the animals get into the hands of PETA and go to Primarily Primates or a similar facility . . . They would not only show the public the horrors of IBR's research but would also use the transfer to 'prove' to the public that Delta was not the right place for the animals . . . they would cite the death of Brooks as further evidence. I believe that would be more damaging to this Center's reputation than any of the charges that have been leveled so far.

After two and a half pages Gerone concluded: " . . . I would hate to see PETA win a battle politically that it was unable to win in the courts . . . If that happens, everyone will believe that they must have been right all along . . . "

Within hours, Pacheco was on Capitol Hill with the APS memo and Bob Smith's staff was on the phone with William Raub. Raub claimed he knew nothing of the secret plan, but the memo's reference to negotiations between the scientific community and "governmental agencies" cast a black shadow of doubt on Raub's declaration of innocence.

Smith and Charlie Rose sent Raub a written demand for a "full and immediate explanation," but didn't hold out much hope for a sudden repentance. If the negotiations with NIH wound up nowhere, and it looked like that's where they were heading, the Supreme Court's decision was crucial. If the Justices upheld the Appeals Court ruling that PETA lacked standing to sue, their only option was to introduce legislation. Smith had threatened several times to draft a bill mandating the monkeys' release, most recently after Brooks's mysterious death, but both HHS and NIH had asked him to hold off until they discussed the case further.

Both Congressmen also believed, on a more fundamental level, that individuals should have the right to bring suit against government agencies like the U.S. Department of Agriculture if they weren't providing even the ineffective protection for animals required by law. They could give citizens that right by amending the Animal Welfare Act.

After seeing the APS memo, Charlie Rose introduced H.R. 1770 in the House of Representatives, giving "any person" the right to sue "on his own behalf or on behalf of any animal" those people responsible for enforcing the Animal Welfare Act. If the bill were passed, PETA would at least be able to file against the USDA and finally have its day in court.

Two weeks later, on April 6, the U.S. Supreme Court, without comment, refused to hear PETA's lawsuit.

The Supreme Court's decision followed PETA's most successful winter anti-fur campaign to date. The newspapers were full of the fur industry's woes: plummeting sales and an increasingly tainted reputation. Celebrities had publicly donated their furs to PETA for use in protests, and fur-wearers on the street were likely to be confronted by activists offended by the deaths that the coats represented.

The last seven months had been hectic and exhilarating for Pacheco and Newkirk. As the demand for furs plunged, fur farms closed and applications for trapping licenses decreased. They felt that they were making a tangible difference in the lives of animals. At times like these, Pacheco felt a renewed hope in his work at PETA. He was glad that he was young, that he had so many years left to devote to the fight for animals rights. His energy soared. He slept less and worked harder.

But his successes made the setbacks in the Silver Spring Monkeys case seem all the more heartbreaking. And NIH seemed to take a cruel pleasure in doling them out.

The day following the Supreme Court's dismissal, Raub sent a letter to Smith in which he stated that due to "pathology in the spine" euthanasia for the deafferented monkeys was still under consideration.

The Supreme Court's dismissal left Newkirk and Pacheco nowhere to go with the suit unless Rose's bill passed, but they had little hope the justice system would protect the Silver Spring Monkeys any more than it already had. Congressional intervention and public pressure became even more crucial. Fortunately their support on Capitol Hill was solid. Dornan, Rose, Lantos, Chandler, Roe and Smith had never flagged in their efforts, despite the setbacks and frustrations of failed talks.

Smith even offered to buy the monkeys after the Supreme Court turned down the case. Although his resolution already had more than 200 co-signers, he was fed up with NIH's broken promises and wanted a resolution, even if it meant taking custody of the primates himself.

Public outrage was mounting as well. Activists in Louisiana bombarded Governor Edwin Edwards with letters urging him to investigate Delta's claim that the monkeys' health was deteriorating. Actress Doris Day, who had begun her own animal protection organization, wrote to her former colleague Ronald Reagan for help. But by far the most effective boost to their efforts came from columnist Jack Anderson, known for his inside-the-beltway exposés.

After taking the "confidential" APS memo to Congress, Pacheco, Newkirk and PETA's media department debated the next step. Should they issue a press release? Or should they just send copies to grassroots groups around the country? They finally decided that the people who most needed to know what NIH had cooked up were right in Washington—the elected representatives who authorized NIH's budget. They took the memo and packet of background material to Anderson's office and hoped for the best.

On April 25, the secret memo of the American Physiological Society was suddenly very public news. Pacheco, Smith, Rose, Raub and an American Psychological Association representative were interviewed for the column, and the result was acutely embarrassing for the National Institutes of Health. Smith lambasted the agency for its "bureaucratic bullheadedness." Rose accused NIH of misleading Congress with promises that appeared to have been forgotten. Raub denied involvement in the clandestine negotiations, but the APA spokesperson contradicted his claim.

The unexpected airing of NIH's dirty linen gave Dornan's San Diego Zoo negotiations a jump start. Suddenly, both NIH and HHS were ready to placate Congress by at least talking about transferring some of the primates to Donald Lindburg's care.

Delta, by contrast, was steadfast in its resolve. The deafferented monkeys would have to be destroyed. While Gerone apparently made these claims to anyone who would listen, he refused to allow an independent exam to confirm his statements. He still refused visitation requests from Smith and Pacheco, and had not begun the socialization process for the physically normal monkeys, even though nearly a year had passed since the primates were moved to Louisiana.

Just a month after Anderson's column, the *New York Times* ran a front-page article headlined "Fate of Monkeys a source of Pain for 6 Years" in which the Delta director advocated euthanasia. "It's the humane thing to do," Gerone was quoted as saying.

Gerone also voiced his true fear by accusing PETA of caring less about the monkeys than about its effort to stop all experiments on animals, but ultimately the article added to the pressure on NIH to follow through with its earlier vows.

Chapter Seventeen

Waves of Panic

"I have obtained a confidential memorandum, Mr. Speaker, from the American Psychological Association . . . Mr. Speaker, NIH should think twice before they let something like this happen. If this goes through, the Department of Health and Human Services will not only have lied to Congress, but to the Chairman of the Committee on Energy and Commerce . . . "
—Congressman Charlie Rose on the floor of the House of Representatives, March 25, 1987

On September 1, 1987, five of the normal monkeys, Montaigne, Adidas, Sisyphus, Chester and Haydn, were removed from their individual steel cages at the Delta Regional Primate Research Center and loaded onto a waiting van. After a short ride they were lifted aboard an airplane and flown to their new home at the San Diego Zoo's Center for the Reproduction of Endangered Species.

For the first time in at least a decade, they would bask in the sunlight, and when they were warmed, recline on a shady perch and nibble the juicy pulp from a fresh California orange. Their enclosures were large—enormous compared to the packing trunk-sized cages in which they had existed for years—and entirely outdoors in San Diego's mild climate. They would have a fresh, deep layer of straw to sleep on, their first soft beds since their capture from the jungle. They would make friends with their caretakers and willingly offer themselves to be groomed and petted. Eventually, three of them would learn to trust each other and would live together, enjoying the close physical companionship of other macaques for the first time since infancy.

They were oblivious to the arguments and controversy that marked the months preceding their transfer to their new way of life. In fact, had Bob Dornan been less persistent and had the scientific community not been caught hatching a plot to kill the deafferented monkeys, the relocation might never have occurred.

The zoo board's initial interest in taking all of the primates was considerably dampened by late spring, 1987. Although NIH was embarrassed by its apparent involvement in the proposal outlined in the secret APS memo, it stood by Delta's recommendation that euthanasia was the best course of action for the disabled macaques. Pacheco suspected that the zoo trustees were being lobbied by Peter Gerone or some of the members of the scientific organizations. He and Dornan wrote letters assuring the trustees that PETA would not create problems for the zoo and would cooperate fully in the smooth relocation. Eventually, the zoo's executive director, Douglas Myers, and the board declined to accept both the deafferented primates and Sarah, as they did not have a group of rhesus monkeys for her to live with.

Pacheco felt that Donald Lindburg, who would oversee the monkeys' care, would reconsider this decision later. He liked the quiet, sandy-haired Lindburg, who had been highly recommended by Jane Goodall, and trusted him when he promised an open-door policy. He knew he would be able to visit the macaques and see for himself how they were adapting.

On June 26, Dornan issued a news release:

> San Diego Zoo To Accept 5 Silver Spring Monkeys—After a phone call from congressman Robert K. Dornan . . . the San Diego Zoo has now officially agreed to accept five of fourteen 'Silver Spring Monkeys' currently incarcerated at the Delta Regional Primate Research Center in Louisiana.

It was a day for celebration at the PETA office, where the staff was planning the next fall's anti-fur campaign and compiling experts' statements on the conditions at the SEMA laboratory.

Pacheco felt a sense of relief he hadn't known in a very long time. Half of his task was now complete.

He didn't know that on that very day, Peter Gerone was hammering another nail in the coffin-lid over the eight crippled monkeys who were to remain in his care.

By this time Edwin Edwards, the governor of Louisiana, had received so much public pressure about the Silver Spring Monkeys that he was compelled to take some sort of action. The case was out of his control, he explained in a form letter sent to all who wrote; he had referred the complaints to the Louisiana Society for the Prevention of Cruelty to Animals in New Orleans, and asked the SPCA to prepare a report for him.

On June 26, the same day Dornan released his statement to the press, two representatives of the SPCA drove to the Delta and observed the monkeys.

Exactly how this visit came about remains a mystery. For a year, Congressman Smith, Newkirk, Pacheco, Roger Galvin and others who had followed the case for years and had visited the primates at the Poolesville animal center, had been denied entry to Delta. They had proposed an independent exam by veterinarians of their choice to verify or dispute the claims of Delta's Ad Hoc Committee. All their requests were turned down.

Gerone did seem to understand the damage his denials might add to his growing public relations problems. He even made a point of inviting three representatives of the animal protection movement to attend the special meeting of the Delta Committee on Care and Use of Laboratory Animals to consider recommendations for the monkeys. However, the people he chose were young, unfamiliar with primatology, and had not been involved directly in the case. Two of them, Sean Hawkins and Merry Caplan, were suspicious enough not accept Gerone's offer.

In his letter of refusal, Hawkins wrote:

As you know, I am a 20-year-old college student who has been employed in private veterinary practices (limited dogs and cats) for three years. I have no experience with primates. With this in mind, I find it absurd that my requests for an independent veterinarian or primate expert to accompany me on my visit to Delta to lend me professional and medical advice have repeatedly denied . . . why would Delta elect a non-credentialed person to the committee unless it is an insurance that, should I disagree with Delta, my opinion would not carry any weight?

Hawkins had also heard that the third animal protection representative, who did attend the meeting, served on the board of the local humane society. Also on the board was Robert Wolf, Delta's veterinarian.

" . . . this local humane society," Hawkins wrote, "is the only one in Louisiana which has actively fought moderate animal welfare legislation, including a bill to require minimum standards for the operation of dog pounds."

It was difficult for Hawkins, Caplan, Newkirk and Pacheco to conclude that Gerone and the Delta staff really wanted an honest evaluation of the monkeys' condition from the humane community.

How the Louisiana SPCA's president, Stanley Muller, and executive director, Gary Frazell, were chosen is unclear. One thing is certain—not all members of the SPCA board were privy to the invitation or the subsequent report. Merry Caplan served on the board and knew nothing of the visit until Frazell and Muller had issued an official statement that the SPCA concurred with the Delta's recommendation "that the eight monkeys be euthanized without further delay."

The SPCA's report was a powerful tool for Delta and NIH. Even animal protectionists thought the monkeys should be destroyed, Gerone could—and did—argue; PETA cared more about winning than about these animals.

It was certainly conceivable to Newkirk and Pacheco that the monkeys might very well be suffering. How could they not be, at the very least, uncomfortable? It was reasonable to suggest that imprisonment in a puny space might be a leading contributor to their ill health. They sat in Newkirk's cubicle at the PETA office and discussed possible responses to the report. It was difficult *not* to wonder if they had let the case drag on too long.

If they were in bad shape, Pacheco told Congressman Smith the next day, they would agree to immediate euthanasia, but they wanted to see for themselves how the monkeys were. They didn't trust Delta, NIH or HHS officials. Furthermore, there was the report of Janis Ott-Joslin.

Reportedly, the SPCA representatives invited the veterinarian, who had once been helpful to PETA in the early days of the case, to accompany them on their visit to Delta. Janis Ott, as she was known in 1981, had examined the monkeys in Lori Lehner's basement. She was by no means a PETA supporter and hadn't been in contact with the organization for some time. It was not known what her relationship to Delta, if there was one, was at the time of her visit.

In any case, Ott-Joslin did not recommend euthanasia for seven of the deafferented macaques, but suggested that amputation and possible resocialization be considered on an individual basis. Only for Billy did she suggest "that the time has come to make a decision."

When the SPCA findings were released to the Associated Press on August 13, two weeks before the transfer of the control monkeys to the zoo, Pacheco and Newkirk were startled to read in Ott-Joslin's report that Delta veterinarians were "concerned that the animals may be experiencing 'phantom pain,' " the very condition that Taub and his experts had denied so vigorously in court in Rockville, Md.

Despite the ultimate success of the zoo transfer negotiations, Bob Smith had enough of NIH's failure to keep its promise to resocialize the disabled monkeys. When he learned that Health and Human Services Secretary Otis Bowen had elected to back Delta's plan to destroy the monkeys, he decided that at least he could keep his promise to NIH and PETA. In July, he introduced H.R. 2883, co-signed by Charlie Rose, Tom Lantos, Patricia Schroeder and several other members:

> ... [T]he Secretary of Health and Human Services ... shall
> take such steps as are necessary to enter into an agreement
> with the sanctuary known as Primarily Primates ...

More than 130 Representatives signed on to the bill in the next few months, but like its counterpart in the Senate introduced by Steve Symms of Idaho, and an identical bill introduced by Smith in 1989, it never got out of committee. In spite of widespread bipartisan support, there were some Representatives sympathetic to NIH's position. Smith now believes political maneuvering by some members of the various committees the bills were referred to kept them from ending up on the floor for a vote by the full House and Senate—where they probably would have passed.

Still, the introduction of binding legislation sent waves of panic through much of the scientific world. Two months later, when five of the monkeys were sent to their new and happier home at the zoo, some researchers began talking about a tactical change in their fight against the growing animal rights movement.

One was Frederick Goodwin, M.D., then the director of Intramural Research at the National Institutes of Mental Health (NIMH). NIMH, like NIH, annually funds and conducts hundreds of experiments involving animals and is administered by the Department of Health and Human Services. Goodwin, an outspoken proponent of the use of animals in laboratories, had already, in his words, "developed four clinical investigators who have been trained in the arguments of the animal rights people and who have had media training."

Goodwin was ready for an all-out assault.

On September 28, Goodwin attended a meeting to discuss the animal rights movement with the directors of NIH and representatives of HHS. The following day, in a memo to the HHS deputy assistant secretary for health, he wrote:

> The stakes are enormous. The animal rights' [sic] movement threatens the very core of what the Public Health Service is all about . . . The health community must participate in a more pro-active posture, working in concert with patient groups, voluntary health organizations, the American Medical Association, and other groups of health professionals.

Goodwin was apparently nervous about how this "pro-active posture" would appear to the public: "Wherever feasible, the research institutions should leave the 'out front' activities to the other groups."

But he wasn't opposed to paying for it, presumably with tax money: "The PHS and its agencies should find some acceptable way to provide funding for some of these efforts and technical support for others."

Goodwin proposed a two-pronged approach. First, he suggested touting "health advances directly dependent upon animal research. Here we should draw liberally from those health areas that already enjoy wide public and congressional support, i.e., AIDS, dementia, schizophrenia, various childhood disorders, etc."

Second, they should attack the "philosophical underpinnings" of animal rights and illustrate "how the movement's philosophy is based on a degradation of the concept of human nature."

When Ingrid Newkirk later read this memo, it struck her that Goodwin was just plain scared, as well as mistaken about animal rights philosophy. She did not understand how extending respect to other living beings degraded human nature. Didn't bashing an improperly anesthetized baboon in the head degrade human nature? Or keeping crippled monkeys locked away in tiny cages for years on end?

By the end of 1987, Congressmen Smith, Rose and Lantos requested the General Accounting Office to provide a report on the amount of money the government had spent on the Silver Spring Monkeys case so far. They also attempted to continue negotiations on transferring the remaining nine primates at Delta to the San Diego Zoo.

Pacheco devoted himself to this plan with increased intensity. He saw the five monkeys living at the zoo in December and could hardly believe how well and happy they looked. They were housed away from the public zoo area and weren't disturbed by a parade of strangers each day. They had gained weight and their reddish-brown coats were thick and glossy. Donald Lindburg guessed they were 13 or 14 years old. Lindburg and Susan Clark, an animal psychologist, were working methodically toward the day when the monkeys would be placed together for the first time.

Pacheco sat down with Lindburg and his supervisor, Werner Heuschele, a veterinarian and the director of research for the zoo's Center for the Reproduction of Endangered Species, after viewing the monkeys. If the zoo board agreed, Pacheco was told, they would happily discuss how they could help. They were already learning what they hoped would be valuable information about resocializing primates and planned to apply their knowledge to their work with populations of endangered lion-tailed macaques.

They would need money for a facility to house the monkeys and to pay a small staff to care for them. Pacheco promised that all costs would be covered by an endowment fund set up by animal protection groups. PETA would also agree to publicly portray the transfer as the result of good faith efforts on all sides, including Delta's. Or they would say nothing, if that was preferred. Just to prove it, PETA would post a bond and enter into a voluntary court-ordered injunction enjoining the organization and its representatives from violating the agreement. PETA was also willing to agree to the release of the primates' bodies, upon their natural death, to the scientific community.

It was a good meeting, and a nice way to spend the day. Back home, the Washington weather was cold and rainy, while here in San Diego it was sunny, the temperature in the mid-70s. He was reassured by Lindburg's and Heuschele's enthusiasm, and by the condition of the monkeys already in the zoo's care. Who could argue with their plan? Everybody would win—the monkeys would be rescued but would remain in the hands of researchers. Even William Raub at NIH seemed to be in favor of the move. Pacheco began to fantasize about the transfer. He imagined loading the monkeys into a van and driving to the airport. He wondered if Billy still used his hands as pillows. Did Augustus still cradle his withered arm with his healthy hand? He could picture them, tired from their trip, curling up on a pile of straw— their first soft bed since they were taken from Lori Lehner's basement. The monkeys would grow old here together, he thought, happy to groom each other and eat fresh fruit in the warmth of the California sunshine.

On February 4, 1988, Bob Smith met with HHS Secretary Otis Bowen. Just two days earlier the zoo's board of trustees had officially authorized their executive director, Douglas Myers, to continue negotiations with Representative Bob Dornan and NIH. In light of this, Bowen was agreeable, and Smith, for the first time in many months, felt that they had made some progress.

It wasn't until NIH decided to convene yet another panel of experts to assess the monkeys' health that Pacheco began to have serious doubts about the agency's intentions. He knew from previous experience that the committee's findings could be influenced by factors other than the primates' conditions, and since the report that came out of the exam was likely to influence the

San Diego Zoo board's decision, it was crucial that the evaluation be fair.

This must have occurred to Dornan, too. He insisted that a member of his staff, Jerry Gideon, be present. But the other observers—Joseph Brady from IBR's board, Gerone, Raub, Louis Sibal from NIH and Delta veterinarian Robert Wolf—tipped the scale a bit too far in the other direction to ease Pacheco's mind. At least the panel itself would include Donald Lindburg and Dave Rehnquist, the veterinarian responsible for the monkeys at NIH's animal center. Pacheco's relationship with Rehnquist was cordial, and even though he knew Rehnquest wasn't keen on keeping experimental animals around if they weren't being used in the laboratory, he trusted the veterinarian's medical judgment.

The other four members of the panel were more worrisome. There were three professors of medicine, including one from Washington University, whose president, William Danforth, had volunteered to raise funds to buy the Silver Spring Monkeys so they could be experimented on and killed.

And there was Douglas M. Bowden, M.D., the director of the Regional Primate Research Center in Seattle. A colleague of Gerone's, Bowden's views became obvious in a letter he sent to Raub later that year, after he accepted a macaque considered unusable for experimentation from the University of Oregon. He had the animal euthanized even though Primarily Primates had offered to take the monkey.

"Our experience," Bowden wrote, "illustrates the kind of harassment and media event that is likely to occur repeatedly throughout the country if NIH establishes a precedent that lesioned research animals be sold or donated for nonscientific purposes. Every surplus lesioned animal in which PETA or any other anti-research organization registers an interest would become the potential subject of a bitter and protracted debate . . . for the U.S. biomedical research community as a whole, it would be disastrous."

When Pacheco read a copy of this letter many months later, he would wonder, as he had throughout the last seven years, what was wrong with providing a life for an animal labeled "surplus." If someone was willing to do it, and do it humanely, within the bounds of the law, at their own cost, why should it frighten the scientific community so much?

The panel's report, issued after three days of exams and conferences, caught Pacheco and Newkirk off guard in one respect—suddenly, the monkeys were again deemed a "unique scientific resource." The panel recommended, contrary to repeated promises made by NIH, HHS and Delta, that when the monkeys' health deteriorated to the point that euthanasia became necessary, they be subjected to a final experiment under anesthesia before being killed.

Pacheco demanded to know exactly who would determine when euthanasia was necessary. He hadn't been allowed to see the monkeys even once in the 21 months since they were moved to Louisiana, and Gerone had refused entry to any of the veterinarians Pacheco trusted. Besides, it was becoming pretty obvious that the recommendation to euthanize depended on who was doing the examining. Doctors Koltun and Biundo weren't convinced that euthenasia was necessary for any of the monkeys in 1986, but just a few months later the Ad Hoc Committee advised it for all of them.

The current panel held yet another view: Domitian and Augustus should be killed; Nero, Allen and Sarah "are reasonably good candidates for resocialization"; Billy, Paul and Titus should be "maintained in their present states."

Amputation was not suggested, and phantom pain was not even mentioned.

This latest report presented some difficult questions for Pacheco and Newkirk. Pacheco had been particularly concerned about Domitian for some time. The monkey who had once been docile, who had willingly offered his furry back to Pacheco for grooming, had become aggressive and angry. He was reportedly thin and had continued to attack his disabled left arm, so that it was covered with lacerations and scars. Augustus, too, was in poor shape, according to the physical exam report. Euthanasia probably would be best, they concluded.

But they could not agree to keeping four of the monkeys in two feet by two feet prisons for the rest of their lives. They had to be given a chance. Then, if amputation and resocialization didn't make a difference in their lives, if these original plans utterly failed, they could look at other options.

Congressman Smith wrote to Raub on March 30. He would agree to euthanasia for Domitian and Augustus, but he wanted a witness present when it happened. He also insisted that all seven of the remaining monkeys be transferred to the zoo.

Just a month later, while Smith waited for a response, the San Diego Zoo inexplicably refused to take any of the monkeys.

Chapter Eighteen

Plotting To Kill

"My view is the animal rights people make too much money on these monkeys to let them die."
—Peter Gerone, director, Delta Regional Primate Research Center, the Shreveport Journal, *December 20, 1988*

The official reason, according to zoo president Betty Jo Williams, was that "taking these macaques would constitute an unacceptable departure from the conservation, education and recreation missions of our non-profit zoological society."

What Williams's April 27 letter didn't say was that her board of trustees had been heavily influenced by what Pacheco was told by one zoo official were "certain members of the hard-core neurological scientific community."

"In other words," Pacheco asked his contact, "they would rather condemn the monkeys to solitary confinement than see this Congressional plan work?"

"It would be perceived as a 'moral victory for the humane movement,' " he was told.

Apparently the letters of reference for PETA and offers of assistance in the relocation from researchers like LEMSIP's Moor-Jankowski were not enough to counteract the influence of Taub's associates.

Bob Smith sent another "Dear Colleague" letter to members of Congress, again asking them to support his bill. He was blunt in his characterization of the "Silver Spring Monkey Saga (continued), : What is standing in the way of this transfer is an unreasonable degree of resentment on the part of the biomedical research community toward any and all animal welfare groups, and the influence of the biomedical community on NIH."

By June, the General Accounting Office's report on the cost of the case to the government was complete—except that most of the expenses were not included. The $105,084 net federal cost did not include HHS or NIH public relations employee time, or inspections by the USDA, because records on these were not maintained. The cost of the lawsuits to HHS and the Department of Justice were estimated because again, for some reason, no records were kept.

One thing was clear: IBR's reimbursement to the government covered only about 10 percent of what was owed. As far as Smith was concerned, any tax money spent on the monkeys was too much when a better alternative had been available all along.

Furthermore, despite Smith's request that Domitian and Augustus not be allowed to suffer, a request with which PETA concurred, the monkeys continued to sit in the tiny cages in Louisiana. NIH offered no explanation.

Raub and his colleagues, it turns out, were hatching yet another plan for the monkeys.

On July 1, 1988, just as Congress was preparing to recess for the Independence Day holiday, Raub wrote a letter to Bob Dornan in which he stated that because "the surgically disabled Silver Spring monkeys are likely to require euthanasia eventually and that some almost surely would reach that stage this year . . . Staff of the Department of Health and Human Services (HHS) and collaborators therefore have prepared a plan for euthanasia."

The plan included a four-hour experiment in which portions of the monkeys' skulls would be sawed off and their brains repeatedly probed with an electrode. Then the monkeys would be killed.

The experiment would be conducted "[w]hen, for purely humane reasons independent of any scientific consideration, the attending veterinarians at the Delta Primate Center decide that a particular deafferented animal must be euthanized . . . "

Pacheco's anger exploded when Dornan's assistant called with the news. How could they talk about "purely humane reasons" when they had refused to euthanize Domitian and Augustus? Had they kept these two monkeys deteriorating in their steel boxes while they threw together an experiment? Or were the monkeys in better shape than he'd been led to believe?

Within hours of receiving the four-page protocol for the experiment, Newkirk and Pacheco, with help from Neal Barnard, distributed copies to physicians and veterinarians for evaluation. Their analyses indicated that the outline of the experiment submitted to Congress was not typical of scientific protocols. For one thing, Barnard noted, it just wasn't put together according to the accepted standards. No principal investigator was listed; the protocol was not dated; there was no mention of where the experiment would be conducted; there was no hypothesis.

But even more disturbing, the procedure did not appear to many researchers to have any scientific value. The protocol proposed three areas of study. First, by measuring electrical activity in the part of the brain that would have been connected to the monkeys' arms had their nerves not been cut, the experimenters hoped to see if the brain had reorganized to allow this particular portion to receive information from normal parts of the body.

Second, they would preserve the spinal cord to see if any "sprouting" of the severed nerve fibers had occurred. Finally, they would examine the neurotransmitter chemicals in the crippled limbs. The information gathered, they grandly claimed, could help with "the development of physical therapies and pharmacological agents that will optimize recovery" of people with spinal cord injuries.

But according to neurological surgeon Carrie Walters, "They cannot link the experimental design of this particular protocol with spinal cord injury. These monkeys have peripheral nerve injury and not spinal cord damage. The giant leap from peripheral nerve dorsal roots to spinal cord injury does not work."

Susan Clay, a pediatric neurologist, commented: "Their stated goals and suggestions and correlations to the human model are not based on the injuries that the Silver Spring monkeys have incurred . . . These researchers have no experience in rehabilitation. Their work is not cited or referred to by anyone caring directly for patients (humans) or studying humans for rehabilitation . . . I see no value in this work . . . "

All of the scientists Barnard asked to review the protocol noted that the treatment of the monkeys during the last decade was not even mentioned in the brief document. In fact, the four investigators listed, two from Vanderbilt University, one from a Veterans Administration hospital, and one, not surprisingly, from the National Institutes of Mental Health, had not been involved in any way in the primates' care. As psychologist Roger Fouts pointed out, "The Silver Spring monkeys have been subjected to an experimentally uncontrolled environment over the past seven years with many unknown and uncontrolled variables affecting their lives and nervous systems."

When Newkirk read the analyses, she was disgusted that Raub and HHS officials had stamped their approval on such an embarrassing document. It had obviously been written hastily, possibly to forestall any other transfer PETA or Congress might propose.

Gerone would later claim that the protocol did not describe an "experiment" in the true sense of the word, but rather an "observation" of animals who had a particular condition. But the projected outcome of the procedure, obviously meant to impress Congressional readers, was a bit grandiose for a simple observation of crippled primates.

The odd thing was, the only facility under consideration for possible relocation had been proposed by William Raub of NIH.

Pacheco and Newkirk were skeptical. They didn't trust NIH to begin with, and they weren't reassured when they learned that Moorpark College was a school for "people seeking careers in the fields of zoo keeping, animal training and wildlife education." PETA was opposed to the use of wild animals in TV, films and circuses, because many of these exotic cats, orangutans, chimps and birds led such dismal lives, confined in small cages and forced to perform unnatural acts. PETA's research and investigation department had responded to numerous complaints involving such bizarre sideshows as boxing kangaroos; bears, whose teeth and claws had been pulled, forced to wrestle men in bars; and mules compelled to dive from 30-foot platforms into shallow pools. Now NIH was suggesting that the Silver Spring Monkeys be turned over to an institution founded to promote animal acts.

But what Pacheco found when he visited Moorpark's program director, Gary Wilson, on the southern California campus, was different from what he expected. Wilson was willing to examine the monkeys, along with a veterinarian who served on Moorpark's advisory board, to consult with Donald Lindburg at the San Diego Zoo, and to give an honest opinion. He would need a facility built for the monkeys, if he accepted them, and a caretaker. He thought he could get to Delta in late August or September.

In July, Adidas, one of the five monkeys living at the San Diego Zoo, died of an intestinal infection that had also hit a number of the other animal colonies at the park.

Adidas had been one of the playful monkeys, curious about the people around him. His death was not as traumatic for Pacheco as it might have been. At least he'd spent his last months in a comfortable and roomy enclosure. The zoo officials were also refreshingly open about the circumstances of his illness. There were no mysteries surrounding Adidas's final weeks as there had been with Brooks's.

Not long after, Montaigne, also at the zoo, tested positive for the Herpes B virus. Because this potentially fatal disease is easily transmissable, Montaigne could not be part of the resocialization project, but would have to remain separate from the other monkeys.

Just a few months later, Sisyphus, Chester and Haydn were placed together for the first time in a large sunny enclosure, where they have lived compatibly ever since. Their resocialization was a complete success.

In the meantime, with the new protocol hanging over his head, Smith angrily demanded once again to see the monkeys in Louisiana. He'd been pushing for visitation rights for two years, only to have the door repeatedly slammed in his face. The proposal to experiment on and kill the monkeys was intolerable, given NIH's promise never to conduct invasive procedures. He wanted to see for himself what the monkeys looked like. Until he did, he withdrew his authorization for the euthanasia of Domitian and Augustus.

Raub wrote to assure him that no monkeys would be destroyed until Wilson had seen the animals. But two or three of the monkeys, Raub warned, "are so seriously disabled that an indefinite deferral of euthanasia would be inhumane."

Finally, in August, after 26 months of waiting, Smith was allowed inside the Delta Regional Primate Research Center.

It was a depressing sight.

In the bank of cages before him, each of the eight deafferented monkeys sat hunched over in his own steel cell, without even enough space to walk a few feet to stretch the muscles in his legs. Billy was the most pitiful, his two deafferented arms hanging loosely at his sides, but he still had the gentle personality Smith remembered from his visit to the Poolesville facility a few years earlier.

The place was clean, Smith later commented. "The part that bothered me was the small caging . . . There was barely enough room to stand up."

"If you think," Pacheco had said to Smith earlier, "that the monkeys are suffering, and should be euthanized, I'll agree to it."

But Smith wasn't convinced that the animals were in pain. And neither were Gary Wilson or James Peddie, the veterinarian from Moorpark, who saw the primates a month later, on September 26.

Pacheco was there, too, thanks to Smith's demands, to represent Congress and PETA. He didn't know what to expect from Wilson and Peddie. There was no way of predicting how they would react to the monkeys' conditions. Delta's various panels and committees had given so many different recommendations that it was impossible to know what the truth was any longer.

Raub was there, too, representing NIH. Pacheco wondered whether or not he would live up to his commitment. Despite their recently proposed experimental protocol, HHS and NIH had guaranteed Smith that if Moorpark agreed to accept the primates, they would agree to release them—as long as PETA and Congress would agree to the final invasive procedure when the monkeys required euthanasia. Pacheco and Newkirk finally agreed to this condition. It seemed to be the only way to give the monkeys a chance. At least someone other than Gerone and his experts would decide when the animals were close to death.

Wilson and Peddie were taken in the colony room to look at the eight deafferented monkeys. They saw Sarah. They looked at the X rays and discussed with Peter Gerone the various abnormalities of the macaques' spines, arms and shoulders. When they left they took with them copies of the health records.

Then they flew back to California, after promising a decision within the next few weeks.

When Wilson's report arrived in early October, Pacheco was elated. Peddie had not found the monkeys in as poor shape as he expected. Moorpark was willing to take all of the monkeys except Paul, who had tested positive for the Herpes B virus. They could be safely transported by air with an attending veterinarian or in specially-equipped vans. Once at Moorpark, they would initially be housed in cages similar those at Delta, but would gradually be placed in larger enclosures.

Moorpark was even willing to take the control monkeys from the San Diego Zoo, if Lindburg and his board wished to place them permanently in a different facility.

With any luck, Pacheco thought, the Silver Spring Monkeys would be in California by Christmas.

Wilson's report was sent to Bob Smith, Bob Dornan and Charlie Rose in Congress, and to William Raub at NIH. Newkirk and Pacheco thought a compromise had finally been reached.

But Raub didn't like Wilson's conclusions.

"The report," he wrote Wilson on October 11, "is inaccurate, incomplete, and otherwise seriously misleading . . . As it stands, the report is far from a satisfactory basis upon which the NIH and Moorpark College could negotiate a custody agreement for any of the monkeys, either those at the Delta Center or those at the San Diego Zoo."

Raub accused Wilson of misrepresenting Donald Lindburg's views and Peddie's recommendations, and suggested that his decisions about the monkeys were not based on fact, and therefore played into the hands of animal rights activists. Raub proposed a visit to Moorpark in November so that they could "reach a consensus on what a realistic role for Moorpark College would be."

Despite Raub's offer to meet with Wilson, his letter couldn't have made his wishes more obvious. "I hope," he wrote, "you will reconsider your analysis and rethink your conclusion."

Wilson bristled at Raub's charges.

"Although I believe you meant no offense," he wrote to Raub a few days later, "I cannot help resenting the implication you make that I was somehow manipulated by others to disregard the evidence . . . We have no desire to make any kind of 'statement' about research with animals, animal rights, or anything else." He reminded Raub that Moorpark had no burning desire to "provide a home for animals previously utilized in research." If they could help NIH out they were happy to do it and they'd take one monkey or eight—it was up to others to decide how they wished to accept or refuse Moorpark's offer. But Wilson was standing by his report. He confirmed his conclusions with both Peddie and Lindburg and he wasn't changing anything.

Wilson also sent a copy of Raub's letter and his response to Bob Smith. Smith was outraged. He'd been purposely misled, he felt, by all the government officials, from everyone at NIH he dealt with all the way up the line to HHS Secretary Otis Bowen.

"We were being told things they never were going to commit on, policy-wise," Smith said years later.

He and Dornan again turned to President Reagan for help and demanded an explanation from HHS. Reagan did nothing, and HHS put them off until the year was almost over.

For Pacheco, Raub's response to Wilson's report was a declaration of war. They had been negotiating warily, but in good faith. They'd also been talking quietly, without press releases or public demonstrations. Now, with pretty straightforward evidence that Raub, at least, never intended to follow through with his latest promise, and had obviously believed Wilson and Moorpark College would make the "right" decision, all that would change.

Pacheco and PETA staff member Ilene Cohen began calling celebrities and asking them sign onto a letter of support to Reagan. Newkirk, with the help of graphic artists, worked on an ad to run in major newspapers if NIH didn't accept Moorpark's offer after Raub visited the campus.

Raub's final judgment was predictable: Moorpark was inadequate, and while their discussions dragged on several of the monkeys were rapidly deteriorating.

On December 26, PETA's full-page ads ran in the *New York Times*, the *Washington Times*, and the *Los Angeles Times*, and in the *Washington Post* on December 27.

Above a picture of Domitian, taped spread-eagled in Edward Taub's custom-made restraint chair—the photo that ran on the front page of the *Post* in 1981—ran this headline: "Dear President Reagan, one phone call from you will save this animal's life." The letter beneath asked Reagan to call Otis Bowen "and make HHS keep its promise, end the years of waste and suffering, and allow these animals to live in peace."

Pacheco's signature was at the bottom, along with the names of 50 actors, directors, musicians and writers, including Paul and Linda McCartney, Angie Dickinson, Mary Stuart Masterson, James Coburn, Sir John Gielgud, Rue McClanahan, Debbie Reynolds, River Phoenix, James Woods, Ryan O'Neal and Kim Basinger.

The original letter delivered to the White House included the signatures of more than 250 physicians and veterinarians. Doris Day personally phoned the Oval Office, but her call was not returned.

The day after the ad ran in the *Post*, Smith met with HHS Undersecretary Don Newman. Smith was told, and believed, the purpose of the meeting was "to continue discussing the transfer of the monkeys to two private, non-profit primate care organizations." But when he sat down across from Newman, the two men did not talk about relocating the primates. Instead, HHS officially reneged on its promise to send the animals to Moorpark.

The same day, NIH announced that three of the Silver Spring Monkeys, Domitian, Augustus, and Paul, would be experimented on and killed within 24 hours.

Chapter Nineteen

Another Death

"The mushroom shaped surgical light is out, now that the devices are in place. In the room, three scientists are attending to the monkey lying anesthetized on the operating table . . . Off in the distance a light rock radio station is playing."
—*"Silver Spring Monkeys, Archives of the Future,"* Tulane Medicine, *autumn, 1991*

Margaret Woodward was somewhat skeptical of PETA when she got a telephone call from Alex Pacheco on December 28. She knew little about the Silver Spring Monkeys case and even less about the animal rights movement. Now the Tulane alumnus was being asked to file a lawsuit against her alma mater and seek an immediate temporary restraining order to prevent the killing of a monkey. Surely the scientists knew what was best for this animal, she thought.

But the referral was legitimate. It came through another New Orleans attorney who conveyed to Woodward his regard for PETA's Washington, D.C., legal counsel, Phil Hirschkop. So Woodward put her doubts on the back burner and dashed to the Civil District Court of St. Tammany Parish.

Woodward—"Peggy" to her friends—had been a lawyer for more than a dozen years by 1988. She had a small, successful practice and had not handled so much as a single case involving animals. She could not know that Pacheco's request would lead her through more than five years of almost daily battles, or that she would one day become the first attorney to argue a case involving animals to the United States Supreme Court.

Eventually, as Woodward came to know Newkirk and Pacheco, she thought them decent people and appreciated their exhaustive research and attention to detail. "But it was the behavior of my opponents at NIH, HHS and Delta that convinced me I was on the right side," she said later.

During the next few years, as she tried to stave off the monkey killings, she was shocked by the lengths the government would go to in order to succeed. They staunchly denied the existence of documents, only to produce them in court once Woodward had obtained them through different sources. They twisted the facts surrounding custody of ownership. They touted their openness yet consistently denied her or her clients entry to the Delta center.

Worst of all, they seemed to care nothing about the monkeys themselves or about maintaining the integrity of science, though this was their constant battle cry. If the primates' lives had to be sacrificed to prevent PETA from winning a tactical victory, they apparently had no pangs of conscience. If they had to pass off a sloppily written experimental protocol as groundbreaking science just to get rid of their source of embarrassment, then so be it. Woodward came to the conclusion that NIH officials had dug themselves into a hole they couldn't get out of—they had lied to Congress, to the Administration and to the public. Now they had to fend off any inquiry that this new lawsuit mandated.

Woodward would later say that the scales fell from her eyes slowly, that she didn't really want to find out what was becoming impossible to deny. She was a normal American kid, maybe a bit brighter and spunkier than most, and she had grown up believing that science and the people who practiced it were beyond reproach, beyond question. As she discovered they were capable of deception and exploitation, it became even more important to her to dig out the facts, no matter how long it took and or how many hoops she had to jump through. At least then, when the truth came out, they wouldn't be able to hide behind their claims of altruism.

The restraining order was granted just in the nick of time, on the day the macaques were to be destroyed. Woodward and

PETA had until January 6, 1989 to come up with something more permanent. The only option seemed to be the courts; NIH clearly was not swayed by Congressional negotiations.

Woodward filed *International Primate Protection League, PETA, Louisiana in Support of Animals (LISA) and Alex Pacheco v. the Administrators of Tulane University, IBR and NIH,* and the long months of depositions, motions and courtroom appearances began again. This suit was similar to PETA's earlier case, dismissed by the Supreme Court in 1987, but Woodward was careful to word it to address the concerns of the judges who had ruled that PETA did not have standing to sue. The demands of the new suit were stronger, too. This time, PETA and its co-plaintiffs, including LISA, a local animal rights group, asked for full custody of the monkeys.

It was cold and dark by 5 p.m., New Year's Eve, as Pacheco, Newkirk and dozens of activists gathered at the "Ellipse" on E Street behind the White House. They held candles, as they had in 1986 at James Wyngaarden's house on the NIH campus, tiny beacons of hope that the President would respond to their request and call Otis Bowen.

Their presence at the White House was largely symbolic. Ronald Reagan was spending the holiday, his last as President, at the Walter Annenberg Estate in Rancho Mirage, Calif. There, too, at the corner of Bob Hope and Frank Sinatra Drives, activists gathered with candles in their hands.

Earlier that day, PETA held press conferences in both places to announce the filing of the suit, to publicly censure NIH for breaking its promise, and to call on the President to perform a final simple act of compassion. These events launched a fresh round of editorials and renewed interest in Sisyphus, Chester and Haydn, still doing well at the San Diego Zoo. (A photo of two of these monkeys, sitting peacefully together on a pile of fresh straw, accompanied a long article in the *San Diego Union* a few days later. Chester, the story confirms, is still the leader of the troupe.)

Pacheco's and Newkirk's organization, now nearly a decade old, had a quarter of a million members, income approaching nine million dollars and more than 60 employees. They had exchanged their Kensington warehouse for a larger one a few miles away in

Rockville, which they again turned into a suite of offices and meeting rooms.

By now PETA was the most visible representative of a changing attitude toward animals in the United States. Millions of people all over the country now shopped for cruelty-free cosmetics and requested vegetarian entrees on the menus of their favorite restaurants. High school students regularly refused to dissect the corpses of dead animals; veterinary students demanded that practice surgeries be done under the supervision of experienced doctors on animals who really needed the procedures, rather than cutting open and then killing healthy animals. Cities banned horses from their hot, polluted streets. Anti-hunting activists followed hunters through the woods, shouting and clanging pans together to warn deer of the approaching danger. When PETA sponsored an animal rights music festival featuring rock musician Howard Jones on Washington, D.C.'s National Mall, more than 100,000 people showed up.

Society had dramatically changed since the Silver Spring Monkeys made headlines in 1981.

In the days following NIH's announcement, Pacheco sat in his corner windowless office in the rear of the building and frantically tried to reach a list of physicians and veterinarians who could be called as expert witnesses. It took several calls to reach each person—everyone seemed to have left town for the holidays.

The most important was Thomas Vice, the consulting veterinarian for Primarily Primates. In early November, at the insistence of Congressmen Smith and Dornan after Raub's letter chastising Gary Wilson was sent to them, Vice was allowed to see the monkeys at Delta. He looked at each of the animals, talked to Peter Gerone and two of Delta's vets.

"It is my professional opinion," he stated in his January 4 affidavit, "that the health care needs and medical management of all the Silver Spring monkeys, including Billy but excluding Paul [who carried the Herpes B virus], can be adequately handled at Primarily Primates."

Of all the monkeys, Billy, with his crippled arms and spinal arthritis, was the most handicapped, Vice found. But he was "bright and alert and responsive to strangers." Clearly Billy had special needs, but they could be met at the Texas sanctuary. Vice concluded that euthanasia was not warranted for Billy or for any of the others.

While Pacheco and his assistant put together a list of potential witnesses, Newkirk and PETA's outreach staff began dialling the numbers of the four hundred grassroots animal protection organizations located all over the country. They would bombard outgoing President Reagan with letters and phone calls, and if that didn't work, they would keep it up when George and Barbara Bush moved to Pennsylvania Avenue.

Pacheco also began the enormous task of bringing Woodward up to date on the case. Copies of all relevant letters, memos, evaluations of the monkeys' health and other paperwork had to be sent to her office in New Orleans. Fortunately, Pacheco had continued his habit of keeping extensive notes on the events of the case and kept updated timelines with the dates NIH made and broke each of its promises.

There were dozens of conference calls over the telephone, and gradually Pacheco and Newkirk came to trust Woodward and to appreciate the speed and humor with which she grasped the relevant aspects of the case.

By this time, though the contents of the protocol for the experiment had not been improved, NIH at least had the sense to list a principal investigator—even if it was difficult to see the addition of Peter Gerone's name as anything other than a convenient political move. Gerone, meanwhile, was telling the press that killing the monkeys was "the humane thing to do to put these animals out of their misery."

Neal Barnard was so disgusted with the protocol and NIH's thinly veiled attempt to hoodwink Congress with grandiose claims that poking at these monkeys' brains would "lead to treatments for strokes or trauma not even envisioned now," that he lodged a complaint with the NIH Office of Scientific Integrity. But even though OSI was set up to investigate just such charges of fraud, it was unwilling to challenge its own director, William Raub. So OSI passed the buck to the Office of Scientific Integrity Review (OSIR) at HHS.

OSIR officials hardly blinked. Barnard's allegations didn't fall within their jurisdiction, they said.

Barnard demanded to know what exactly *did* fall within their realm. What Barnard was talking about, he was told, was bad science; that didn't have anything to do with scientific integrity.

"They don't give a tinker's damn," Barnard later told Newkirk. "What they're telling me is that there is no one in all of NIH and HHS who can even look into a charge of scientific misconduct."

After this frustrating trail to nowhere, Barnard and the Physicians Committee for Responsible Medicine joined the legal fray and filed suit against Otis Bowen's replacement, HHS Secretary Louis Sullivan. They would take him to court to force him to investigate their charges.

Domitian, Augustus, Paul and Billy lived on despite NIH's claim that they were close to death, unaware of the controversy raging in the Louisiana courts.

In early January, the restraining order was extended another three weeks and the case was moved at the request of NIH and the Justice Department to federal court. This was bad luck for PETA. It would be much more difficult for Woodward to establish her clients' right to sue NIH in a federal court. But early maneuvering by the government agencies to bump the suit up to that level also proved to be a turning point in the case.

Although NIH had maintained for years that IBR was the legal owner of the monkeys, they now claimed custody pursuant to an earlier court order. They neglected to mention that this court order, issued back in 1981 when the primates were removed from IBR the second time, had expired years ago. Because it helped them move the case to a higher court, it was expedient not to mention this fact.

More importantly, the government's attorneys invoked a pre-Civil War law to bolster their argument for a move to the federal level. The century-old law, drafted to protect tax collectors, allowed for the removal of a suit against an officer of a government agency from state to federal court. As Woodward saw it, this statute was meant to protect individuals, not entire agencies. This difference in the interpretation of the law was crucial, as it turned out, and led them slowly, and somewhat haltingly, to the U.S. Supreme Court.

The new Administration offered a fresh opportunity. Nobody knew how the incoming President would respond to a public appeal, but Pacheco and Newkirk were sure it couldn't be worse than it had been during the last eight years.

By February, so many people were phoning President Bush to urge him to free the Silver Spring Monkeys that White House telephones were nearly constantly jammed. By fall, it was reported on "Good Morning America" that abortion, catastrophic health care and the Silver Spring Monkeys were the top three subjects on which the White House was receiving mail. Bob Smith, Charlie Rose and Bob Dornan also appealed to Bush in a letter signed by 40 members of Congress.

Congress focused as well on Louis Sullivan, but the new HHS secretary's response was noncommittal. He used PETA's pending lawsuit as a reason not to take decisive action even though his release of the macaques would have made the suit unnecessary. Buddy Roemer, who had taken Edwin Edwards's place as Governor of Louisiana, was unhappy that the primates were being, in his words, "warehoused" in his state, and also wrote to Sullivan.

It soon became clear, however, that the new Administration was going to maintain the standards of the old. Louis Sullivan became an outspoken opponent of the animal rights movement and defender of animal experimentation, while William Raub was promoted to the Presidential advisory staff in 1991.

PETA's lawsuit, in the meantime, worked its way through pre-trial hearings and conferences. Federal Judge Veronica Wicker refused to dismiss the case, as NIH's Bob Lanman and Justice Department attorney Ruth Morris Force requested. The defendants had filed no compelling evidence, Wicker pointed out, that the physical conditions of the animals warranted euthanasia and frankly didn't understand why NIH wanted to kill them.

"The issues that I have before me are legal issues," she said at a February hearing, "and I want that very clear, but I don't understand why NIH just doesn't turn them over [to PETA], if, as you say, all you want to do is kill them . . . "

"But there is research," Force countered, "although plaintiffs–"

"Well, that is something that has not been made specifically clear to this court."

Wicker felt that PETA was on shaky legal ground, too, but nevertheless extended indefinitely the restraining order prohibiting euthanasia. At a later hearing, she scheduled a November trial date. The Justice Department immediately appealed her decision not to dismiss the case, and suddenly the suit was bumped up again, this time to the Fifth Circuit Court of Appeals in New Orleans.

As Pacheco and Woodward prepared for the next hearing, the debate on the use of animals in experimentation heated up in the press. Dozens of editorials, endorsing one side or the other, appeared in newspapers and scientific journals.

"The animal rights people are using these monkeys to make their case that animal research is cruel," Peter Gerone told the *Christian Science Monitor*, suggesting that PETA would oppose euthanasia for political reasons.

"It's a shrewd campaign on [their] part," Pacheco responded, "but we'd never be opposed to euthanasia if the animal were in pain."

By August, Gerone was involved in organizing a new group called Foundation for Animal Use in Society ("it sounds intriguingly Faustian," Barnard remarked when he heard the acronym), whose goal was to protect the interests of experimenters, hunters, trappers, meat processors and furriers. Gerone was to be in charge of fundraising and membership.

Pacheco was also organizing an alliance to lend strength to PETA's fight for custody. People Protecting Primates (PPP), chaired by Doris Day, brought together 80 international animal protection groups with a combined membership that topped three million.

Taub's staunch defender Adrian Morrison climbed into the pit again, too, speaking out publicly against the animal rights movement and criticizing PETA's philosophy.

Pacheco had no idea that his debate with Morrison, scheduled for August 22 on WOSU radio in Ohio, would be exceptional in any way. He was unaware that Morrison was deeply involved in deciding the monkeys' fates. (In a later Animal Liberation Front break-in at the University of Pennsylvania, handwritten notes concerning the Silver Spring Monkeys were removed from Morrison's office: "Euthanize them . . . then decided to euth 2 right away and delay others . . . so PETA wouldn't descend.") Pacheco was stunned when Morrison announced over the air that Paul had lost over 40 percent of his body weight, was being fed by stomach tube and was close to death. PETA's lawsuit prevented Delta veterinarians from putting the monkey out of his misery, Morrison said.

Within hours, PETA delivered letters to Peter Gerone and William Raub. If Morrison's statements were true, Pacheco demanded, why had NIH not informed PETA or the courts?

"If this information is accurate," Pacheco wrote, "and Paul has been permitted to deteriorate to the point that he is *in extremis,* the only humane course of action is euthanasia . . . All we ask is independent confirmation by any of our veterinarians or by me... Please do not let this animal suffer if indeed he is . . . "

Smith and Dornan also wrote to Raub: " . . . we are deeply concerned that Paul has been forced to suffer while no attempt has been made to contact the courts, the litigants, or members of Congress who have repeatedly expressed our concern about the plight of these monkeys."

Raub confirmed Paul's condition but refused to allow an independent examination or to order euthanasia. Pacheco was nearly frantic. He knew from the reports of the Moorpark and Primarily Primates veterinarians that Paul, the oldest of the monkeys, grey-haired even in 1981, was as healthy as could be expected only a few months earlier. He hadn't been in pain in November, so Raub's claim that "Paul has been candidate for euthanasia since at least December" sounded like an excuse for keeping his failing health secret. Were they hoping that he would fade away and die so that they could blame PETA for his suffering?

After a hurried discussion with Peggy Woodward, Pacheco and Newkirk decided to file a motion with the court. It was an action they had never imagined themselves taking— they were asking a judge to force NIH to destroy one of the monkeys. The motion also required Delta to preserve Paul's body for an independent exam.

The Saturday before the August 28 hearing was to take place, Paul, pitifully thin, his tail scalded by his own urine, slipped into a coma and died. Delta incinerated his body the same day.

From the evidence that surfaced later, it appeared that Paul's condition in the final weeks of his life, like Brooks's in 1986, was carefully guarded information. On New Year's Eve, 1988, while more than 50 candles lit the Ellipse behind the White House, Delta's nighttime crew "discover[ed] that Paul had severely traumatized his left arm," according to Tulane's clinical report. Following this injury, which would never have occurred had Paul's arm been amputated in 1986, as promised by NIH, his health began to decline rapidly.

Six weeks later, Paul's deafferented left arm was "severely lacerated." The report does not indicate how, in his tiny barren cage, the laceration occurred. This time, Delta veterinarians Marian Ratterree and James Blanchard felt that amputation was necessary, but they removed the arm not at the shoulder, like Nero's, but at the middle of the humerus. Within a few months, the stump was infected and rotting, and when it finally ruptured, what was left of the arm was cut off at the shoulder.

But Paul never recovered. For four weeks he deteriorated before the Delta staffs' eyes. By August 17, "Paul was extremely anorexic, severely depressed, weak." When he was again examined on August 24, while Pacheco was demanding his euthanasia, the Delta vets found it "was not necessary to anesthetize Paul for this physical exam due to his weakened condition." Forty-eight hours later he was dead and his body burned.

It had been NIH's practice over the years, every time the agency had been publicly exposed for withholding information, to offer to renegotiate the monkeys' future. It was no different when Paul died and his pitiful condition was revealed.

First, Delta officials moved Sarah to a larger indoor/outdoor enclosure with younger monkeys, finally coming close to fulfilling its promise of resocialization for at least one of the monkeys. Then, the Justice Department attorneys arranged a meeting to discuss a tentative plan to evaluate the remaining seven macaques.

Before the meeting took place, while Congress was in recess for the Christmas holidays, NIH announced that Billy was to be destroyed.

Chapter Twenty

The Supreme Court

"There is no doubt in my mind that this research protocol is solid science."
—William Raub, NIH, *the* New York Times, *January 18, 1990*

"To represent this as science is an affront to science itself."
—Daniel Robinson, chairman, Georgetown University psychology department, Nature, *January 25, 1990*

On Sunday, January 14, 1990, Billy was anesthetized, the top of his skull was removed, and his brain was repeatedly prodded with a tiny electrode. He was then destroyed.

The procedure followed two weeks of arguments and hearings, during which Pacheco barely slept or ate. Next to Domitian, Billy was the monkey he was closest to—who could resist his gentle helplessness? Of all the primates, it was Billy who most affected those who visited them. Roger Galvin, Lori Lehner, Dave Rehnquist, Bob Smith, Gary Francione, Annette Lantos—all remembered Billy in particular when they spoke of the monkeys years later. It may have been because he was so accepting of humans, or because, as the most disabled, he was a heart-rending reminder of what people do to animals.

In the final days of 1989, Pacheco and Newkirk agreed to Billy's euthanasia on the condition that a veterinarian of their choice be allowed to examine him first. They would not agree to the final experiment. It was sham science, as far as they were concerned. It might have been different if NIH had kept its bargain with Moorpark College. Then Billy would have had at least *one* decent year in his life, and allowing the procedure would have been a compromise they might have been willing to make.

On New Year's Eve, Primarily Primates veterinarian Thomas Vice again flew to Louisiana to examine Billy, but his report put Pacheco in a quandary. Vice felt Billy's spine curvature and generally poor health warranted euthanasia, but he also told Peggy Woodward, who spoke to him by telephone several times that day, that Billy was not in unrelievable pain.

The decision was agonizing for Pacheco. He wanted to prevent the kind of suffering Paul had endured, but if Billy wasn't in pain . . . Should he hold out, in the hope that PETA might soon rescue Billy from the government's clutches? Or should he agree to have Billy killed only if his condition worsened and he did begin to suffer?

Several hours later he made his decision. He could not kill Billy. The deciding factors: Billy's pain could be relieved, and they might win their case and finally move all the monkeys, including Billy, to a place where they could heal and really enjoy life. There was still hope.

Pacheco knew, of course, that he was giving NIH ammunition and that they would call foul loudly and clearly. He agonized over whether he had done the right thing—it was impossible to know. But he knew one thing beyond any doubt. He was thinking first and foremost of the monkeys themselves.

Within 10 days, on January 9, the Fifth Circuit Court of Appeals in New Orleans partially lifted the restraining order to allow Billy to be killed. The same day, the Physicians Committee for Responsible Medicine filed for another restraining order in U.S. District Court in Washington, D.C. It was granted on Friday, January 12, by Judge John Penn.

On Sunday, with Judge Penn off for the weekend, Justice Department attorneys requested an emergency hearing, claiming that Billy was near death.

This hearing was held in Judge Stanley Sporkin's chambers and Neal Barnard remembers that Peter Gerone, who spoke via telephone from Louisiana, admitted that Billy might not die immediately, that he could go on for some time. But if he did die, Gerone added dramatically, they would not have been able to harvest valuable information from his brain in a final experiment.

Sporkin lifted the restraining order. This time not a minute was wasted at Delta. Billy was dead within hours.

In February, hard on the heels of Billy's death, PETA was dealt another blow—one from which it would take months to recover. *Washingtonian*, a magazine about personalities and events in the D.C. area, printed an article about PETA entitled "Beyond Cruelty." In it, author Katie McCabe stated that Pacheco had admitted in court to staging some of the photographs of the monkeys at IBR. The accusation stemmed from the unsuccessful attempts by Taub's lawyers to suggest that pulling the fecal trays from the bottoms of the cages in order to photograph the accumulated waste constituted staging. Another of the article's allegations was that PETA mishandled donations.

Pacheco and Newkirk immediately filed suit against McCabe and the magazine's publishers.

Not surprisingly, the article was widely circulated by Gerone and others in the scientific community. It provided a handy weapon for the public relations battle that had raged since 1981.

Eventually, as a result of the suit, *Washingtonian* printed a two-page apology and retraction admitting, among other things, that the photos were not staged and that there was no basis for the charge of mishandling funds.

The year 1990 didn't get any better. In March, the Fifth Circuit Court of Appeals dismissed PETA's case. Woodward immediately filed an appeal with the United States Supreme Court, arguing that the case had been illegally moved from state to federal court.

On June 25, NIH announced that Domitian, Big Boy and Augustus would be experimented on and killed within 48 hours.

Domitian and Augustus had already lived two years beyond the time Delta and NIH officials had earnestly pronounced they were near death. It was impossible for Newkirk and Pacheco to believe that suddenly all three monkeys simultaneously required euthanasia. They forestalled the killings for several days by seeking another temporary restraining order, but when that proved futile, their only hope, once again, was Congress. Smith, Dornan, Lantos, Rose, Roe and several others wrote to Raub immediately, asking him to delay the procedures until they had a chance to talk. A meeting was arranged for Tuesday, July 10.

Pacheco was nervous about the delay. NIH had a habit of making decisions during Congressional recesses, and the Fourth of July holiday was just days away.

As it turned out, Pacheco's fears were valid. On Friday, July 6, with Congress out of session, the three monkeys were put through the same procedure as Billy and then destroyed.

Raub issued a statement denying that he had agreed to meet with the Representatives, but his version of the story was contradicted in the *Washington Post* by Greg Simon, a staff member of the House Science and Technology Committee. An agreement had indeed been reached, Simon asserted, and NIH violated it.

Soon after, Pacheco and animal rights artist Greg Metz erected a 10-foot-tall sculpture of a monkey, electrodes in his head, bound to a metal cross, in front of the Department of Health and Human Services.

"NIH is just crucifying them for political reasons," Pacheco told the *New York Times*.

Newkirk didn't even lift an eyebrow when Timothy Pons from NIMH, who participated in the experiments on the three primates, claimed to have made an astounding discovery. As Bob Smith wryly commented, "I've never seen any research done by the federal government where they would say, after spending thousands and thousands, sometimes millions, that the results were negative and they didn't get anything out of it."

Pons's "remarkable" find was that the area of the monkeys' brain that had reorganized itself following deafferentation was much larger than he'd expected. Barnard and the neurosurgeons he had consulted weren't impressed. Reorganization of the brain was a well-known phenomenon, they pointed out. How could Pons and Raub claim, as they were loudly doing, that this knowledge would help them in the development of drugs or surgery, particularly when the animals' life experiences, which affect the reorganization process, were not known, recorded or accounted for?

But Pacheco and Newkirk were less concerned about the blustering of the neuroscientists than about the four remaining monkeys.

Sarah, Nero, Titus and Allen were the only Silver Spring Monkeys left at Delta. Would NIH sign their death warrants before the Supreme Court made a decision about hearing the case? The waiting was almost too much for Pacheco to stand. In the space of a year, Paul, Billy, Augustus, Big Boy and Domitian were lost. The litigation hadn't been able to save them anymore than the bills introduced in Congress or the thousands of phone calls and letters to President Bush.

Pacheco and Newkirk decided to try an appeal to one more person who might be able to help—Barbara Bush. In November, thanks largely to an appeal in the *National Enquirer*, PETA deposited 46,000 letters on the White House steps, all addressed to the First Lady, and seeking the Silver Spring Monkeys' release.

A few days later, on November 27, the Supreme Court agreed to decide whether or not PETA's lawsuit had been improperly transferred from state to federal court.

March 27, 1991. Peggy Woodward had prepared for this appearance before the U.S. Supreme Court as well as any attorney could, but it was still terrifying. As if arguing before the highest court in the land weren't daunting enough in itself, she knew that this was the end of the line for the Silver Spring Monkeys. If she lost here, at least three of the remaining four primates would perish, and there would be nothing that she could do about it.

During the last three years, she tried every legal maneuver she could think of just to get the chance to argue PETA's case in court. She had worked hard—and had been matched every step of the way by Pacheco. She was amazed at Pacheco's energy, at the way he was willing to spend hours or days following a course of action he knew might not lead anywhere because he wanted to make sure he'd exhausted every possibility. There were nights when she had finally said, "I can't do anymore. I'm too tired."

"Just a little longer," Pacheco would say.

Gary Francione and Anna Charleton also spent most of the last month preparing for this day. Francione sent eight of the students in his Animal Rights Law Clinic at Rutgers to the law library to research cases that might have even the remotest relevance. They worked from early morning until midnight, every day for three weeks.

The week before, Francione set up a mock Supreme Court and law professors, playing the parts of the Justices, grilled Woodward for hours, asking question after question.

Woodward was also helped by Jonathan Mook, a former partner of PETA's D.C. attorney, Phil Hirschkop.

For weeks, Woodward ate, breathed, slept and lived the case, going over every detail, every possible turning point in her mind. Now, dressed not in the expected "power" suit, but in a plain skirt, print jacket and blouse, with Francione at the table next to her, she sat before the Justices, waiting for her chance to make history.

It couldn't have gone better.

The questions were tough and fast coming, but to her surprise she answered each one succinctly. She felt herself relax as Justice Antonin Scalia joked about the jurisdictional language of the statute in dispute.

"She is brilliant," Newkirk whispered to Pacheco and clasped his hand in hers.

Francione recalls that Richard Seamon from the Justice Department, who represented NIH, seemed less sure of himself than Woodward, and was unable to answer every question put to him. But if Woodward agreed, she also knew that that in itself didn't mean the Court would rule in her favor.

When it was over, the feelings of relief at having gotten it over with and the euphoria at having done a difficult task well lasted exactly nine days. Even as the activists took photos on the white marble steps of the Supreme Court building, Pacheco could almost feel NIH plotting away. On April 5, another bomb dropped: NIH announced that Titus and Allen were failing and would soon be destroyed.

NIH's motives in ordering the euthanasia were so transparent that Newkirk and Pacheco would have found them laughable if the consequences hadn't been so final. Killing off the subjects of the case before the Supreme Court issued its ruling would be expedient, but surely, they prayed, the Court would see through it.

The lower courts apparently weren't so clear-sighted. Restraining orders were denied PETA in both New Orleans and in Washington, D.C.

On Wednesday, April 10, Supreme Court Justice Anthony Kennedy stepped in and barred the killing temporarily. He ordered the Justice Department to file its argument by 2 p.m. the following day.

Bob Smith, now a Senator, demanded Titus's and Allen's clinical records, which Pacheco than sent to veterinarians for analysis.

"The document calls for euthanasia of the monkeys in question," veterinary professor and former primate researcher Nedim Buyukmihci wrote. "The document falls short, however, of making an adequate case for euthanasia. It is comprised of five paragraphs that are riddled with imprecise information leaving more questions than they answer. A great deal of pertinent information that is necessary for proper evaluation of the need for euthanasia is not contained anywhere in this document."

Despite the evidence submitted by PETA, the Supreme Court lifted the restraining order on Friday, April 12.

Within hours, Titus and Allen were dead.

Monday, May 20, 1991. Justice Thurgood Marshall, already a personal hero to many in the PETA office who felt a strong connection between the civil and animal rights movements, would deliver the Court's opinion. The lives of just two monkeys, Sarah and Nero, would be irrevocably affected by what happened in the next few minutes.

So, too, would the careers of thousands of animal experimenters. If NIH couldn't demolish cases like PETA's, how many more lawsuits would be filed? Removal of the case to a higher court was a legal wall surrounding the government. If the Court ruled in PETA's favor, the wall would begin to crumble. NIH would have to account for its actions.

The moments of waiting were almost unbearable for Newkirk and Pacheco, but while Pacheco was silent, clenching and unclenching his jaws, Newkirk nervously cracked jokes with Woodward.

Justice Marshall cleared his throat, and in the next five minutes gave Newkirk and Pacheco the right to argue the case for custody of the monkeys in a lower court.

They had won!

While Newkirk wrote as fast as she could, Pacheco missed most of what was said next, his mind racing ahead to the next court date.

"We therefore reverse the decision of the Court of Appeals and remand the case to the District Court with instructions that the case be remanded to the Civil District Court for the Parish of [New] Orleans, Louisiana."

Justice Scalia, who had agreed to teach a course for Tulane University, abstained, but the rest of the Justices were unanimous in their decision. The first case concerning animals in laboratories ever argued before the U.S. Supreme Court had been won, not by the government, but by an animal rights organization considered by many to be representative of the "radical fringe."

For Pacheco and Newkirk it was a bittersweet victory. Brooks, Paul, Billy, Domitian, Big Boy, Augustus, and now Allen and Titus, for years denied the chance to sit in the sunshine, to feel a warm breeze, for years condemned to solitary confinement, were gone forever, unaware of the trail blazed by their sad case. The long battle that paralleled the growth of the animal rights movement had not been able to prevent their suffering.

Now Newkirk and Pacheco prepared to begin a new fight. In spite of everything—the government's many deceptions, its broken promises, the thousands of dollars and thousands of hours spent—they were ready to start all over again. They could only hope that Nero and Sarah would live long enough to benefit from their day in court.

Epilogue

" . . . [T]he monkeys became to the two opposing camps something like children in the worst of bad divorces—living symbols of everything you hate about your opposite."
—*the* Globe and Mail, *March 17, 1990*

This year, more than a decade after the Silver Spring Monkeys were captured in the jungles of the Philippines, that country's government has banned the sale of wild-caught monkeys, effective in 1994.

But Sarah and Nero live on at Delta (now called the Tulane Regional Primate Research Center).

Although the U.S. Supreme Court found that PETA had a right to be heard in the court in which the suit was filed, the animal rights organization was again denied the chance to speak. In late 1992, despite the ruling of the Highest Court in the Land, the Civil District Court judge dismissed the case.

PETA has filed another appeal.

Sarah is the more fortunate of the two monkeys. She serves as a surrogate mother to younger rhesus monkeys in an outdoor enclosure. Nero remains in the two foot by two foot steel cage in which he has been confined for more than seven years.

Edward Taub now teaches in the psychology department at the University of Alabama in Birmingham. He no longer conducts experiments on animals.

William Raub left the White House after Bill Clinton was elected and now works at the Environmental Protection Agency.

Senator Bob Smith and Congressmen Charlie Rose, Bob Dornan and Tom Lantos have been targeted by animal experimentation lobbying groups as anti-human animal rights activists. In spite of the political backlash they have suffered from this inaccurate and unfair characterization, they have stood by their conviction that the Silver Spring Monkeys should be released to a sanctuary.

People for the Ethical Treatment of Animals has continued to flourish. The organization that was once just two people planning to change the way the world perceives animals now has 400,000 members, a $10 million budget and 70 employees. PETA has continued to conduct undercover investigations and to release to the public copies of materials taken by the Animal Liberation Front during its break-ins. Consequently, the FBI has investigated PETA employees, as well as members of Earth First! and the Sea Shepherd Society who have spoken out publicly for animal rights. Despite the FBI's inability to locate ALF members or to link any evidence from the ALF raids to PETA, the organization's employees and supporters have been subpoenaed to testify before grand juries convened in five states, their homes have been raided, and their garbage sifted through. In the fall of 1992, FBI agents claimed to have uncovered evidence of what they believe is a plot to rescue the Silver Spring Monkeys from Delta.

Alex Pacheco and Ingrid Newkirk continue to battle government agencies. In early 1993 they sued NIH for concealing large sections of a protocol for a new head wound experiment—involving guinea pigs rather than baboons—at the University if Pennsylvania. As a result of the suit, the entire protocol was made public on May 1, 1993.

References

Introduction and Chapter One

Affidavit in support of an application for an arrest warrant, Sergeant Richard W. Swain, September 10, 1981.
Christopher Anderson, "NIH loses a legal shield," *Nature*, May 30, 1991.
Carleton R. Bryant, "Activists' tactics hinder research, Sullivan warns," *Washington Times*, July 31, 1992.
Peter Carlson, "The Strange Ordeal of the Silver Spring Monkeys," *Washington Post Magazine*, February 24, 1991.
Peter Gerone, "The Real Story of the Silver Spring Monkeys" (unpublished), August, 1992.
Ingrid Newkirk interview, January 21, 1993.
Alex Pacheco interview, January 22, 1993.
Alex Pacheco, "The Choice of a Lifetime," *Between the Species*, Winter, 1990.
Andrew Rowan, "The Silver Spring 17," *International Journal for the Study of Animal Problems*, 3 (3) 1982.
State of Maryland vs. Edward Taub, John Kunz, official audio recording, October 27-31, 1981.
State of Maryland vs. Edward Taub, John Kunz, photographs introduced by state's attorney, October 27-31, 1981.
Edward Taub, "The Silver Spring Monkeys Incident: The Untold Story," transcript of lecture, September 6, 1990.
Paul W. Valentine, "Open House at NIH Makes a Pitch to the Coming Generation, *Washington Post*, September 13, 1992.

Chapter Two

Karin Chenoweth and Mike Ahlers, "Monkey Lab Loses U.S. Funding," the *Montgomery Journal*, October 9, 1981.
John G. Gianutsos, "Feedback Contributions to Recovery in the Deafferented Primate Forelimb" (Doctoral Dissertation), February, 1975.
Ingrid Newkirk interview, January 21, 1993.
Ingrid Newkirk, "The Darker Side," *Washingtonian*, October, 1986.
Neurological Sciences Study Section Review Group (NIH) Disapproval for Funding of Edward Taub's project proposal entitled "Fetal Origins of Primate Sensory-Motor Integration," October/November, 1979.
NIH Grant Application NS16685 for the period April 1, 1980 through March 31, 1983.
Alex Pacheco interview, January 22, 1993.
Alex Pacheco, "The Choice of a Lifetime," *Between the Species*,Winter, 1990.
Report and Recommendations of the NIH Committee to Investigate Alleged Animal Care Violations at the Institute for Behavioral Research, October 5, 1981.
Peter Singer, *Animal Liberation, New York Review of Books*, 1975.
State of Maryland vs. Taub, Kunz, official audio recording, October 27-31, 1981.
State of Maryland vs. Taub, official transcript, June 15-July 3, 1982.
Edward Taub, "Motor Function in Deafferented Animals," draft of chapter for *Handbook of Physiology, The American Physiological Society*, 1980.
Ibid., "The Silver Spring Monkey Incident: The Untold Story," transcript of lecture given September 6, 1990.
Ibid., "Somatosensory Deafferentation Research with Monkeys: Implications for Rehabilitation Medicine," *Behavioral Psychology in Rehabilitation Medicine: Clinical Applications*, L.P. Ince, ed., Williams and Wilkins, 1980.
Edward Taub, *et al.*, "Some Anatomical Observations Following Chronic Dorsal Rhizotomy in Monkeys," *Neuroscience*, Vol. 5, 1980.

Chapter Three

Donald Barnes affidavit, August 25, 1981.
Donald Barnes interview, February 9, 1993.
Michael Fox affidavit, August 31, 1981.
Michael Fox interview, January 28, 1993.
Michael Fox, *Laboratory Animal Husbandry*, State University of New York Press, 1986.
Ronnie Hawkins affidavit, September 6, 1981.
Ronnie Hawkins interview, February 24, 1993.
John McArdle affidavit, September 1, 1981.
John McArdle interview, February 18, 1993.
Shirley McGreal interview, February 18, 1993.
Ingrid Newkirk interview, January 21, 1993.
Alex Pacheco interview, January 22, 1993.
State of Maryland vs. Taub, Kunz, official audio recording, October 27-31, 1981.
Geza Teleki affidavit, August 28, 1981.
Geza Teleki interview, February 4, 1993.

Chapter Four

"Congress Urged to Require Better Treatment of Animals Used in Scientific Research," *Congressional Quarterly*, November 13, 1982.
Roger Galvin interview, January 26, 1993.
Lori Lehner interview, February 25, 1993.
Ingrid Newkirk interview, January 21, 1993.

Alex Pacheco interview, January 22, 1993.
State of Maryland vs. Taub, Kunz, official audio recording, October 27-31, 1981.
Richard Swain affidavit, September 10, 1981.
Richard Swain interview, January 31, 1993.
Geza Teleki interview, February 4, 1993.
Robert Weitzman interview, March 12, 1993.
Ronald D. White, "Police Raid Lab, Seize Animals," *Washington Post*, September 12, 1981.

Chapter Five

Mike Ahlers, "Calls Driving Them Bananas," *Montgomery Journal*, September 29, 1981.
Ibid., "Crusader Plotted Monkey Exposé," September 13, 1981.
Ibid., "Fate of 17 Confiscated Monkeys Argued in Court," September 18, 1981.
Ibid., " 'Stolen' Picture Charges Stir Monkey Controversy," September 21, 1981.
Michael Fox interview, January 28, 1981.
Lori Lehner interview, February 25, 1993.
Memorandum from Charles R. McCarthy to William Raub, October 7, 1981.
"Monkeys Transferred After Abuse Charges," *New York Times*, September 13, 1981.
Alison Muscatine, "Animal Lab Official Says Whistle Blower Sought Publicity," *Washington Post*, September 13, 1981.
Ingrid Newkirk interview, January 21, 1993.
Alex Pacheco interview, January 22, 1981.
William Raub deposition, January 27, 1989.
Report and Recommendations of the NIH Committee to Investigate Alleged Animal Care Violations at the Institute for Behavioral Research, October 5, 1981.
Phillip Robinson, Janis Ott affidavit, September 18, 1981.
Richard Swain, affidavit in support of an application for an arrest warrant, September 27, 1981.
Richard Swain interview, January 31, 1993.
Geza Teleki interview, February 4, 1993.
USDA Animal and Plant Health Inspection Service site reports, April 24, 1981; July 13, 1981; September 15, 1981; September 17, 1981.
Ronald D. White, "Judge Orders Return of Monkeys," *Washington Post*, September 19, 1981.
Ibid., "NIH Conducting Probe of Alleged Animal Abuse at Research Facility," September 17, 1981.

Chapter Six

Mike Ahlers, "3 Women Arrested in Case of 17 Monkeys," *Montgomery Journal*, September 25, 1981.
Ibid., "Calls Driving Them Bananas," September 29, 1981.
Ibid., "Monkeys' Return Opposed," October 5, 1981.
Ibid., "The 17 Monkeys Are Kidnaped," September 24, 1981.
Court Order, Circuit Court for Montgomery County, Maryland, Misc. Pet. No. 5821, Judge David Cahoon, October 2, 1981.
David Michael Ettlin, "NIH suspends animal lab's $115,000 grant," *Sun* (Baltimore), October 9, 1981.
Michael Fox affidavit, October 3, 1981. Lori Lehner interview, February 25, 1993.
Letter to Joseph Vasapoli from Thomas Malone, October 8, 1981.
Ingrid Newkirk interview, January 21, 1993.
Alex Pacheco interview, January22, 1993.
"Police Are Unable to Find Stolen Research Monkeys," *Washington Post*, September 25, 1981.
Report and Recommendations of the NIH Committee to Investigate Alleged Animal Care Violations at the Institute for Behavioral Research, October 5, 1981.
Saundra Saperstein, "17 Monkeys Returned to Md. Lab," *Washington Post*, October 1, 1981.
Ibid., "After Delicate Negotiations, the 17 Missing Monkeys Are Back," September 27, 1981.
Ibid., "Scientist Is Charged With Cruelty," September 28, 1981.
State of Maryland vs. Taub, Kunz, official audio recording, October 27-31, 1981.
Richard Swain interview, January 31, 1993.
Geza Teleki affidavit, October 3, 1981.
Geza Teleki interview, February 4, 1993.
Ronald White, "NIH Cuts Off 'Monkey Lab' Federal Fund," *Washington Post*, October 8, 1981.

Chapter Seven

Mike Ahlers, "Bills Before Congress," *Montgomery Journal*, October 14, 1981.
Ibid., "Congress Eyes Lab Animals," October 9, 1981.
Complaint and Petition for Ex Parte or Preliminary or Interlocutory and Final or Permanent Injunction, filed by IPPL, *et al.*, in the Circuit Court for Montgomery County, Maryland, December 3, 1981.
"Congress urged to curb testing," *Toronto Sun*, October 14, 1981.
Court Order, Circuit Court for Montgomery County, Maryland, Misc. Pet. No. 5821, Judge David Cahoon, October 8, 1981.
David Michael Ettlin, "House to hear about monkeys," *Sun* (Baltimore), October 11, 1981.

References

Ibid., "Judge orders monkeys taken from laboratory after one dies," October 10, 1981.
Ibid., "NIH plans surprise animal-lab inspections," October 14, 1981.
Ann Cottrell Free, "Animal Lovers are Not People Haters," *Washington Post*, October 17, 1981.
Roger Galvin interview, January 26, 1993.
Letter to William Raub from Joseph Vasapoli, July 28, 1982.
Ingrid Newkirk interview, January 21, 1981.
Alex Pacheco interview, January 22, 1981.
Dave Rehnquist interview, March 15, 1993.
Saundra Saperstein, "The Monkeys: A Rally for Animal Lovers," *Washington Post*, October 11, 1981.
Richard Swain interview, January 31, 1993.
Geza Teleki interview, February 4, 1993.
USDA Animal and Plant Health Inspection Service site report, October 21, 1981
Laura B. Weiss, "Scientists Oppose Legislation: Congress Urged to Require Better Treatment of Animals Used in Scientific Research," *Congressional Quarterly*, November 13, 1982.

Chapter Eight

Mike Ahlers, "Monkey Trial Ends with Verdict in Air," *Montgomery Journal*, November 2, 1981.
David Michael Ettlin, "Scientist, aide go on trial on animal cruelty charges," *Sun* (Baltimore), January 28, 1981.
Michael Fox interview, January 28, 1993.
Roger Galvin interview, January 26, 1993.
John McArdle interview, February 18, 1993.
Shirley McGreal interview, February 18, 1993.
Ingrid Newkirk interview, January 21, 1993.
Alex Pacheco interview, January 22, 1993.
Dave Rehnquist interview, March 15, 1993.
Saundra Saperstein, "Graphic Film Shown at Scientist's Cruelty Trial," *Washington Post*, October 28, 1981.
State of Maryland vs. Taub, Kunz, official audio recording, October 27-31, 1981.
Geza Teleki interview, February 4, 1993.

Chapter Nine

Mike Ahlers, "Psychologists Split On Monkey Money," *Montgomery Journal*, August 25, 1982.
Ibid., "Scientist Found Guilty of Cruelty To Lab Monkeys," November 24, 1981.
Donald Barnes interview, February 9, 1993.
Laura Bird, "Corporate Critic Complain Companies Hide Behind 'Grass-roots' Campaigns," *Wall Street Journal*, July 8, 1992.
Complaint for Declaratory Relief, *The Fund for Animals vs. Dr. Thomas Malone, et al.*, filed U.S. District Court, December 7, 1981.
Complaint for Declaratory Relief, *The Humane Society of the United States, et al. vs. John R. Block, et al.*, filed U.S. District Court, November 9, 1981.
David Michael Ettlin, "Taub denies allegations of cruelty," *Sun* (Baltimore), November 1, 1981.
Michael Fox interview, January 28, 1993.
Roger Galvin interview, January 26, 1993.
Annette Lantos interview, March 8, 1993.
Letter to Edward Taub from Michael Pallak, May 25, 1982.
Letter to Shirley McGreal from Michael Pallak, August 19, 1982.
Mailgram to American Psychological Association from Edward Taub, June 7, 1982.
John McArdle interview, February 18, 1993.
Adrian R. Morrison, "What's With 'Animal Rights,'" *American School Board Journal*, January, 1992.
Ingrid Newkirk interviews, January 22, 1993; March 18, 1993.
Alex Pacheco interview, January 22, 1993.
Keith B. Richburg, "Scientist Convicted, Fined $3,015 for Cruelty to Monkeys," *Washington Post*, November 24, 1981.
Saundra Saperstein, "Taub Pledges to Fight to Save His Laboratory," *Washington Post*, November 27, 1981.
Ibid., "Scientist on Trial Denies Lab Animals Mistreated," November 1, 1981.
Ken Shapiro interview, January 27, 1993.
State of Maryland vs. Taub, Kunz, official audio recording, October 27-31, 1981.
Brad Stertz, "Lab Chief's Trial on Animal Cruelty May Affect U.S. Research," *Los Angeles Times*, October 27, 1981.
Geza Teleki interview, February 4, 1993.
Kenneth Weiss, "Lawyer Forsakes Meat," *Montgomery Journal*, August 17, 1983.

Chapter Ten

Mike Ahlers, "Custody of Monkeys Is Now the Issue," *Montgomery Journal*, July 6, 1982.
Ibid., "Groups Say Monkeys Need Friend in Court," December 11, 1981.
Ibid., "Monkey Case Jurors Stay In the Fray," July 22, 1982.
Bill Ahrens, "Two protection groups sue for custody of lab monkeys," *Washington Times*, July 8, 1982.
"Doctor fined $500 for animal cruelty," *Plain Dealer*, September 2, 1982.

Roger Galvin interview, January 26, 1993.
Annette Lantos interview, March 8, 1993.
Walter Goodman, "Of Mice, Monkeys and Men," *Newsweek*, August 9, 1982.
IPPL, et al., vs. IBR, et al., filed in the Circuit Court for Montgomery County, Maryland, December 3, 1981.
Letter to Edward Genn from Ingrid Newkirk, February 18, 1982.
Letter to Thomas Malone from Tom Lantos, *et al.*, November 25, 1981.
Letter to Thomas Malone from Edward Taub, December 30, 1981.
Letter to William Raub from Alan Cranston, July 30, 1982.
Letter to Edward Taub and Joseph Vasapoli from James Wyngaarden, August 30, 1982.
Letter to James Wyngaarden from Joe Biden, *et al.* August 9, 1982.
Shirley McGreal interview, February 18, 1993.
Ingrid Newkirk interview, January 21, 1993.
"Nightline" transcript, July 19, 1982.
Timothy Noah, "Monkey Business," *New Republic*, June 2, 1982.
Alex Pacheco interview, January 22, 1993.
Dave Rehnquist interview, March 15, 1993.
"Researcher convicted in monkey case," *Sun* (Baltimore), July 3, 1982.
Keith B. Richburg, "Jury Finds a Silver Spring Researcher Guilty of Cruelty to One of His Monkeys," *Washington Post*, July 3, 1982.
"Scientists Fear Animal Lovers May Stifle Research," *News & Courier* (Charleston), July 6, 1982.
State of Maryland vs. Taub, official transcript, June 15-30, 1982.
State of Maryland vs. Taub, pre-trial hearing, official transcript, 1982.
Arlo Wagner, "Psychologist pays $500 fine for abuse of research animal," *Washington Times*, September 2, 1982.

Chapter Eleven

Marc Adams, "Researcher loses appeal on withdrawal of grant," *Washington Times*, June 15, 1984.
Mike Ahlers, "Monkey researcher loses final grant appeal," *Montgomery Journal*, June 14, 1984.
The Animal League Defense Fund fact sheet, July, 1986.
Annotated Code of Maryland, Article 27, Section 59.
J.S. Bainbridge, Jr., "Animal researcher wins cruelty appeal," *Sun* (Baltimore), August 11, 1983.
Arthur Brisbane, "HHS Sanction Against Animal Researcher Upheld," *Washington Post*, June 16, 1984.
Court Order, Civil No. HAR 81-3246, Judge John R. Hargrove, filed April 19, 1985.
Departmental Grant Appeals Board Decision, Department of Health and Human Services, May 31, 1984.
Federal Defendants' Combined Motion to Dismiss, *IPPL, et al., vs. IBR, et al.*, filed by U.S. Attorneys J. Frederick Motza and James P. Ulwick, November 4, 1982.
Roger Galvin interview, January 26, 1993.
Erica Goode, "Researcher Takes On the Animal Lovers," *San Francisco Chronicle*, August 29, 1983.
Annette Lantos interview, March 8, 1993.
Letter to the editor, *Neuroscience Newsletter*, from William Raub and Joe Held, April 11, 1983.
Ingrid Newkirk interview, January 21, 1993.
Objections and Opposition to Magistrate's Report and Recommendations, *IPPL, et al. vs. IBR, et al.*, filed U.S. District Court, January 30, 1985.
Alex Pacheco interview, January 22, 1993.
Dave Rehnquist interview, March 15, 1993.
Robert Smith interview, February 17, 1993.
Richard Swain interview, January 31, 1993.
"Who's Who in Laboratory Animal Science," *Lab Animal*, July/August, 1983.
Graham R. Wiemer, "Animal Rights Group Holds Vigil to Focus on Plight of Monkeys," *Idaho State Journal*, May 22, 1986.
"Unnecessary Fuss," PETA videotape, 1984.

Chapter Twelve

"Britches," PETA videotape, 1985.
Gary Francione interview, May 4, 1993.
Paul Houston, "Senate Votes Tighter Safeguards for Lab Animals," *Los Angeles Times*, October 29, 1985.
Letter to Edward Genn from John Hargrove, June 26, 1984.
Letter to William Raub from Joseph Vasapoli, September 24, 1985.
Letter to Joseph Vasapoli from William Raub, October 2, 1985.
Letter to James Wyngaarden from Gary Francione, May 13, 1986.
Magistrate's Report and Recommendations, *IPPL, et al., vs. IBR et al.*, U.S. Magistrate Frederic N. Smalkin, filed January 17, 1985.
Adrian R. Morrison, "What's Wrong With 'Animal Rights,'" *American School Board Journal*, January, 1992.
Motion for Order Altering or Amending Judgment and for Order Reconsidering and Setting Order of Dismissal Aside, and Memorandum of Points and Authorities, filed in U.S. District Court by Edward Genn, April 19, 1985.
Ingrid Newkirk, *Free the Animals*, Noble Press, 1992.
Ingrid Newkirk interview, January 21, 1993.

References

Objections and Opposition to Magistrate's Report and Recommendations, filed in U.S. District Court by Edward Genn, January 30, 1985.

Chapter Thirteen

"67 Major Medical Groups and Natn'l Inst. Health Battle Animal Rights Case," PETA press release, May 7, 1986.
"Animal Rights Group Set Up Vigil at NIH," *Washington Post*, April 29, 1986.
Neal Barnard interview, March 26, 1993.
Neal Barnard, et al., "NIH Research Protocol for Silver Spring Monkeys: A Case of Scientific Misconduct," *Perspectives on Medical Research*, Vol. 2, 1990.
Carolyn Click, "PETA wants its day in court in monkey case," *Montgomery Journal*, May 9, 1986.
Gary Francione interview, May 4, 1993.
Mike Grim, "Use of monkeys is issue in appeal," *Richmond Times-Dispatch*, May 9, 1986.
Jaleh Hagigh, "Group wants monkeys freed," *Montgomery Journal*, April 29, 1986.
James Kilpatrick, "Appalling tale of animal abuse," *Kansas City Times*, May 9, 1986.
Ibid., "Caged in Poolesvile," *Washington Post*, May 12, 1986.
Ibid., "Federal Monkey Business," *Chicago Sun-Times*, May 12, 1986.
Mary Knudson, "Rally demands release of 15 monkeys maimed in research, mired in litigations," *Sun* (Baltimore), May 18, 1986.
Letters to Emmett Barkley from Gary Francione, April 16, 1986; April 24, 1986; April 25, 1986; May 29, 1986.
Letter to Robert Lanman from Gary Francione, May 28, 1986.
Letter to Senate and House of Representatives from the American College of Neuropsychopharmacology, et al., April 30, 1986.
Letter to Robert Smith from William Raub, May 2, 1986.
Letter to Robert Smith from William Raub, May 20, 1986.
Letter to Mr. O.D. Sweat from Gary Francione, April 4, 1986.
Letter to James Wyngaarden from Gary Francione, April 17, 1989.
Letter to James Wyngaarden from Charles Mathias, May 5, 1986.
Letters to James Wyngaarden from Robert Smith, et al., April 21, 1986; May 27, 1986.
Letters to Joseph Vasapoli from William Raub, October 2, 1985.
Ingrid Newkirk interview, January 21, 1993.
"NIH Fights Groups' Claim To Animals," Associated Press, May 9, 1986.
Alex Pacheco interview, January 22, 1993; April 15, 1993.
"PETA holds candlelight vigil at NIH," *Montgomery Journal*, May 2, 1986.
Robert Smith interview, February 17, 1993.
Arlo Wagner, "Animal rights group pitches tent at NIH," *Washington Times*, April 29, 1986.

Chapter Fourteen

"1985 Primate Center Mortality Rates," PETA fact sheet, 1986.
Karlyn Barker and Eve Zibart, "NIH Willing to Transfer Lab Monkeys," *Washington Post*, June 14, 1986.
Barbara Boxer's statement, Congressional Record, June 26, 1986.
Alan Cranston's statement, Congressional Record, June 11, 1986.
Bob Dart, "Movement to free captive monkeys grows," *Atlanta Journal Constitution*, June 14, 1986.
Department of Health and Human Services press release, June 13, 1986.
Gary Francione interview, May 4, 1993.
David Fyten, "Of Mice & Men," *Tulanian*, Spring, 1987.
Peter Gerone interview, June 11, 1993.
Peter Gerone resumé and biographical data, July 17, 1991.
House Concurrent Resolution 351, introduced June 11, 1986.
Judi Hymel, "Monkey transfer sparks 2nd day of protest at TU center," *Times-Picayune*, June 26, 1986.
Ibid., "Transfer of monkeys to La. center protested," June 25, 1986.
James Kilpatrick, "Why Can't They Just Let Those Monkeys Go?" *Washington Post*, May 27, 1986.
Letter to Joseph Brady from William Raub, June 23, 1986.
Letter to House of Representatives from Lawrence J. DeNardis, June 24, 1986.
Letters to Robert Lanman from Edward Genn, July 23, 1986; August 4, 1986.
Letter to Donald Newman from Robert Smith, June 10, 1986.
Letter to Robert Smith from James Wyngaarden, June 9, 1986.
Letter to James Wyngaarden from Robert Smith, May 27, 1986.
Letter to John J. Walsh from William Raub, June 23, 1986.
Lawrence Maddrey, "Monkeys' case has a humane, simple answer," *Virginian Pilot and Ledger Star*, June 10, 1986.
"Maimed monkeys cause D.C. stir," United Press International, May 27, 1986.
"Negotiation On 'Silver Spring Monkeys Case' Break Down," Robert Smith press release, June 11, 1986.
Ingrid Newkirk interview, January 21, 1993.
Alex Pacheco interview, January 22, 1993.
"PETA denounces proposal for monkeys," *Montgomery Journal*, June 16, 1986.
"The Real Delta Death Rates," PETA fact sheet, 1986.
Dave Rehnquist interview, March 15, 1993.
Charlie Rose's statement, Congressional Record, June 26, 1993.

Robert Smith interview, February 17, 1993.
"Vigil 'Til Victory," *PETA News,* Winter, 1986.

Chapter Fifteen

"15 Monkeys Cause a Stir," *New York Times,* June 29, 1986.
"Animal Rights Protesters Arrested," *Washington Post,* August 6, 1986.
Neal Barnard, *et al.,* "NIH Research Protocol for Silver Spring Monkeys: A Case of Scientific Misconduct," *Perspectives on Medical Research,* Vol. 2, 1990.
Fourth Circuit Court of Appeals Decision by Judges Widener, Ervin and Wilkinson, September 4, 1986.
Gary Francione interview, May 4, 1993.
Bridget Kauber, "See No Evil, Hear No Evil: The Federal Courts and the Silver Spring Monkeys," *University of Colorado Law Review,* Vol. 63, Issue 2, 1992.
Letter to Joseph Brady from William Raub, June 23, 1986.
Letter to Robert Lanman from Edward Genn, July 23, 1986.
Letter to Ronald Reagan from Robert Smith, Charlie Rose, and Rod Chandler, September 25, 1986.
Letters to Robert Smith from Peter Gerone, January 12, 1987; July 15, 1986.
Phil McCombs, "Life and Death On the Cutting Edge," *Washington Post,* June 2, 1986.
Ingrid Newkirk interview, January 21, 1993.
Ingrid Newkirk, notes on conversation with Peter Gerone, June 25, 1986.
Alex Pacheco interview, January 22, 1993.
"Primate Protest," *Richmond Times-Dispatch,* August 6, 1986.
Silver Spring Monkeys fact sheet, Delta Regional Primate Research Center, July 3, 1989.
Robert Smith interview, February 17, 1993.
Debbie Stone, "NIH ships 15 monkeys to facility in Louisiana," *Montgomery Journal,* June 25, 1986.
Katie Tyndall, "Animal Rights and Research Woes," *Washington Times,* August 4, 1986.

Chapter Sixteen

Jack Anderson and Joseph Spear, "Washington merry-go-round," syndicated, April 25, 1987.
Neal Barnard, *et al.,* "NIH Research Protocol for Silver Spring Monkeys: A Case of Scientific Misconduct," *Perspectives on Medical Research,* Vol. 2, 1990.
"Discussion Notes for Council," American Physiological Society memorandum, March 17, 1987.
Gary Francione interview, May 4, 1993.
Jane Goodall, *Through a Window,* Houghton Mifflin, 1990.
Jane Goodall and Dale Peterson, *Visions of Caliban,* Houghton Mifflin, 1993.
Jaleh Hagigh, "Monkey confiscated from lab dies five years later," *Montgomery Journal,* November 18, 1986.
"High court denies appeal in animal rights case," *Boston Globe,* April 7, 1987.
House of Representatives Bill 1770, introduced March 24, 1987.
Letter to Peter Gerone from Robert Smith, February 18, 1987.
Letter to William Raub from Charlie Rose and Robert Smith, March 25, 1987.
Letter to Robert Smith from William Raub, February 26, 1987.
Letter to Betty Jo Williams from Jan Moor-Jankowski, April 25, 1988.
Letter to Robert Windom from Robert Smith, January 23, 1987.
Memorandum to John J. Walsh from Peter Gerone, January 5, 1987.
Minutes, Committee on Care and Use of Laboratory Animals, Delta, February 16, 1987.
Alex Pacheco interview, May 6, 1993.
"New Paltz monkeys in Mexico," *Times-Herald Record* (Middletown, NY), August 20, 1987.
"NIH Receives Recommendations for Silver Spring Monkeys," Tulane Medical Center press release, February 25, 1987.
Robert Reinhold, "Fate of Monkeys a Source of Pain for 6 Years," *New York Times,* May 23, 1987.
Charlie Rose's statement, Congressional Record, March 25, 1987.
James H. Rubin, "Court bars suits on animals rights at U.S.-aided lab," *San Francisco Examiner,* April 6, 1987.
Silver Spring Monkeys fact sheet, Delta, July 3, 1989.
Robert Smith interview, February 17, 1993.
Brenda Spinks, written statement following telephone conversation with Peter Gerone, January 7, 1987.
Geza Teleki interview, February 4, 1993.

Chapter Seventeen

Neal Barnard, *et al.,* "NIH Research Protocol for Silver Spring Monkeys: A Case of Scientific Misconduct," *Perspectives on Medical Research,* Vol. 2, 1990.
House of Representatives Bill 2883, introduced July1, 1987.
"Inspection Report of the Louisiana Society for the Protection of Animals of the Silver Spring Monkeys, Delta Regional Primate Center," August 5, 1987.
Letter to Charles A. Bowsher from Robert Smith, Charlie Rose, and Tom Lantos, November 9, 1987.
Letter to Peter Gerone from Sean Hawkins, February 13, 1987.
Letter and report to Stanley Muller from Janis Ott Joslin, June 28, 1987.
Letter to Douglas Myers from Bob Dornan and Robert Smith, January 8, 1988.

References

Letter to Douglas Myers from Charlie Rose, January 13, 1988.
Letter to William Raub from Douglas Bowden, November 14, 1988.
Letter to William Raub from Peter Gerone, August 13, 1987.
Letter to William Raub from Robert Smith, March 30, 1988.
Letter to Robert Smith from Donald Newman, September 23, 1987.
Memorandum to Lowell T. Harmison from Frederick Goodwin, September 29, 1987.
Ingrid Newkirk interview, January 21, 1993.
Alex Pacheco interview, May 6, 1993.
Senate Bill 2707, introduced August 10, 1988.
"San Diego Zoo To Accept 5 Silver Spring Monkeys," Bob Dornan press release, June 26, 1987.
"Seized Laboratory Monkeys Get Home in California," United Press International, July 4, 1987.
Silver Spring Monkeys fact sheet, Delta, July 3, 1989.
Robert Smith interview, February 17, 1993.

Chapter Eighteen

Agreement with Ventura County Community College District for the Care of the Silver Spring Monkeys, 1988.
Neal Barnard, et al., "NIH Research Protocol for Silver Spring Monkeys: A Case of Scientific Misconduct," Perspectives on Medical Research, Vol. 2, 1990.
"Dear Colleague" letter from Robert Smith, June 16, 1988.
GAO report HRD-88-89 Silver Spring Monkeys, June 3, 1988.
"HHS' monkey business," Washington Times, January 4, 1989.
Letter from Susan Clay, July 20, 1988.
Letter from Roger Fouts, July 12, 1988.
Letter from Carrie Walters, (undated).
Letter to Bob Dornan from William Raub, July 1, 1988.
Letter to William Raub from Betty Jo Williams, April 27, 1988.
Letter to William Raub from Gary Wilson, October 15, 1988.
Letter to Ronald Reagan from Robert Smith and Bob Dornan, December 14, 1988.
Letter to Robert Smith from William Raub, July 19, 1988; October 13, 1988.
Letter to Robert Smith from Gary Wilson, October 16, 1988.
Letter to Gary Wilson from William Raub, October 11, 1988.
Alex Pacheco interview, May 6, 1993.
Robert Smith interview, February 17, 1993.
John Wilkens, "Macaques are back in social swing," San Diego Union, January 3, 1989.
Gary Wilson, "Evaluation of the Silver Spring Monkeys as Regards Relocation to Moorpark College and Subsequent Care," September 26, 1988.

Chapter Nineteen

Neal Barnard, "The Case of the 'Silver Spring Monkeys,' " Washington Post, February 25, 1989.
Neal Barnard interview, March 26, 1993.
Neal Barnard, et al., "NIH Research Protocol for Silver Spring Monkeys: A Case of Scientific Misconduct," Perspectives on Medical Research, Vol. 2, 1990.
"Clinical Report for G791 (Paul)," Delta Regional Primate Research Center, August 25, 1989.
Peter Gerone interview, June 11, 1993.
Howard LaFranchi, "Animal Research Debate Heats Up," Christian Science Monitor, March 10, 1989.
IPPL, et al., vs. Administrators of the Tulane Educational Fund, et al., transcript of proceedings in U.S. District Court before Judge Veronica Wicker, February 1, 1989.
"Lab Monkeys Get 'Reprieve,'" Washington Post, January 5, 1989.
Letters to George Bush from Robert Smith, et al., May 25, 1989; July 21, 1989; August 9, 1989.
Letter to Ruth Morris Force from Margaret Woodward, August 25, 1989.
Letter to Peter Gerone from Alex Pacheco, August 22, 1989.
Letter to William Raub from Robert Smith and Bob Dornan, August 25, 1989.
Letter to Robert Smith from William Raub, August 25, 1989.
Letter to Louis Sullivan from Buddy Roemer, March 22, 1989.
Alex Pacheco interview, May 6, 1993.
PETA Press Release, December 30, 1988.
Thomas Vice affidavit, January 4, 1989.
Margaret Woodward interview, March 23, 1993.

Chapter Twenty

"46,000 Enquirer Readers Plead With Barbara Bush: Help Stop Cruel Tests on Monkeys," November 27, 1990.
Neal Barnard, et al., "NIH Research Protocol for Silver Spring Monkeys: A Case of Scientific Misconduct," Perspectives on Medical Research, Vol. 2, 1990.
David Braaten, "Congressmen seek to save 'Silver Spring Monkeys,' " Washington Times, July 6, 1990.
Steve Cannizaro, "Judge allows disabled monkey to be put to death in Tammany," Times-Picayune, January 17, 1990.

"Court Blocks Killing of Research Monkeys," *New York Times,* April 12, 1991.
Mike Folks, "Judge allows killing of lab monkey 'Billy,' " *Washington Times,* January 16, 1990.
Gary Francione interview, May 4, 1993.
Roger Galvin interview, January 26, 1993.
Peter Gerone interview, June 11, 1993.
Amy Goldstein, "A 'Silver Spring Monkey' Undergoes Final Experiment," *Washington Post,* January 22, 1990.
"Government Scientists Put Monkeys to Death," *New York Times,* July 8, 1990.
Veronica T. Jennings, "Monkey Case Evolves Into New Battle," *Washington Post,* April 10, 1991.
"Judge Refuses to Prevent Deaths of Monkeys in Federal Laboratory," *New York Times,* July 1, 1990.
"Lawmakers to Appeal on Monkeys' Behalf," *Washington Post,* July 6, 1990.
Annette Lantos interview, March 8, 1993.
Lori Lehner interview, February 25, 1993.
Letter to Robert Lanman from Margaret Woodward, December 29, 1989.
Letter to William Raub from Robert Smith, June 28, 1990.
Letter to Robert Smith from Nedim Buyukmihci, April 9, 1991.
Letter to Robert Smith from William Raub, June 25, 1990.
Katie McCabe, "Beyond Cruelty," *Washingtonian,* February, 1990.
"Mourning Monkeys," *Washington Times,* July 11, 1990.
Alex Pacheco interview, January 22, 1993.
Daniel H. Pink, " 'Silver Spring Monkeys' die in La. Experiment," *Washington Post,* July 7, 1990.
Tim P. Pons, *et al.,* "Massive Cortical Reorganization After Sensory Deafferentation in Adult Macaques," *Science,* June 28, 1991.
Dave Rehnquist interview, March 15, 1993.
Robert Smith interview, February 17, 1993.
Tim Stephens, "High Court to Hear PETA vs. NIH," *Journal of NIH Research,* March, 1991.
Supreme Court of the United States Syllabus and Opinion, IPPL, et al., vs. Administrators of Tulane Educational Fund, et al., May 20, 1991.